Business Management

Business Management

Rowan Sutherland

Clanrye International
www.clanryeinternational.com

Clanrye International,
750 Third Avenue, 9th Floor,
New York, NY 10017, USA

ISBN: 978-1-64726-076-7

Cataloging-in-Publication Data

Business management / Rowan Sutherland.
p. cm.
Includes bibliographical references and index.
ISBN: 978-1-64726-076-7
1. Industrial management. 2. Management. 3. Business. I. Sutherland, Rowan.
HD31.2 .B87 2021
658--dc23

For information on all Clanrye International publications visit our website at www.clanryeinternational.com

Clanrye International

Table of Contents

Preface VII

Chapter 1 Introduction to Business Management 1
- Business 1
- Business Management 3
- Business Management System 8

Chapter 2 Types of Organizations 10
- Organization 10
- Company 11
- Non-Profit Organization 16

Chapter 3 Organizational Hierarchy 20
- Upper Management 23
- Middle Management 27
- Lower Management 30

Chapter 4 Fundamental Business Processes 32
- Planning 32
- Organizing 34
- Coordinating 35
- Commanding 37
- Controlling 37

Chapter 5 Branches of Business Management 39
- Business and Information Technology 39
- Human Resource Management 44
- Financial Management 49
- Marketing Management 57

- Operations Management 80
- Production Management 101

Chapter 6 Diverse Aspects of Business Management 105

- Business Operations 105
- Business Intelligence 106
- Asset Management 110
- Change Management 111
- Conflict Management 116
- Constraint Management 120
- Corporate Governance 131
- Design Management 132
- Organization Development 137
- Benchmarking 142
- Lean Dynamics 147
- Business Process Management 149
- Market Research 159

Chapter 7 Business Strategy: An Integrated Study 161

- Business Strategy 162
- Strategic Management 164
- Business Analysis 190
- Planning 207
- Approaches 212
- Business Process Modeling 219

Chapter 8 Entrepreneurship and Small Business Management 222

- Entrepreneurship 222
- Small Business 224
- Small Business Management 237
- Benefits of Small Business Management 238

Permissions

Index

Preface

This book has been written, keeping in view that students want more practical information. Thus, my aim has been to make it as comprehensive as possible for the readers. I would like to extend my thanks to my family and co-workers for their knowledge, support and encouragement all along.

The administration of a business organization is known as business management. It involves the setting of strategies of the organization as well as coordinating the efforts of its employees for the successful accomplishment of its objectives. The management of most large organizations is divided into three levels, which are arranged in a hierarchal, pyramidal structure. These levels consist of senior managers, middle managers and lower managers. The board of directors and the CEO generally constitute the senior managers. The middle managers are the branch managers and regional managers. Lower managers include the team leaders and supervisors who oversee the work of regular employees. This book elucidates the concepts and innovative models around prospective developments with respect to business management. Most of the topics introduced in this book cover new techniques and the applications of this field. It aims to serve as a resource guide for students and experts alike and contribute to the growth of the discipline.

A brief description of the chapters is provided below for further understanding:

Chapter - Introduction to Business Management

Business refers to the activity of producing or buying and selling either products or services, which is done in order to make a profit. The act of organizing people for the purpose of accomplishing the objectives and goals of a business is known as business management. This chapter has been carefully written to provide an easy understanding of the varied facets of business management.

Chapter - Types of Organizations

An entity which is made up of multiple people and which has a specific purpose is known as an organization. There are numerous types of organizations such as corporations and nonprofit organizations. The topics elaborated in this chapter will help in gaining a better perspective about these types of organizations.

Chapter - Organizational Hierarchy

Organizational hierarchy refers to a power structure where a person or a group has the most authority or power. Each successive level which lies below it has lesser authority than its predecessor. These levels can be broadly divided into upper, middle and lower management levels. This chapter has been carefully written to provide an easy understanding of the varied facets of organizational hierarchy.

Chapter - Fundamental Business Processes

A business process refers to a collection of tasks which are aimed at producing a service or a product for a particular customer or a group of customers. Some of the basic business processes are planning, organizing and coordinating. The chapter closely examines these key business processes to provide an extensive understanding of the subject.

Chapter - Branches of Business Management

The set of activities associated with running a company is known as business management. Some of the branches of business management are human resource management, financial management and marketing management. This chapter discusses in detail the theories and concepts related to these branches of business management.

Chapter - Diverse Aspects of Business Management

There are varied aspects which are studied under business management. Some of these are business operations, business intelligence, business process, asset management, change management, conflict management and constraint management. The topics elaborated in this chapter will help in gaining a better perspective about these aspects of business management.

Chapter - Business Strategy: An Integrated Study

The combination of all the decisions which are taken by a business to achieve their goals is known as business strategy. There are a number of areas which fall under the umbrella of this field such as planning and strategic management analysis. All the diverse concepts related to business strategies have been carefully analyzed in this chapter.

Chapter - Entrepreneurship and Small Business Management

The process of designing, launching and then running a new business is known as entrepreneurship. The new business is generally a small business, with lesser number of employees than a regular-sized business. This chapter closely examines the key concepts related to entrepreneurship and the management of small businesses to provide an extensive understanding of the subject.

Rowan Sutherland

1

Introduction to Business Management

Business refers to the activity of producing or buying and selling either products or services, which is done in order to make a profit. The act of organizing people for the purpose of accomplishing the objectives and goals of a business is known as business management. This chapter has been carefully written to provide an easy understanding of the varied facets of business management.

BUSINESS

A business is defined as an organization or enterprising entity engaged in commercial, industrial, or professional activities. Businesses can be for-profit entities or non-profit organizations that operate to fulfill a charitable mission or further a social cause.

The term business also refers to the organized efforts and activities of individuals to produce and sell goods and services for profit. Businesses range in scale from a sole proprietorship to an international corporation. Several lines of theory are engaged with understanding business administration including organizational behavior, organization theory, and strategic management.

Generally, a business begins with a business concept (the idea) and a name. Depending on the nature of the business, extensive market research may be necessary to determine whether turning the idea into a business is feasible and if the business can deliver value to consumers. The business name can be one of the most valuable assets of a firm; careful consideration should thus be given when choosing it. Businesses operating under fictitious names must be registered with the state.

Businesses most often form after the development of a business plan, which is a formal document detailing a business's goals and objectives, and its strategies of how it will achieve the goals and objectives. Business plans are almost essential when borrowing capital to begin operations.

It is also important to determine the legal structure of the business. Depending on the type of business, it may need to secure permits, adhere to registration requirements, and obtain licenses to legally operate. In many countries, corporations are considered to be juridical persons, meaning that the business can own property, take on debt, and be sued in court.

Business Structures

Many businesses organize themselves around some sort of hierarchy or bureaucracy, where positions in a company have established roles and responsibilities. The most common structures include sole proprietorships, partnerships, corporations, and limited liability companies, with sole proprietorships being the most prevalent.

A sole proprietorship, as its name suggests, is a business owned and operated by a single natural person. There is no legal separation between the business and the owner; the tax and legal liabilities of the business are thus that of the owner.

A partnership is a business relationship between two or more people who join to conduct business. Each partner contributes resources and money to the business and shares in the profits and losses of the business. The shared profits and losses are recorded on each partner's tax return.

A corporation is a business in which a group of people acts together as a single entity; most commonly, owners of a corporation are shareholders who exchange consideration for the corporation's common stock. Incorporating a business releases owners of financial liability of business obligations; however, a corporation has unfavorable taxation rules for the owners of the business.

For this reason, a relatively new business structure, a limited liability company (LLC), is available; this structure combines the pass-through taxation benefits of a partnership with the limited-liability benefits of a corporation.

Business Sizes

Business sizes range from small owner-operated companies, such as family restaurants, to multinational conglomerates such as General Electric. Larger businesses may issue corporate stock to finance operations. In this case, the company is publicly traded and has reporting and operating restrictions. Alternatively, smaller businesses may operate more independently of regulators.

Industries

A company may describe its business by communicating the industry in which it operates. For example, the real estate business, advertising business, or mattress production business are industries in which a business can exist. Because the term "business" can be interchanged with day-to-day operations as well as the overall formation of a company, the term is often used to indicate transactions regarding an underlying product or service. For example, ExxonMobil transacts business by providing oil.

BUSINESS MANAGEMENT

Business management is the act of organizing people to accomplish the desired goals and objectives of a business. Business management requires the utilization of the entity's resources in the most efficient manner possible.

Business management comprises organizing, planning, leading, staffing or controlling and directing a business effort for the purpose of accomplishing the entity's listed goals. In a for-profit business model, business management focuses on the satisfaction of a range of stakeholders, including the officers of the business, its employees, shareholders and the general public (consumers). In this regard, business management's primary function is to secure a profit, (for shareholders) create valuable and innovative products at a reasonable cost (consumers) and provide employment opportunities. In a nonprofit scope, business management will focus on keeping the faith of its supporters and donors.

Basic Functions of Business Management

Business management operates through a series of functions, typically classified as organizing, staffing, planning, leading, monitoring, controlling and motivating.

1. Planning: This area of business management decides what needs to happen in the future and subsequently generates plans for action. Planning is the foundation for effective business management; by deciding what needs to happen next week, next year or over the next five years, a business can develop a strategy to meet its listed goals.

2. Organizing: This portion of business management implements a pattern of relationships among its employees to encourage the optimum use of the entity's resources. Organizing is needed to utilize the businesses' finite resources; effective use of resources is the foundation for reaching a desired level of productivity.

3. Staffing: This area of business management focuses on recruiting, analyzing and hiring individuals for appropriate employment posts.

4. Leading: Also referred to as "directing" in the business management model, leading requires the entity's executives to determine what needs to be accomplished in a situation and what employees are best to fulfill such expectations.

5. Monitoring/Controlling: This phase of the business management process requires the leaders of the entity to monitor progress in relation to the plans and business of the business.

6. Motivation: A key aspect to the business management model, motivation is a basic function to maximize employment efficiency. By boosting morale, employees will carry-out their specific tasks in an effective manner.

Basic Roles of the Business Management Process

1. Decisional Roles: Carried out by the entity's executives, the decisional roles are required for decision-making purposes.

2. Interpersonal: These roles are necessary to effectively coordinate and interact with the employee base. Interpersonal roles are used to bridge the gap between the businesses' executives and their employees; interpersonal roles are used to create a sense of uniformity and a team environment.

3. Informational: These roles are implemented to handle, analyze and share information that is important to the business.

Management Skills Needed for the Business Management Process

1. Diagnostic: These skills are essential to the business management process because they analyze the appropriate course of action/responses to situations that may affect the business's stability or health.

2. Political: These skills are used to build a foundation for the business; political skills are needed to establish connections with public bodies, the public and other companies.

3. Conceptual: These skills are required to effectively evaluate complex situations.

4. Interpersonal: A series of skills needed to bolster motivation and communication among the executives and employee-base of a company. Interpersonal skills are a fundamental aspect of the business management process because they enable executives to mentor employees and delegate tasks.

Formation of a Business Management Plan

In the business management process, the mission of the entity is the most fundamental purpose. The vision of the company's goals reflects its overall aspirations; this portion of the business management process specifies the intended direction of the company. The business management process also requires the entity to list its objectives. By listing objectives, the business will refer to the ends at which a certain activity is aimed—this gives the purpose's tangible actions a means.

The business's management plan is a guide that stipulates regulations and objectives; the management plan may be used by executives in the decision-making process and may be followed by the entity's employees to bolster transparency and motivation.

Regardless of its particular use, the business plan must be flexible and easily interpreted by all employees of the business.

The business management plan refers to the construction of a coordinated plan of action that lists the goals and the resources used to engage these goals in relation to the company's long-term objectives. The business management plan provides guidelines for all members of the business; these instructions or regulations stipulate how the employees and managers ought to utilize and allocate the entity's factors of production.

The Implementation of the Business Management Plan

To effectively implement a business management plan, the following strategies and relationships must be formed:

- The policies must be discussed with all executives, managerial staff and general employees of the business model.
- All managers must understand how and where they can implement their strategies and policies.
- A formal plan of action must be constructed for each department of the management plan.
- All strategies and policies must be reviewed at least quarterly—the review of the business management plan will be evaluated to ensure that the provisions of the plan are properly aligned with the broader goals of the business.
- Contingency plans must be developed to meet changes in the macro-economy or the environment.
- The business management plan must actively assess the progress of the company as well as the actions carried-out by the top executives of the company.
- The construction of a sound environment and palpable team spirit is required for the business to be efficient.
- The objectives, missions, strengths and weaknesses of each sector of the business must be evaluated to determine their roles in achieving the broader mission.
- A planning strategy must be created to ensure that all initiatives are consistent and that strategies are aimed at achieving the same objectives.

The above policies must be discussed with all executives and managerial personnel that are required in the execution of any department's policy. Organizational alteration is achieved through the implementation of succinct plans. An example of a common business management plan will include the following steps: Increase the corporation's urgency, create a vision, bolster communication, empower action, create short-term goals and victories, keep pushing towards the final objective and make changes stick.

Important Players in the Business Management Process

The majority of business entities have three distinct management levels: first-level, mid-level and top-level executives or managers. These executives are classified in a distinct hierarchy of authority to perform different tasks aligned with the business model. In a number of organizations, these managers provide the business model with the following tasks:

Top-level Managers

This classification is comprised of a board of directors, a president, a vice-president, CEO's, CFO's, CLO's etc. These executives are responsible for controlling, directing and overseeing the entire organization. The top-level management of corporations develops goals, strategies, and company policies and renders decisions on the direction of the business. Moreover, top-level managers will play a primary role in the mobilization and utilization of outside resources to effectively produce or supply the company's product or service. Because of these roles, top-level managers are accountable to the general public and shareholders.

Middle-level Managers

This classification consists of general managers, branch managers and the company's department managers. Middle-level managers are accountable to top-level managers for their department's function. A middle-level manager must devote more time to directional and organizational functions of the business model. These individuals execute organizational plans in accordance with the entity's policies and objectives of the above-listed executives. Middle-level managers discuss information and policies from executives and regurgitate the orders derived from these conservations to lower management workers. Most importantly, because of their everyday interaction with the general employee base, middle-level managers inspire and provide guidance to employees to promote more efficient performance.

Common functions of the Middle-level Managers are given below:

- Middle level managers will design and implement effective group work and information systems to bolster productivity in the business model.
- Middle level managers define and monitor group-level performance indicators.
- Middle level managers pinpoint and resolve problems among workers.
- Middle level managers implement reward systems to support cooperative behavior.

First-level Managers

This group of the business management system consists of supervisors, foremen and the everyday experienced employee—individuals in this group are typically in charge of a few fellow employees. First-level managers focus on directing and controlling ground-level employees to effectively carry-out their work. First-level managers assign employee tasks and supervise these workers on day-to-day activities. These individuals ensure quality and quantity production; they will make suggestions and implement regulations to ensure proper compliance. A first-level manager will provide the following to employees:

- Motivate employees.
- Supervise employees.
- Provide career planning services.
- Offer performance feedback.

Process Management

Business process management is an approach to business management that believes that all aspects of the organization should be aligned with meeting the wants, needs, and desires of the business' clients. Business process management is a holistic management approach. This approach to business management strives for innovation, flexibility, and integrating technology, while promoting business efficiency and effectiveness.

A manager or company that subscribes the business process management approach to business management believes that the processes should be improved upon on a continual basis. Proponents of the business process management approach believe that this approach allows a company to be more efficient and effective, which in turn, leaves them more capable of changing to accommodate new conditions in a traditional, hierarchical management approach that is focused on function.

On a more general level, business management is the process by which the operation of a business is made possible through planning, organizing, staffing, leading or directing, and controlling a corporation, organization, or effort with the intent of accomplishing a specific goal. Often, at the highest level of a corporation, business management will involve setting these goals in the first place.

Business process management enables a company to abstract business processes from software or technology infrastructure; business process management goes far beyond automating business software or solving the entity's problems. Business process management enables the entity to respond to changing market and consumer regulatory demands faster than its competitors—this effectively creates a competitive advantage.

This form of management is made tangible through the use of business process management software. Business process management software is a computer program that organizes a company's business model; the software will align the company's goals with its available resources to create a detailed business management plan.

When utilized business process management software or tolls will allow a business to engage in the following:

- Business process management software or tools enable users to strategize processes and functions.
- Business process management software or tools to develop a baseline for the process improvement.
- Business process management software or tools to develop a model, which will stimulate the change to the process.
- The tools enable users to analyze simulations to determine optimal improvements.
- The tools enable users to select and implement the suggested improvements.

To deploy this maneuver, the business process management software will provide user defined dashboards to monitor the improvement in real time. Business process management software will relay the performance information back to the user for the subsequent iteration.

BUSINESS MANAGEMENT SYSTEM

Business Management System, or BMS, is a toolset that's used for tactical implementation and strategic planning of practices, processes, policies, guidelines, and procedures to use in the deployment, execution, and development of business strategies and plans, as well as any associated management activities. They provide a foundation for both tactical and strategic business decisions when it comes to current processes, tasks, activities, and procedures with the goal of meeting all objectives an organization has and satisfying the customer expectations and needs.

The main idea of Business Management System is to give management the tools for monitoring, planning, and controlling their activities and measure the performance of a business. They also aim to put into effect continuous improvement processes in the company. This system finds the principles of the organization's existence and is linked closely to business success criteria. It is a multi-level hierarchy of different business solutions that show how an organization that's profit-oriented will perform different functions, such as marketing, sales, staffing, and purchasing to complete a task successfully.

Business Management Tactics

The functional group of a BMS finds what the tactical techniques and approaches are when it comes to implementing business plans that are linked to their business strategies. Tactical solutions should only be brought up during the decision-making part. They should be executed based on the timeframes that are in the document for the business management strategy. Extra business schedules can be formed and assigned to this tactical implementation practice as well.

Business Management Tactics are defined as activities that follow the business standards that were identified in the company's policies. They put into effect business tasks and plans so they can meet the goals that have been prioritized.

There are also processes and guidelines in this functional group to develop business management plans. The guidelines have practical instructions and directions to show how decision makers can control all the tactical solutions. They include operations and procedures that show how performers get daily tasks and activities accomplished. This group also directs the staff towards the completion of business solutions and recognizing implementation plans that are aligned with the management tactics.

Management Styles

There are several types of management that are common, including democratic, autocratic, paternalistic, and laissez-faire. Democratic management style is used when employees are able to give feedback or input on business decisions. Autocratic management lets the business owner be the person in charge of making all decisions and leading the company through the business environment. When the best work environment possible is created for each employee, it's known as paternalistic management. Laissez-faire has the most employee autonomy and lets decisions be made with little to no business owner oversight.

Traditional management is a hierarchy of employees, with low, mid, and senior-level management. The manager creates expectations for the goals employees need to make.

2

Types of Organizations

An entity which is made up of multiple people and which has a specific purpose is known as an organization. There are numerous types of organizations such as corporations and nonprofit organizations. The topics elaborated in this chapter will help in gaining a better perspective about these types of organizations.

ORGANIZATION

A social unit of people that is structured and managed to meet a need or to pursue collective goals. All organizations have a management structure that determines relationships between the different activities and the members, and subdivides and assigns roles, responsibilities, and authority to carry out different tasks. Organizations are open systems-they affect and are affected by their environment.

Organization's Purpose and Priorities

Mission

All of the people in an organization should be working toward a common purpose. That purpose is often referred to as the mission. The mission might be implied to its members or explicitly expressed to them. When explicitly expressed, it is often in the form of a mission statement. The statement is often reviewed during a process called strategic planning.

Vision

The organization's vision is an image of what success would look like at some point in the future, both for the people that the organizations serves and for the organization itself. It can be very inspirational and motivational to explicitly articulate that vision in a statement like the mission statement during strategic planning.

Values

The organization's values are the overall priorities in the nature of how the organization wants to work toward its mission. Values can be reflected in how the people in the organization are actually working together. These might be referred to as real or enacted values. Values can also be about how the organization wants it members to work together. These might be referred to as desired values.

Strategic Priorities

These are the overall, most important matters and activities for members to attend to, when working toward the mission. Similar to the mission, vision and values, they might be implied or explicit among members. The priorities might be associated with assignments for who is address which ones and by when. The priorities are often referred as "strategic goals" during a strategic planning process.

Thus, it could seem to be a major challenge when working to lead, manage or improve an organization. Fortunately, there are some things in common to all types of organizations because they all are systems.

COMPANY

A company, abbreviated as co., is a legal entity made up of an association of people, be they natural, legal, or a mixture of both, for carrying on a commercial or industrial enterprise. Company members share a common purpose, and unite to focus their various talents and organize their collectively available skills or resources to achieve specific, declared goals. Companies take various forms, such as:

- Voluntary associations, which may include nonprofit organizations.
- Business entities with an aim of gaining a profit.
- Financial entities and banks.

A company or association of persons can be created at law as a legal person so that the company in itself can accept limited liability for civil responsibility and taxation incurred as members perform (or fail to discharge) their duty within the publicly declared "birth certificate" or published policy.

Companies as legal persons may associate and register themselves collectively as other companies – often known as a corporate group. When a company closes, it may need a "death certificate" to avoid further legal obligations.

Types

- A company limited by guarantee: Commonly used where companies are formed for non-commercial purposes, such as clubs or charities. The members guarantee the payment of certain (usually nominal) amounts if the company goes into insolvent liquidation, but otherwise, they have no economic rights in relation to the company. This type of company is common in England. A company limited by guarantee may be with or without having share capital.

- A company limited by shares: The most common form of the company used for business ventures. Specifically, a limited company is a "company in which the liability of each shareholder is limited to the amount individually invested" with corporations being "the most common example of a limited company." This type of company is common in England and many English-speaking countries. A company limited by shares may be a:
    - Publicly traded company.
    - Privately held company.
- A company limited by guarantee with a share capital: A hybrid entity, usually used where the company is formed for non-commercial purposes, but the activities of the company are partly funded by investors who expect a return. This type of company may no longer be formed in the UK, although provisions still exist in law for them to exist.
- A limited liability company: "A company—statutorily authorized in certain states—that is characterized by limited liability, management by members or managers, and limitations on ownership transfer", i.e., L.L.C. LLC structure has been called "hybrid" in that it "combines the characteristics of a corporation and of a partnership or sole proprietorship". Like a corporation, it has limited liability for members of the company, and like a partnership it has "flow-through taxation to the members" and must be "dissolved upon the death or bankruptcy of a member".
- An unlimited company with or without a share capital: A hybrid entity, a company where the liability of members or shareholders for the debts (if any) of the company are not limited. In this case doctrine of a veil of incorporation does not apply.

Less common types of companies are:

- Companies formed by letters patent: Most corporations by letters patent are corporations sole and not companies as the term is commonly understood today.
- Charter corporations: Before the passing of modern companies legislation, these were the only types of companies. Now they are relatively rare, except for very old companies that still survive (of which there are still many, particularly many British banks), or modern societies that fulfill a quasi-regulatory function.
- Statutory companies: Relatively rare today, certain companies have been formed by a private statute passed in the relevant jurisdiction.

Note that "Ltd" after the company's name signifies a limited company, and "PLC" (public limited company) indicates that its shares are widely held.

In the legal context, the owners of a company are normally referred to as the "members". In a company limited or unlimited by shares (formed or incorporated with a share capital), this will be the shareholders. In a company limited by guarantee, this will be the guarantors. Some offshore jurisdictions have created special forms of offshore company in a bid to attract business for their jurisdictions. Examples include "segregated portfolio companies" and restricted purpose companies.

There are, however, many, many sub-categories of types of company that can be formed in various jurisdictions in the world.

Companies are also sometimes distinguished for legal and regulatory purposes between public companies and private companies. Public companies are companies whose shares can be publicly traded, often (although not always) on a stock exchange which imposes listing requirements/Listing Rules as to the issued shares, the trading of shares and future issue of shares to help bolster the reputation of the exchange or particular market of an exchange. Private companies do not have publicly traded shares, and often contain restrictions on transfers of shares. In some jurisdictions, private companies have maximum numbers of shareholders.

A parent company is a company that owns enough voting stock in another firm to control management and operations by influencing or electing its board of directors; the second company being deemed as a subsidiary of the parent company. The definition of a parent company differs by jurisdiction, with the definition normally being defined by way of laws dealing with companies in that jurisdiction.

Corporation

A corporation is an organization-usually a group of people or a company—authorized by the state to act as a single entity (a legal entity; a legal person in legal context) and recognized as such in law for certain purposes. Early incorporated entities were established by charter (i.e. by an ad hoc act granted by a monarch or passed by a parliament or legislature). Most jurisdictions now allow the creation of new corporations through registration.

Corporations come in many different types but are usually divided by the law of the jurisdiction where they are chartered into two kinds: by whether they can issue stock or not, or by whether they are formed to make a profit or not. Corporations can be divided by the number of owners: corporation aggregate or corporation sole. A corporation sole is a legal entity consisting of a single ("sole") incorporated office, occupied by a single ("sole") natural person.

Where local law distinguishes corporations by the ability to issue stock, corporations allowed to do so are referred to as "stock corporations", ownership of the corporation is through stock, and owners of stock are referred to as "stockholders" or "shareholders". Corporations not allowed to issue stock are referred to as "non-stock" corporations; those who are considered the owners of a non-stock corporation are persons (or other entities) who have obtained membership in the corporation and are referred to as a "member" of the corporation.

Corporations chartered in regions where they are distinguished by whether they are allowed to be for profit or not are referred to as "for profit" and "not-for-profit" corporations, respectively.

There is some overlap between stock/non-stock and for-profit/not-for-profit in that not-for-profit corporations are always non-stock as well. A for-profit corporation is almost always a stock corporation, but some for-profit corporations may choose to be non-stock.

Registered corporations have legal personality and their shares are owned by shareholders whose liability is generally limited to their investment. Shareholders do not typically actively manage a corporation; shareholders instead elect or appoint a board of directors to control the corporation in a fiduciary capacity. In most circumstances, a shareholder may also serve as a director or officer of a corporation.

In American English, the word corporation is most often used to describe large business corporations. In British English and in the Commonwealth countries, the term company is more widely used to describe the same sort of entity while the word corporation encompasses all incorporated entities. In American English, the word company can include entities such as partnerships that would not be referred to as companies in British English as they are not a separate legal entity.

Late in the 19th century, a new form of company having the limited liability protections of a corporation, and the more favorable tax treatment of either a sole proprietorship or partnership was developed. While not a corporation, this new type of entity became very attractive as an alternative for corporations not needing to issue stock. In Germany, the organization was referred to as Gesellschaft mit beschränkter Haftung or GmbH. In the last quarter of the 20th Century this new form of non-corporate organization became available in the United States and other countries, and was known as the limited liability company or LLC.

Ownership and Control

A corporation is, at least in theory, owned and controlled by its members. In a joint-stock company the members are known as shareholders and each of their shares in the ownership, control, and profits of the corporation is determined by the portion of shares in the company that they own. Thus a person who owns a quarter of the shares of a joint-stock company owns a quarter of the company, is entitled to a quarter of the profit (or at least a quarter of the profit given to shareholders as dividends) and has a quarter of the votes capable of being cast at general meetings.

In another kind of corporation, the legal document which established the corporation or which contains its current rules will determine who the corporation's members are. Who a member is depends on what kind of corporation is involved. In a worker cooperative, the members are people who work for the cooperative. In a credit union, the members are people who have accounts with the credit union.

The day-to-day activities of a corporation are typically controlled by individuals appointed by the members. In some cases, this will be a single individual but more commonly corporations are controlled by a committee or by committees. Broadly speaking, there are two kinds of committee structure.

- A single committee known as a board of directors is the method favored in most common law countries. Under this model, the board of directors is composed of both executive and non-executive directors, the latter being meant to supervise the former's management of the company.
- A two-tiered committee structure with a supervisory board and a managing board is common in civil law countries.

Formation

Historically, corporations were created by a charter granted by government. Today, corporations are usually registered with the state, province, or national government and regulated by the laws enacted by that government. Registration is the main prerequisite to the corporation's assumption of limited liability. The law sometimes requires the corporation to designate its principal address, as well as a registered agent (a person or company designated to receive legal service of process). It may also be required to designate an agent or other legal representative of the corporation.

Generally, a corporation files articles of incorporation with the government, laying out the general nature of the corporation, the amount of stock it is authorized to issue, and the names and addresses of directors. Once the articles are approved, the corporation's directors meet to create bylaws that govern the internal functions of the corporation, such as meeting procedures and officer positions.

The law of the jurisdiction in which a corporation operates will regulate most of its internal activities, as well as its finances. If a corporation operates outside its home state, it is often required to register with other governments as a foreign corporation, and is almost always subject to laws of its host state pertaining to employment, crimes, contracts, civil actions, and the like.

Naming

Corporations generally have a distinct name. Historically, some corporations were named after their membership: for instance, "The President and Fellows of Harvard College". Nowadays, corporations in most jurisdictions have a distinct name that does not need to make reference to their membership. In Canada, this possibility is taken to its logical extreme: Many smaller Canadian corporations have no names at all, merely numbers based on a registration number, which is assigned by the provincial or territorial government where the corporation incorporates.

In most countries, corporate names include a term or an abbreviation that denotes the corporate status of the entity (for example, “Incorporated” or “Inc.” in the United States) or the limited liability of its members (for example, “Limited” or “Ltd.”). These terms vary by jurisdiction and language. In some jurisdictions, they are mandatory, and in others they are not. Their use puts everybody on constructive notice that they are dealing with an entity whose liability is limited: one can only collect from whatever assets the entity still controls when one obtains a judgment against it.

Some jurisdictions do not allow the use of the word “company” alone to denote corporate status, since the word “company” may refer to a partnership or some other form of collective ownership (in the United States it can be used by a sole proprietorship but this is not generally the case elsewhere).

Personhood

Despite not being individual human beings, corporations, as far as US law is concerned, are legal persons, and have many of the same rights and responsibilities as natural persons do. For example, a corporation can own property, and can sue or be sued. Corporations can exercise human rights against real individuals and the state, and they can themselves be responsible for human rights violations. Corporations can be “dissolved” either by statutory operation, order of court, or voluntary action on the part of shareholders. Insolvency may result in a form of corporate failure, when creditors force the liquidation and dissolution of the corporation under court order, but it most often results in a restructuring of corporate holdings. Corporations can even be convicted of criminal offenses, such as fraud and manslaughter. However, corporations are not considered living entities in the way that humans are.

NON-PROFIT ORGANIZATION

A non-profit organization (abbreviated “NPO,” or “non-profit” or “not-for-profit”) is an organization whose primary objective is to support an issue or matter of private interest or public concern for non-commercial purposes, without concern for monetary profit. NPOs are active in a wide range of areas, including the environment, the arts, social issues, charities, early childhood education, health care, religion, research, sports and other endeavors. In many cases, those who have acquired excess of wealth turn to philanthropy and establish or provide support to such organizations.

Since those involved in running a non-profit organization must pursue goals that benefit the community, rather than personal profit, they are not bound by the competition of the business sector. In this way, NPOs serve the whole purpose of society, advancing goodness in diverse areas for the benefit of many.

A non-profit corporation is a corporation created by statute, government, or judicial authority that is not intended to provide a profit to the owners or members. A corporation that is organized to provide profits to its owners or members is a for-profit corporation. A non-profit corporation is always organized as a non-stock corporation.

A non-profit corporation is usually created with a specific purpose, such as for educational, charitable, or related to other enumerated purposes, it may be a foundation, a charity or other type of non-profit organization. In some cases it may also be a public corporation. In many countries these entities are subject to exemption from various tax laws, with certain restrictions.

The use of the term "not-for-profit" rather than "non-profit" has been debated within the field. While there are definitive preferences for one term or the other, there is no broad consensus.

For-profit Distinction

The legal and ethical restrictions on the distribution of profits to owners or shareholders as what fundamentally distinguishes NPOs from commercial enterprises.

NPOs generally do not operate to generate profit, a characteristic widely considered to be defining of such organizations. However, an NPO may accept, hold, and disburse money and other things of value. It may also legally and ethically trade at a profit. The extent to which it can generate income may be constrained, or the use of those profits may be restricted. NPOs therefore are typically funded by donations from the private or public sector, and often have tax exempt status. Donations may sometimes be tax deductible.

Some 'non-profits' are operated by volunteers and/or paid positions. Additionally, an NPO may have members or participants or beneficiaries or students as opposed to customers in a for-profit organization. One should not generalize about the comparative cost of a 'non-profit' verses 'for profit' organization; there may be a significant internalized profit in a non-profit organization.

Legal aspects

Most countries have laws which regulate the establishment and management of NPOs, and which require compliance with corporate governance regimes. Most larger organizations are required to publish their financial reports detailing their income and expenditure for the public. In many aspects they are similar to business entities though there are often significant differences. Both non-profit and for-profit entities must have board members, steering committee members, or trustees who owe the organization a fiduciary duty of loyalty and trust. A notable exception to this involves churches, which are often not required to disclose finances to anyone, not even its own members if the leadership chooses.

Formation and Structure

In the United States, non-profit organizations are normally formed by incorporating in the state in which they expect to operate and carry out their activities. The act of incorporating creates a legal entity enabling the organization to be treated as a corporation under law and to enter into business dealings, form contracts, and property as any other individual or for-profit corporation may do.

Non-profits can have members but many do not. The non-profit may also be a trust or association of members. The organization may be controlled by its members who elect the Board of Directors, Board of Governors or Board of Trustees. Non-profits may have a delegate structure to allow for the representation of groups or corporations as members. Alternately, it may be a non-membership organization and the board of directors may elect its own successors.

A primary difference between a non-profit and a for-profit corporation is that a non-profit does not issue stock or pay dividends, (for example, The Code of the Commonwealth of Virginia includes the Non-Stock Corporation Act that is used to incorporate non-profit entities) and may not enrich its directors. However, like for-profit corporations, non-profits may still have employees and can compensate their directors within reasonable bounds.

Tax Exemption

In many countries, non-profits may apply for tax exempt status, so that the organization itself may be exempt from income tax and other taxes, and (in some cases) so that financial donors may claim back any income tax paid on donations, or deduct from their own tax liability the amount of the donation. Only limited types of tax exempt, non-profit organizations offer to donors the advantage of deductions for the amount donated.

If an organization is to qualify for tax exempt status, the organization must specify that no part of its assets shall benefit any of persons who are members, directors, officers or agents (its principals). Also, the organization must have a legal charitable purpose, such that the organization was created to support educational, religious, or charitable activities. These elements do not mean that the organization cannot pay employees or contractors for work or services they render to the organization. This limitation means that as long as the organization operates within its exempt purposes and it maintains an endowment or uses any excess revenue to further develop its activities it will not be taxed by the Internal Revenue Service.

Not only must the organization meet the requirements the state where it is organized sets for non-profits, but it must also meet complex IRS regulations. These regulations are used not only to determine if the organization is exempt from tax under the organization's activities as a non-profit organization. It may apply for a ruling that donations to it are tax deductible to the persons or business entities who make them. The organization itself will be exempt from taxation as long as it does not engage in unrelated business activities. As well the IRS has enacted intermediate sanctions should the members of the organization engage in practices that may excessively benefit any of the organizations members (or officers, directors, etc.) rather than revoking the organization's exempt status (which was the only option available before the adoption of intermediate sanctions) the IRS may now levy a penalty on the organization for engaging in a transaction that resulted in a private inurement or private benefit.

References

- Besley, Scott; Brigham, Eugene (2008). Principles of Finance (4th ed.). Cengage Learning. p. 105. ISBN 978-0-324-65588-9
- Organizations, definition: managementhelp.org, Retrieved 11 April, 2019
- Non-profit-organization, entry: newworldencyclopedia.org, Retrieved 18 August, 2019
- Phelan, Ben (7 January 2013). "Dutch East India Company: The World's First Multinational". PBS.org (PBS Online). Retrieved 13 March, 2018

3

Organizational Hierarchy

Organizational hierarchy refers to a power structure where a person or a group has the most authority or power. Each successive level which lies below it has lesser authority than its predecessor. These levels can be broadly divided into upper, middle and lower management levels. This chapter has been carefully written to provide an easy understanding of the varied facets of organizational hierarchy.

An organization can have many different managers, across many different titles, authority levels, and levels of the management hierarchy.

Management Levels

Most organizations have three management levels:

- Low-level managers;
- Middle-level managers;
- Top-level managers.

These managers are classified in a hierarchy of authority, and perform different tasks. In many organizations, the number of managers in every level resembles a pyramid.

Top-level Managers

The board of directors, president, vice-president, and CEO are all examples of top-level managers.

These managers are responsible for controlling and overseeing the entire organization. They develop goals, strategic plans, company policies, and make decisions on the direction of the business. In addition, top-level managers play a significant role in the mobilization of outside resources. Top-level managers are accountable to the shareholders and general public.

Middle-level Managers

General managers, branch managers, and department managers are all examples of middle-level managers. They are accountable to the top management for their department's function.

Middle-level managers devote more time to organizational and directional functions than top-level managers. Their roles can be emphasized as:

- Executing organizational plans in conformance with the company's policies and the objectives of the top management;
- Defining and discussing information and policies from top management to lower management;
- Inspiring and providing guidance to low-level managers towards better performance.

Some of their functions are as follows:

- Designing and implementing effective group and intergroup work and information systems;
- Defining and monitoring group-level performance indicators;
- Diagnosing and resolving problems within and among work groups;
- Designing and implementing reward systems supporting cooperative behavior.

Low-level Managers

Supervisors, section leads, and foremen are examples of low-level management titles. These managers focus on controlling and directing.

Low-level managers usually have the responsibility of:

- Assigning employees tasks;
- Guiding and supervising employees on day-to-day activities;
- Ensuring the quality and quantity of production;
- Making recommendations and suggestions;
- Upchanneling employee problems.

Also referred to as first-level managers, low-level managers are role models for employees. These managers provide:

- Basic supervision;
- Motivation;
- Career planning;
- Performance feedback;
- Staff supervision.

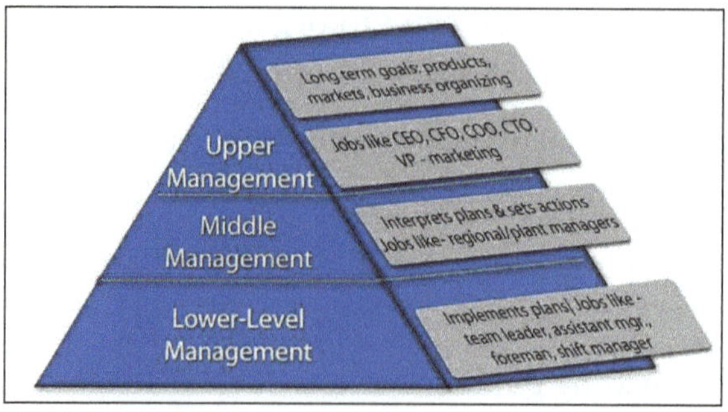

Management Levels: Hierarchical view of management in organizations.

Management Areas: A Functional View

Organizational management is often approached by identifying business functions and assigning leadership to those functions.

Businesses are comprised of a variety of different tasks which, when coordinated properly, create value through producing products and services. Each of these different tasks, or functions, require management and alignment. One approach to management is assigning leadership roles with authority and accountability over these different tasks, or management areas.

This view creates management positions with authority over a given functional department. These management areas can span a wide variety of skills and functions, but the most recognizable and common include marketing, finance, human resources, operations, software development, and IT.

This functional view emphasizes managers who are specialists in their fields who are also capable of leading teams, balancing budgets, and thinking tactically (and sometimes strategically, at the upper levels).

The Role of a Functional Management

Functional management is focused on the execution of a specific organizational task within functional areas, through organizing and leading an organization's talent in a given field. Functional managers have a high level of technical knowledge and skills relative to the area they manage and focus their efforts on achieving best practices.

Let's quickly explore an example of a functional manager to clarify the role and responsibilities. A human resources manager in an organization would be expected to oversee all operations within the scope of human resources. At a medium or larger sized organization, this could include managing specialists in payroll, recruitment, talent development, legal, and a variety of other specializations within the scope of a human resources team.

The manager shouldn't execute each specific task, but instead understand what is required to complete these tasks. The manager must have the broad technical knowledge required to ensure each individual within that functional team has the skills, resources, and alignment necessary to effectively carry out these functions.

Functional Management

A simple way to understand how this all plays out in an organization is a simple organizational chart (org chart, as they are commonly referred to). By taking a look at how the departments are divided, it becomes fairly easy to assume what types of management areas exist from a functional view. As a result, it's fairly common to receive an org chart when you start a job (particularly at larger companies), to understand who reports to whom, and regarding what tasks.

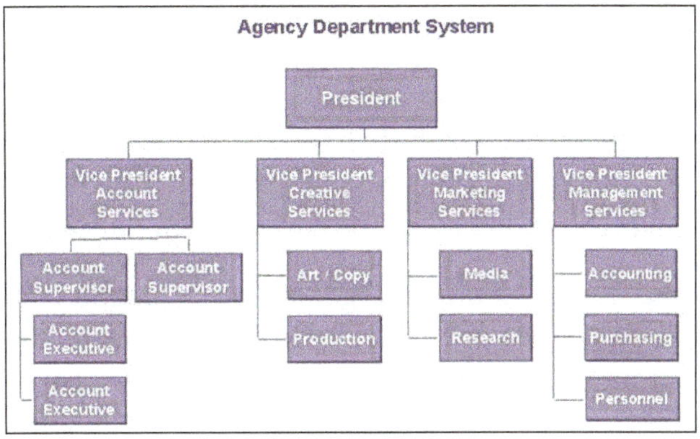

Organizational Chart: This is a simple example of an organizational chart, in this case at an advertising agency. By looking at each functional area, and considering how it relates to broader functional areas, it becomes clear how management areas are divided from a functional perspective.

UPPER MANAGEMENT

Upper management includes individuals and teams that are responsible for making the primary decisions within a company. Personnel considered to be part of a company's upper management are at the top of the corporate ladder and carry a degree of responsibility greater than lower level personnel. Upper management members are imbued with powers given by the company's shareholders or board of directors. Examples of upper management personnel include CEOs, CFOs and COOs.

Shareholders hold a company's upper management responsible for keeping a company profitable and growing. Shareholders do this by exercising their voting power to install boards of directors that will fire underperforming or otherwise disapproved managers. Because upper management personnel members are often not seen by most employees, they are not expected to engage in day-to-day operations.

How Upper Management is Held Accountable

The duties, responsibilities, and careers of upper management are often tied directly to the performance and success of a company. Whereas employees typically are measured against daily goals, such as the flow of the sales at their retail location or the number of customers they served, upper management may face a wholly different degree of criteria.

The overall sales across a division or regional market may be used to gauge the job performance of the executive in upper management who oversees said division.

For instance, a scientist or other researcher working for a drug company can be expected to take a direct, hands-on role in the development of new drug candidates. They will conduct the tests and reformulations to advance the potential product towards submission to regulators. A middle manager might lead their team working on the project, but an executive from upper management will have the prevailing authority on the direction the team takes and bear responsibility for how their efforts affect the company as a whole. If the drug development is a success and furthers the company's strategic plans, the executive who heads the division may be assigned similar projects in the future.

If a company performs below its targeted goals, loses traction compared to its rivals, or its market valuation declines, members of upper management may face the most immediate scrutiny from shareholders. Persistent poor performance of the company could prompt a shakeup of the upper management. This may be focused on one or more individuals such as the CEO or could be a sweeping removal of the executive leadership. The removal of upper management may be done to salvage a company's business and operations and introduce a new direction to follow. A new upper management team might be brought in to correct the course of the company and prepare it to pursue a new direction, which may include a sale of the business.

C-Suite Roles and Titles

C-suite, or C-level, is widely-used vernacular describing a cluster of a corporation's most important senior executives. C-suite gets its name from the titles of top senior staffers, which tend to start with the letter C, for "chief", as in chief executive officer (CEO), chief financial officer (CFO), chief operating officer (COO), and chief information officer (CIO).

- Chief Executive Officer (CEO) – Invariably the highest level corporate executive, the CEO traditionally serves as the face of the company, and frequently consults other C-suite members for advice on major decisions. CEOs can come from any career background, as long as they have cultivated substantial leadership and decision-making skills along their career paths.
- Chief Financial Officer (CFO) – In the financial industry, the CFO position represents the top of the corporate ladder for financial analysts and accountants

striving for upward mobility. Portfolio management, accounting, investment research, and financial analysis are prime skills that CFOs must have learned over the years. CFOs have global mind sets and work closely with CEOs to source new business opportunities while weighing the financial risks and benefits of each potential venture.

- Chief Information Officer (CIO) – A leader in information technology, the CIO usually gets his or her start as a business analyst, then works towards C-level glory, while developing technical skills in disciplines such as programming, coding, project management, MS Office and mapping. CIOs are usually skilled at applying these functional skills to risk management, business strategy, and finance activities. In many companies, CIOs are referred to as the Chief Technology Officers.
- Chief Operating Officer (COO) – The Human Resources (HR), C-level of executive, the COO ensures a company's operations run smoothly in areas such as recruitment, training, payroll, legal, and administrative services. The COO is usually second in command to the CEO.
- Chief Marketing Officer (CMO) – CMOs typically work their way up to the C-suite from sales and/or marketing roles. These execs are skilled at managing social innovation and product development initiatives across both brick-and-mortar establishments and electronic platforms - the latter of which is highly essential in today's digital era.

Other C-Suite officers include the Chief Compliance Officer (CCO), Chief Human Resources Manager (CHRM), Chief Security Officer (CSO), Chief Green Officer (CGO), Chief Analytics Officer (CAO), Chief Medical Officer (CMO), and Chief Data Officer (CDO).

The number of C-level positions varies, depending on variables such as a company's size, mission, and sector. While larger companies may require both a CHRM and a COO, smaller operations may only need a COO to oversee human resources activities.

The role of top management is more than making decisions that affect all employees. It's also to set the bar for the way managers treat the staff and relate to each other, which also affect the success of the company. Understanding the effects of their role helps the top management team make changes as necessary to the way they make decisions, the way they interact with other managers and teams, and how they are perceived by the staff. When employees feel their input is valued, they're more likely to do their jobs enthusiastically and improve the achievement of the company.

Setting Corporate Culture

The corporate policies and acceptable behaviors generally start at the top level of management. The leaders of the company establish procedures and expectations through those policies. The way the company is run day to day, based on those policies, helps establish the corporate culture.

A culture that encourages creativity, innovation and out-of-the-box thinking is likely to result in a company that is successful and continually comes up with new ideas. A stifling corporate culture limits the efforts of the employees, making it difficult for the company to advance. When employees know they have the top management team's support, they contribute without holding back.

Communicating Company Goals

The goals and vision of the company guide the work that is completed by the employees. To reach higher achievements for the company, top management first needs to make sure everyone in the company knows what the company's overall goals and strategy are. It's not enough to know their own goals. They need to understand the direction the company is headed and what management wants to achieve so they can see where their efforts fit into the overall strategy.

Next, top management needs to direct front line managers to establish goals for each employee. These should be achievable but challenging so they push each employee to grow. The goals must take into consideration the company's current situation and its overall strategy and direction. Above all, each employee's goals should be measurable so it's clear when they have been achieved.

Providing Support for Asset Management

A company's financial decisions typically come from the top level of management. This includes each department's budget for the fiscal year. In many cases, the purchase of equipment and other assets must be approved by top management. It's important that top management has confidence in mid-level managers to know what their employees need, and to procure it while keeping within their departments' budgets.

If the employees don't have access to the equipment and resources necessary to complete their jobs, the company's achievement suffers. A management team that supports the staff and has a sense of what they need is better equipped to lead the company to success. Don't let the lack of essential tools for the job hinder the company's success.

Ensuring Management Involvement

The top management of a company leads by example and affects the motivation felt by the employees. A management team that takes a sincere interest and connects with the staff is more likely to inspire the employees to achieve. Transparency from the management team about the company's future aids in motivating the staff because it gives them a better idea of the reasons for their work duties.

Top management needs to also make sure the line of communication and transparency continues throughout the company as well. Make it a company policy that managers meet regularly with each of their employees-weekly, for example-to discuss their progress. Weekly staff meetings are good for keeping everyone informed of coming activities, but they're not a substitute for meeting one-on-one, where each employee has the opportunity to express problems, issues and concerns.

MIDDLE MANAGEMENT

Middle management is the intermediate management level of a hierarchical organisation that is subordinate to the executive management and responsible for 'team leading' line managers and 'specialist' line managers. Middle management is indirectly (through line management) responsible for junior staff performance and productivity.

Unlike line management, middle management is considered to be a senior (or semi-executive) position as middle managers are authorised to speak and act on behalf of the organisation to line managers, junior staff and customers. Middle managers have a huge influence on an organisation's development and success as they often have direct control over 80% of an organisation's workforce.

Middle managers are sub-culture influencers as their personal values and beliefs can result in a culture within a culture, more commonly known as silos within an organisation.

Middle management is revered upwards by line managers and junior managers alike but this reverence is not shared downwards by executives, who are dependent on middle managers to implement company strategy or sideway by support functions, (HR, Marketing, Finance) who are dependent on middle manager support in achieving their goals and objectives.

Since the 20th century, middle management has been reduced in businesses and organisations as a result of reorganization and outsourcing. Such changes include downsizing, delayering and outsourcing. These changes are made in an effort to reduce costs and to make the organisation flatter – subsequently increasing employee's responsibilities and flexibility. In many cases removing the middle manager level resulted in a decrease in line manager performance as senior managers did not have the time available to monitor, manage or develop line manager performance. Since 2010 many organisations have reinstated the middle manager role to address this issue.

Role in an Organization

Functions of a Middle Manager

A middle manager is a link between the senior management and the lower (junior) levels of the organization. Due to involvement into day-to-day running of a business, middle managers have the opportunity to report valuable information and suggestions from the inside of an organization. Moreover, the middle manager is a channel of communication within the organization, as they pass on major decisions of executives and the main goals of an organization to lower levels of employees. This contributes to better coordination between workers and makes a company more united.

Primary responsibility of a middle manager is to implement a strategy, created by the executive level, in the most efficient way possible. In order to reach the target goals, a manager may adjust and interpret the initial plan. Other functions can be divided into three main categories:

- Technical: Middle managers are in charge of facilitating any changes needed in an organization and creating an effective working environment. They administer day-to-day routines, monitors performance and make sure everything is done in compliance with organization's needs.
- Human resources: One of the most important functions of a middle manager is motivating, leading and inspiring their subordinates. This also includes building a team and supporting any team member when necessary.
- Strategic: Strategic functions involve analyzing a subordinate group in terms of productivity and financial effectiveness, creating a strategy of improving the current situation and reporting to the executive management in the form of attending a boardroom meeting or a discussion.

Competencies

A number of competencies critical to become an effective middle manager are given below:

- Leadership: The most important competency that consists of many skills. As an inherent leader, middle managers have to possess sense-making and persuading skills. They must be able to motivate, influence and guide their subordinates, become a role model for them, demonstrate the quality and the level of work contribution necessary for the organization and engage in continuous self-development and learning.
- Decision-making: Ability to quickly solve the problems, make decisions under pressure and take responsibility for the outcome.
- Creativity and Visioning: Managers should have a clear vision of the strategy implementation and be creative in overcoming the possible difficulties.
- Performance management: Involves managing the performance of subordinates and, specifically, the line managers, effectively, by setting clear and measurable objectives for them and provide coaching. Middle managers must be also skilled in presenting, persuading and influencing people.

Middle Manager vs. Line Manager

A middle management position is often mistakenly described as a similar to the line management one. However, there are some differences:

- Middle manager is a semi-executive position – Line managers are promoted to become middle managers. Thus, middle managers enjoy greater salary, benefits and a closer position to a boardroom.
- System of subordination – Line managers are subordinate to middle managers. Middle managers are responsible for large teams and are unable to control performance of every single individual. Thus, direct or line manager measures the team performance and reports to the middle manager.
- Set of duties – Unlike line managers, who have a clear procedure of work and set of duties, middle managers have only target goals. The way of achieving those goals is decided by manager independently.

The role of middle management is subjected to a number of criticisms. This position is often seen as unnecessary and middle managers are blamed for holding back the organization from achieving its full potential and using the influence for their own purposes.

Influence

Middle management is often accused of possessing too much influence. Their centric position in an organization allows to influence strategy and actions in "both upward and downward direction". When supplying information to the executive level, middle managers interpret it subjectively and may insinuate it with their own opinion and evaluation. Further, proximity to the boardroom makes it easy for the manager to promote his or her own interests, by "synthesizing" the information and presenting data from a certain strategic perspective. The same level of influence can be exploited by a middle manager towards the lower staff. Driven by the reasons of maintaining a reputation, strengthening the power and influence, middle manager may introduce company's major strategic decisions in a light, beneficial way for his or her designs.

Resistance

Middle managers' reluctance to lose control in their teams and satisfaction with a settled situation could lead to their resistance in any changes in the strategy or direction of an organization. Usually, the resistance does not take an aggressive form such as refusal to carry out tasks or unconcealed confrontation, but result in a lack of support and eagerness to convey only those tasks, impact of which is clearly visible to the top management. This creates barriers to a growth of a company and lags the overall working process.

Necessity

The overall necessity of middle managers in an organization is questioned. They are said to be too costly, non-effective and constantly underperforming employees. It has been stated that middle managers do not carry out their main duties of linking the organization and reporting effectively, which leads to a block of communication between different levels of staff. Thus, as rapid growth of globalization put pressures on businesses in terms of cost effectiveness and speed of information flow within the organization, middle management make companies less flexible and competitive.

Development of information technology enabled an increase in the span of control and reduced the need for middle management. Moreover, an increasingly big number of modern organizations become flatter and downsized in the pursuit of flexibility, higher competitiveness and innovation. According to David Williams, flat organizations promote greater intercommunication and efficiency of the workers. As a result, many organizations are being restructured, middle management is being reduced and their roles are thought to be out-dated and unnecessary.

At the same time, there is still a need in a middle manager as an employee and they continue playing a significant role in organizations, specifically in setting an overall strategy and targets. Changes in the global market forced them to become more flexible, stress-resistant, acquire new skills.

LOWER MANAGEMENT

This level is the last level of the organizational hierarchy. It represents the operational level and acts as a link between the management and the operational labours. They mainly perform the vital function of supervision and inspection of all activities in order to control them. They are responsible for maintaining better working condition at the workplace as well as for arrangement of the required resources, equipment's and other plans for better performance of the workmen.

Positions: This level consists of Supervisors, Foremen, Inspectors and any other similar position held by any person by whatever name called.

Functions- This level performs the following:

- To act as a communication channel between the management and labours.
- To represent and communicate the feelings of the labours before management.
- To communicate the plans and policies of management to the labours.
- To assist the middle level management in recruitment of new and capable employees.

- To ensure coordination among different levels and department.
- To maintain better human relation.
- To appoint labourers, draft plan for them, and assign them work.
- To sort out the grievances of workmen effectively, as the lower level management are in direct contact with the workmen.
- To arrange and acquire the required resources and equipments etc.
- To provide well working conditions for them.
- To control by minimizing the wastage, controlling cost and maintaining discipline among labours.
- To motivate labours.
- To ensure workers safety and security.

References

- Boundless-business, types-of-management: lumenlearning.com, Retrieved 11 May, 2019
- Connors, J. L.; Rom berg, T. A. (1991). "Middle management and quality control: Strategies for obstructionism". Human Organization. 50: 61–65. doi:10.17730/humo.50.1.2w81h2l600260704
- Upper-management, terms: investopedia.com, Retrieved 30 June, 2019
- Dance, Anthony (2019). Pragmatic Introduction to Middle Management. Amazon: eBookit. pp. 8–14. ISBN ASIN: B07L4D3QB9
- Role-top-management-helping-company-achieve-34052: smallbusiness.chron.com, Retrieved 16 April, 2019
- Balogun, J (2003). "From Blaming the Middle to Harnessing its Potential: Creating Change Intermediaries". British Journal of Management. 14 (1): 69–83. doi:10.1111/1467-8551.00266

4

Fundamental Business Processes

A business process refers to a collection of tasks which are aimed at producing a service or a product for a particular customer or a group of customers. Some of the basic business processes are planning, organizing and coordinating. The chapter closely examines these key business processes to provide an extensive understanding of the subject.

PLANNING

Planning is the process of deciding in advance what is to be done, who is to do it, how it is to be done and when it is to be done. It is the process of determining a course of action, so as to achieve the desired results. It helps to bridge the gap from where we are, to where we want to go. It makes it possible for things to occur which would not otherwise happen. Planning is a higher order mental process requiring the use of intellectual faculties, imagination, and foresight and sound judgment. Accounting to Koontz, O'Donnell and Weihrich, "planning is an intellectually demanding process; it requires the conscious determination of courses of action and the basing of decisions on purpose, knowledge and considered estimates.

Planning is a process, which involves anticipation of future course of events and deciding the best course of action. It is a process of thinking before doing. "To plan is to produce a scheme for future action; to bring about specified results, at specified cost, in a specified period of time. It is deliberate attempt to influence, exploit, bring about, and controls the nature, direction, extent, speed and effects of change. It may even attempt deliberately to create change, remembering always that change (like decision) in any one sector will in the same way affect other sectors". Planning is a deliberate and conscious effort done to formulate the design and orderly sequence actions through which it is expected to reach the objectives. Planning is a systematic attempt to decide a particular course of action for the future; it leads to determination of objectives of the group activity and the steps necessary to achieve them. Thus, it can be concluded that "planning is the selecting and relating of facts and the making and using of assumptions regarding the future in the visualization and formulation of proposed activities believed necessary to achieve desired results.

Other words we can say that Planning is a process of thinking before doing. It involves determinations of goals and the activities required to be performed to achieve the goals. It consists:

- What is to be done?
- How it is to be done?
- Where it is to be done?
- When it is to be done?
- By whom it is to be done?

So planning is a process of shorting out the path for attaining the determined objective of the business. Overall planning is deciding that in present, what is to do in future.

Characteristics of Planning

- Goal oriented: The main purpose of plan is always to determine the goal to be achieved and the activities to be performed to achieve these goals. So planning relates to creative thinking for the solution of various problems.
- Primacy (basic function) of planning: It means planning is the basic function of all other managerial functions. It provides a base for other managerial functions like organizing, staffing, directing and controlling. We can say that structure of all other functions depends on planning.
- Forward looking: Planning is never done for past but is done for the future to achieve certain objective. Therefore, it is said that planning is thinking before doing. Planning is based on estimated future trends of social, economic and technological changes because it has to tackle the future requirements.
- Pervasiveness: Planning is required in all sectors, i.e. business, industry, profession etc. whether it is of large scale or small scale and in all the department of organisation like purchase, production, marketing, finance department etc. however nature of planning differs from one department to another.
- Involving choice (alternative): Planning can be when there are two or more alternatives and the planner can make a choice for the best, in other words, in the absence of choice there will be no planning because then there is a single way of doing something i.e. to be adopted.
- Continuous process: planning is an on-going process, planning starts before performing the job and them goes on with the activities to be performed to do that job and them just after the competition of the job planning regarding starting the new job. Moreover changes take place in business environment and regular plans are made to face such changes.

- Flexible: There must be flexibility in planning, because plans are always based on future, which is uncertain. So flexibility will give a chance to make changes as per future requirements.
- Efficiency of operations: Planning is made with the objective of raising efficiency of operations but it is not necessary that efficiency will raised, if may or may not. So the management should make continuous efforts to minimize the cost of wastage and improving the efficiency by use of latest change in technology.
- Planning is a primary function: Planning is the basis or foundation of the management process. All other functions of management are designed its attain the goals set under planning.
- Planning is the fundamental premise of all management functions: As managerial operations in organizing, staffing, leading, and controlling are designed to support the accomplishment of enterprise objectives, planning logically precedes the execution of all other managerial functions.
- Planning is closely linked to objectives: Each plan specifies the objectives to be attained in the future and the steps necessary to reach them. As Billy E. Goetz said, "plans forecast which actions will tend towards the ultimate objective. Managerial planning seeks to achieve a consistent, coordinated structure of operations focused on desired ends."
- The effectiveness of planning is measured in terms of what it contributes to the objectives: A plan is efficient if it, when put into action, brings about the achievement of the objectives with the minimum of unsought consequences and with positive gains greater than the costs.
- Planning is a pervasive function of management: Planning is a function performed by all managers, although the character and breadth of planning will vary with their authority and with the nature of policies and plans outlined by their superiors.
- Planning is a highly skilful intellectual activity: It involves active use of higher mental process like thinking, innovation or creativity, etc.
- Planning involves selection among the alternatives: It is a highly selective process in which all the alternatives need to be listed and best alternatives are selected or decided.

ORGANIZING

Organizing is the function of management which follows planning. It is a function in which the synchronization and combination of human, physical and financial resources takes place. All the three resources are important to get results. Therefore, organizational function helps in achievement of results which in fact is important for the functioning of a concern. According to *Chester Barnard*, "Organizing is a function by which the concern is able to define the role positions, the jobs related and the co-ordination between authority and responsibility. Hence, a manager always has to organize in order to get results.

A manager performs organizing function with the help of following steps:

1. Identification of activities - All the activities which have to be performed in a concern have to be identified first. For example, preparation of accounts, making sales, record keeping, quality control, inventory control, etc. All these activities have to be grouped and classified into units.

2. Departmentally organizing the activities - In this step, the manager tries to combine and group similar and related activities into units or departments. This organization of dividing the whole concern into independent units and departments is called departmentation.

3. Classifying the authority - Once the departments are made, the manager likes to classify the powers and its extent to the managers. This activity of giving a rank in order to the managerial positions is called hierarchy. The top management is into formulation of policies, the middle level management into departmental supervision and lower level management into supervision of foremen. The clarifications of authority help in bringing efficiency in the running of a concern. This helps in achieving efficiency in the running of a concern. This helps in avoiding wastage of time, money, effort, in avoidance of duplication or overlapping of efforts and this helps in bringing smoothness in a concern's working.

4. Co-ordination between authority and responsibility - Relationships are established among various groups to enable smooth interaction toward the achievement of the organizational goal. Each individual is made aware of his authority and he/she knows whom they have to take orders from and to whom they are accountable and to whom they have to report. A clear organizational structure is drawn and all the employees are made aware of it.

COORDINATING

Coordination is the function of management which ensures that different departments and groups work in sync. Therefore, there is unity of action among the employees, groups, and departments.

It also brings harmony in carrying out the different tasks and activities to achieve the organization's objectives efficiently. Coordination is an important aspect of any group effort. When an individual is working, there is no need for coordination.

Therefore, we can say that the coordination function is an orderly arrangement of efforts providing unity of action in pursuance of a common goal. In an organization, all the departments must operate a part of a cohesive unit to optimize performance.

Coordination implies synchronization of various efforts of different departments to reduce conflict. Multiple departments usually perform the work for which an organization exists.

Therefore, synchronization between them is essential. Lacking coordination, departments might work in different directions or at different timings, creating chaos.

Features of Co-ordination

Coordination is the integration, unification, synchronization of the efforts of the departments to provide unity of action for pursuing common goals. A force that binds all the other functions of management.

The management of an organization endeavours to achieve optimum coordination through its basic functions of planning, organizing, staffing, directing, and controlling.

Therefore, coordination is not a separate function of management because management is successful only if it can achieve harmony between different employees and departments. Here are some important features of coordination:

- It is relevant for group efforts and not for individual efforts: Coordination involves an orderly pattern of group efforts. In the case of individual efforts, since the performance of the individual does not affect the functioning of others, the need for coordination does not arise.
- It is a continuous and dynamic process: Continuous because it is achieved through the performance of different functions. Also, it is dynamic since functions can change according to the stage of work.
- Most organizations have some sort of coordination in place: However, the management can always make special efforts to improve it.
- Coordination emphasizes the unity of efforts: This involves fixing the time and manner in which the various functions are performed in the organization. This allows individuals to integrate with the overall process.
- A higher degree of coordination happens when the degree of integration in the performance of various functions increases.
- It is the responsibility of every manager in the organization: In fact, this is integral to the role of a manager because he synchronizes the efforts of his subordinates with others.

COMMANDING

Employees will know what is expected out of them when working instructions and orders are clear. All the employees will optimize returns when concrete instructions are given with respect to activities carried out by them. Successful managers possess integrity, communicate clearly, and make their decisions based on regular audits. They have the potential to encourage employees to take initiatives or even motivate a team.

Commanding encompasses instructing your team making sure that the team is motivated to complete its task.

Various Aspects of Commanding:

- Understanding and knowing your team members.
- Dealing smartly with incompetency among the teams.
- Being completely aware of the agreements between the organization and the employees; like- being cognizant of employee contracts and human resource policies.
- Leading by example.
- Working together with other managers to achieve common and corporate goals.

CONTROLLING

Controlling consists of verifying whether everything occurs in conformities with the plans adopted, instructions issued and principles established. Controlling ensures that there is effective and efficient utilization of organizational resources so as to achieve the planned goals. Controlling measures the deviation of actual performance from the standard performance, discovers the causes of such deviations and helps in taking corrective actions.

According to Brech, "Controlling is a systematic exercise which is called as a process of checking actual performance against the standards or plans with a view to ensure adequate progress and also recording such experience as is gained as a contribution to possible future needs".

According to Donnell, "Just as a navigator continually takes reading to ensure whether he is relative to a planned action, so should a business manager continually take reading to assure himself that his enterprise is on right course".

Controlling has got two basic purposes:

1. It facilitates co-ordination.
2. It helps in planning.

Features of Controlling Function

Following are the characteristics of controlling function of management:

1. Controlling is an end function- A function which comes once the performances are made in conformities with plans.
2. Controlling is a pervasive function- Which means it is performed by managers at all levels and in all type of concerns.
3. Controlling is forward looking- Because effective control is not possible without past being controlled. Controlling always look to future so that follow-up can be made whenever required.
4. Controlling is a dynamic process- Since controlling requires taking reviewed methods, changes have to be made wherever possible.
5. Controlling is related with planning- Planning and Controlling are two inseparable functions of management. Without planning, controlling is a meaningless exercise and without controlling, planning is useless. Planning presupposes controlling and controlling succeeds planning.

References

- Planning-definition-and-its-features, management-concepts: mbaknol.com, Retrieved 15 May, 2019
- Organizing-function: managementstudyguide.com, Retrieved 09 April, 2019
- Concept-and-features-of-coordination, direction-and-coordination, business-management-and-entrepreneurship: toppr.com, Retrieved 24 August, 2019
- Henri-fayols-functions-of-management: studiousguy.com, Retrieved 18 May, 2019
- Controlling-function: managementstudyguide.com, Retrieved 30 February, 2019

5

Branches of Business Management

The set of activities associated with running a company is known as business management. Some of the branches of business management are human resource management, financial management and marketing management. This chapter discusses in detail the theories and concepts related to these branches of business management.

BUSINESS AND INFORMATION TECHNOLOGY

With more innovation in technology, new businesses are created. With more business, technology comes to the rescue by making things easier. The two exist in something of a symbiotic relationship that ensures they will always coexist.

Business has been around since prehistoric times. It may have begun with nothing more than barter trade, if the history books are to be believed, but it has since morphed into something far more complex, and none of that would have been possible without technology. The major industries of the world would collapse, if the existence and use of information technology were to be snatched suddenly from businesses. That's because most business transactions and operations cannot be conducted in the 21st century without technology.

Need of Technology in Business

Over the years, technology has caused an explosion in commerce and trade. Because of technology, many traditional business models and concepts were revolutionized. Technology gave us the opportunity to see things from a new perspective, and to approach what we were already doing from a new perspective. Technology also gave us greater efficiency for conducting business.

Some of the areas in which technology is crucial to business include point of sales systems, the use of ICT in management, accounting systems, and other complex aspects of everyday business activities. Even something as simple as the calculator, which was revolutionary in its time, came about because of technology. It is tough to imagine going back to performing tasks manually. It would take us back about 100 or so years.

Technology as a Source of Support and Security

Technology enables us to automate numerous processes, which thereby increases our productivity. This is possible because it enables us to use fewer resources, thereby enabling us to improve on quality at a low cost and to improve the speed with which we can deliver to customers. In the process, it has become possible to serve even more clients.

Technology also makes it easy to store more information while maintaining the integrity of that information. We are better able to store sensitive and confidential information in a way that makes it less vulnerable to a data breach. The information can be retrieved instantly when needed, and it can be analyzed not only to study past trends but also to forecast the future. In turn, this can help with the decision-making process.

Technology as a Link to the World

Communication is a part of business. So, transportation and processes make business a web of complicated processes that interplay with each other. With technology, it has been possible to globalize business operations. Now, just about anyone can do business practically anywhere, from any room in their house.

Technology has made it possible for businesses to have a wider reach in the world. The best example of this is the internet and the World Wide Web. The internet is now a crucial part of any businesses' marketing campaign, as it enables the business to attract customers world-wide.

Technology, when well-integrated with business, has made life itself worth living. It would be foolish to deny, however, that there are also threats to business brought about by technology. These include malicious activities by activities and organizations, such as hacking. Because of this, it is important for businesses to exercise responsibility when using technology to conduct business. With the good that technology brings, there is some bad that must also be dealt with. All the same, it is something that's worth all of the baggage, and we must acknowledge and responsibly utilize it to make our businesses better.

Impact of Information Technology in Business

The Industrial Revolution changed things in the business world, making a lot of processes more efficient and increasing productivity a hundred-fold. However, the business world remained somewhat stagnant for a century after. With the technological revolution, and the use of technology in business, however, things changed even more disruptively than during the Industrial Revolution and it would be safe to say that things will never be the same again. The rate at which technology is evolving and adapting is exponential to the point where all businesses are being swept by the wave, whether they are ready for it or not. It might not seem like we've made that much progress, but even just 5 years ago, social media did not have any consumerism, mobile phones weren't used for business, cloud-based solutions did not exist, the App Generation was not born yet, and omni-channel marketing was taking its baby steps.

Technology has just about changed every aspect of business in a big way and this has never happened this fast before in history. To be more specific, here are a few ways in which information technology has affected business.

Advent of Mobile Solutions

Mobility is seen by many as the next great frontier for businesses. Google's algorithms reflect this, as they make mobile websites a priority. Your business and every aspect of it can be handled, using nothing more than a tablet or smartphone. From content marketing to customer relations, to sales, the back-end stuff like invoicing and shipping, all of that power is in your hands.

But mobile solutions aren't just about businesses; they are also about consumers. The millennial generation uses their phones to do everything from buying and selling to sharing their experiences with their friends and finding local businesses.

Phenomenon of Cloud Computing

Cloud computing has made it possible for businesses to outsource many of their functions to third parties using the internet. It makes it possible for variable data packages to be handled but also makes it possible for businesses to expand rapidly and embrace mobility without having to worry about such things as crashes, downtime, and lost data. This has enabled small and medium-sized businesses to gain access to resources that would have cost them a fortune only a few years ago. In effect, the playing field has been leveled.

Increased Customer Segmentation

Since more and more data is flowing, it is now much easier to analyze and gain deep insight into the things that customers are looking for. Analytics services are expanding by the day and are allowing businesses to segment their prospects into more and more specific groups, making it much easier to target them and get more value for their advertising money. Something as simple as having a Google account can let a business know where a user is from, the kind of browser they're using, how they stumbled upon a website, What they do on that website, how long they are likely to stay and at what point they decide to leave. There are even more advanced analytics services that allow businesses to become even more refined with this segmentation in order to improve their conversions drastically.

Increased Connectivity

Technology has made it easier for people to stay in touch. Whether you're looking to communicate with your employees and colleagues via video chat or sending email blasts to leads, mobile technology and the constant innovation that takes place within the space has made it possible for communication to take on a new level of hyper-realism.

Decreasing Costs and Increasing Utility

There are two main things that have come together to make what is called a "buyer's market" possible. These are the fact that both hardware and software that are needed in creating the necessary software solutions have become more affordable and the fact that more and more entrepreneurs who are also tech-savvy are appearing by the day to make use of these technologies. There was a time when it would take a large company about a year to build a back-end inventory system. Now it takes a few college graduates a matter of weeks to build the same thing. Since the solutions are offered affordably and very easy to use, businesses do not have to invest too much money into them and that has made business easier.

A Changing Consumer Base

Millennial have come of age and they are now the force driving the modern economy. Pretty soon, over half the American workforce will consist of millennial and pretty soon they will also be coming into their peak affluence, where they will have a lot of money to spend and very few financial obligations, give them a lot of disposable income. They are greater in number than the baby boomers and are a lot more liberal with their wallets. They are also all about instant gratification. They have also been raised with the internet. They are connected, tech-savvy, and ready to spend. Businesses have to adapt to this new customer base if they are going to thrive.

Greater Consideration for the Social Impact of Business

You can't just assume your business operates in a vacuum anymore. Social networking has made the world a smaller place where users can connect regardless of who they are, where they're from, and how wealthy they are. Only a few years ago you could have gotten by if your customer service was just okay. Now you have to put in the extra effort if you don't want unfavourable ratings on review sites and people going on rants on social media about your service. Businesses, therefore, need to be careful about their online reputation and need to work on their digital footprint.

The End of Downtime

This is actually a negative effect of technology. With increased connectivity, individuals have less and less time to themselves now. Vacation seems to have all but become a thing of the past, with most people working even when they're on vacation. Since we can always access our emails, texts, and social media through our phones and laptops, it is harder and harder to just disconnect and wind down.

Significance of Information Technology to an Organization

It might be a little difficult to fathom the importance of information technology to an organization if you're not an IT professional. However, there are numerous ways in which information technology is crucial to an organization.

Business

The business world changed forever when computers were introduced onto the scene. Businesses can utilize information technology through the use of computers and different software to run their operations in a smoother fashion. They use it in different departments, including finance, manufacturing, human resources, and security.

Education

Education is one of the frontiers of technology and is growing with technology every day. It's important that education be able to keep up with the progress happening in technology by reaching students in a way that adequately helps them to prepare for the future. The students in our classrooms today are meant to be the thought leaders, business people, teachers, and investors of tomorrow, so technology should be used to prepare them. This includes the use of gadgets in teaching, such as computers, mobile phones, and tablets, as well as the use of the internet as a medium of learning.

Finance

With an increasing number of transactions happening online, it is important that financial and security institutions work together to make the internet a safe place. As more transactions are done on the internet, there will be a need for more networks and greater security, making it possible for banks to keep purchases and sales secure.

Health

With improvements in information technology, it is becoming easier to reform the health sector. Medical offices are now able to share medical information with each other, and they can get your health data from your previous doctors. This makes it possible for timely care to be delivered, as well as for costs to be reduced.

Security

With an increasing number of transactions being done online, there is an ever-increasing need for safety. Information technology is what makes it possible to keep your data and information safe and only accessible by you. Through the use of encryption and passwords, your digital data is safely hidden away and can only be accessed by those who have your permission.

HUMAN RESOURCE MANAGEMENT

Human resource management (HRM or HR) is the strategic approach to the effective management of people in a company or organization such that they help their business gain a competitive advantage. It is designed to maximize employee performance in service of an employer's strategic objectives. Human resource management is primarily concerned with the management of people within organizations, focusing on policies and systems. HR departments are responsible for overseeing employee-benefits design, employee recruitment, training and development, performance appraisal, and reward management, such as managing pay and benefit systems. HR also concerns itself with organizational change and industrial relations, or the balancing of organizational practices with requirements arising from collective bargaining and governmental laws.

The overall purpose of human resources (HR) is to ensure that the organization is able to achieve success through people. HR professionals manage the human capital of an organization and focus on implementing policies and processes. They can specialize in finding, recruiting, training, and developing employees, as well as maintaining employee relations or benefits. Training and development professionals ensure that employees are trained and have continuous development. This is done through training programs, performance evaluations, and reward programs. Employee relations deal with the concerns of employees when policies are broken, such as cases involving harassment or discrimination. Managing employee benefits includes developing compensation structures, parental leave programs, discounts, and other benefits for employees. On the other side of the field are HR generalists or business partners. These HR professionals could work in all areas or be labor relations representatives working with unionized employees.

HR is a product of the human relations movement of the early 20th Century, when researchers began documenting ways of creating business value through the strategic management of the workforce. It was initially dominated by transactional work, such as payroll and benefits administration, but due to globalization, company consolidation, technological advances, and further research, HR as of 2015 focuses on strategic initiatives like mergers and acquisitions, talent management, succession planning, industrial and labor relations, and diversity and inclusion. In the current global work environment, most companies focus on lowering employee turnover and on retaining the talent and knowledge held by their workforce. New hiring not only entails a high cost but also increases the risk of a new employee not being able to adequately replace the position of the previous employee. HR departments strive to offer benefits that will appeal to workers, thus reducing the risk of losing employee commitment and psychological ownership.

Antecedent Theoretical Developments

The Human Resources field began to take shape in 18th century Europe. It built on a simple idea by Robert Owen and Charles Babbage during the industrial revolution.

These men concluded that people were crucial to the success of an organization. They expressed the thought that the well-being of employees led to perfect work; without healthy workers, the organization would not survive.

HR emerged as a specific field in the early 20th century, influenced by Frederick Winslow Taylor. Taylor explored what he termed "scientific management" (sometimes referred to as "Taylorism"), striving to improve economic efficiency in manufacturing jobs. He eventually focused on one of the principal inputs into the manufacturing process—labor—sparking inquiry into workforce productivity.

Meanwhile, in England, C S Myers, inspired by unexpected problems among soldiers which had alarmed generals and politicians in the First World War of 1914-1918, co-founded the National Institute of Industrial Psychology (NIIP) in 1921. In doing so, he set seeds for the human relations movement. This movement, on both sides of the Atlantic, built on the research of Elton Mayo and others to document through the Hawthorne studies and other studies how stimuli, unrelated to financial compensation and working conditions, could yield more productive workers. Work by Abraham Maslow , Kurt Lewin, Max Weber, Frederick Herzberg, and David McClelland, forming the basis for studies in industrial and organizational psychology, organizational behavior and organizational theory, was interpreted in such a way as to further claims of legitimacy for an applied discipline.

Birth and Development of the Discipline

By the time enough theoretical evidence existed to make a business case for strategic workforce management, changes in the business landscape (à la Andrew Carnegie, John Rockefeller) and in public policy (à la Sidney and Beatrice Webb, Franklin D. Roosevelt and the New Deal) had transformed the employer-employee relationship, and the discipline became formalized as "industrial and labor relations". In 1913 one of the oldest known professional HR associations—the Chartered Institute of Personnel and Development (CIPD)—started in England as the Welfare Workers' Association; it changed its name a decade later to the Institute of Industrial Welfare Workers, and again the next decade to Institute of Labour Management before settling upon its current name in 2000. Likewise in the United States, the world's first institution of higher education dedicated to workplace studies—the School of Industrial and Labor Relations—formed at Cornell University in 1945. In 1948 what would later become the largest professional HR association—the Society for Human Resource Management (SHRM)—formed as the American Society for Personnel Administration (ASPA).

In the Soviet Union, meanwhile, Stalin's use of patronage exercised through the "HR Department" equivalent in the Bolshevik Party, its Orgburo, demonstrated the effectiveness and influence of human-resource policies and practices, and Stalin himself acknowledged the importance of the human resource, such as in his mass deployment of it in the Gulag system.

During the latter half of the 20th century, union membership declined significantly, while workforce management continued to expand its influence within organizations. In the US, the phrase "industrial and labor relations" came into use to refer specifically to issues concerning collective representation, and many companies began referring to the proto-HR profession as "personnel administration". Many current HR practices originated with the needs of companies in the 1950s to develop and retain talent.

In the late 20th century, advances in transportation and communications greatly facilitated workforce mobility and collaboration. Corporations began viewing employees as assets. "Human resources management" consequently, became the dominant term for the function—the ASPA even changing its name to the Society for Human Resource Management (SHRM) in 1998.

"Human capital management" (HCM) is sometimes used synonymously with "HR", although "human capital" typically refers to a more narrow view of human resources; i.e., the knowledge the individuals embody and can contribute to an organization. Likewise, other terms sometimes used to describe the field include "organizational management", "manpower management", "talent management", "personnel management", and simply "people management".

Business Function

Dave Ulrich lists the functions of HR as: Aligning HR and business strategy, re-engineering organization processes, listening and responding to employees, and managing transformation and change.

At the macro-level, HR is in charge of overseeing organizational leadership and culture. HR also ensures compliance with employment and labor laws, which differ by geography, and often oversees health, safety, and security. Based on the geographic location, there are various laws in place. There are several federal laws that are crucial for HR managers to be familiar with in order to protect both their company and its employees. Important federal laws and regulations include The Fair Labor Standards Act, which includes establishing a minimum wage and protecting the right for certain workers to earn overtime. The Federal Civil Rights Law protects against discrimination and prohibits making any hiring or firing decision based on race, age, sex, and gender. The Family and Medical Leave Act gives eligible employees up to twelve weeks of unpaid leave for family and medical reasons. Ensuring the company is compliant with all laws and regulations is an important aspect of HR and will protect the company from any sort of 'legal liability'. In circumstances where employees desire and are legally authorized to hold a collective bargaining agreement, HR will typically also serve as the company's primary liaison with the employee's representatives (usually a labor union). Consequently, HR, usually through representatives, engages in lobbying efforts with governmental agencies (e.g., in the United States, the United States Department of Labor and the National Labor Relations Board) to further its priorities.

Human Resource Management has four basic functions: staffing, training and development, motivation, and maintenance. Staffing is the recruitment and selection of potential employees, done through interviewing, applications, networking, etc. There are two main factors to staffing: attracting talented recruits and hiring resources. HR Managers must create detailed recruitment strategies and have a plan of action to put forward when recruiting. Next, managers can put strategies into place through hiring resources, by extending out to find the best possible recruits for the team. Recruiting is very competitive since every company wants the best candidates. Using tactics such as mass media can grab the attention of prospective recruits. Training and development is the next step and involves a continuous process of training and developing competent and adapted employees. Here, motivation is seen as key to keeping employees highly productive. This includes employee benefits, performance appraisals, and rewards. Employee benefits, appraisals, and rewards are all encouragements to bring forward the best employees. The last function, maintenance, involves keeping the employees' commitment and loyalty to the organization. Some businesses globalize and form more diverse teams. HR departments have the role of making sure that these teams can function and that people can communicate across cultures and across borders. The discipline may also engage in mobility management, especially for expatriates; and it is frequently involved in the merger and acquisition process. HR is generally viewed as a support function to the business, helping to minimize costs and reduce risk.

In startup companies, trained professionals may perform HR duties. In larger companies, an entire functional group is typically dedicated to the discipline, with staff specializing in various HR tasks and functional leadership engaging in strategic decision-making across the business. To train practitioners for the profession, institutions of higher education, professional associations, and companies have established programs of study dedicated explicitly to the duties of the function. Academic and practitioner organizations may produce field-specific publications. HR is also a field of research study that is popular within the fields of management and industrial/organizational psychology.

One of the frequent challenges of HRM is dealing with the notion of unitarism (seeing a company as a cohesive whole, in which both employers and employees should work together for a common good) and securing a long-term partnership of employees and employers with common interests.

Virtual Human Resources

Technology has a significant impact on HR practices. Utilizing technology makes information more accessible within organizations, eliminates time doing administrative tasks, allows businesses to function globally, and cuts costs. Information technology has improved HR practices in the following areas:

E-recruiting

Recruiting has mostly been influenced by information technology. In the past, recruiters relied on printing in publications and word of mouth to fill open positions. HR professionals were not able to post a job in more than one location and did not have access to millions of people, causing the lead time of new hires to be drawn out and tiresome. With the use of e-recruiting tools, HR professionals can post jobs and track applicants for thousands of jobs in various locations all in one place. Interview feedback, background checks and drug tests, and onboarding can all be viewed online. This helps HR professionals keep track of all of their open jobs and applicants in a way that is faster and easier than before. E-recruiting also helps eliminate limitations of geographic location. Jobs can be posted and seen by anyone with internet access. In addition to recruiting portals, HR professionals often have social media presence through websites such as LinkedIn, allowing them to attract employees through the internet. On social media, they can help build the company's brand by posting company news and photos of company events.

Human Resources Information Systems

HR professionals generally handle large amounts of paperwork on a daily basis, ranging from department transfer requests to confidential employee tax forms. Forms must be on file for a considerable period of time. The use of Human Resources Information Systems (HRIS) has made it possible for companies to store and retrieve files in an electronic format for people within the organization to access when needed, thereby eliminating the need for physical files and freeing up space within the office. HRIS also allows for information to be accessed in a timelier manner; files can be accessible within seconds. Having all of the information in one place also allows for professionals to analyze data quickly and across multiple locations because the information is in a centralized location.

Training

Technology allows HR professionals to train new staff members in a more efficient manner. This gives employees the ability to access onboarding and training programs from virtually anywhere. This eliminates the need for trainers to meet new hires face-to-face when completing necessary paperwork for new employees. Training in virtual classrooms makes it possible for HR professionals to train a large number of employees quickly and to assess their progress through computerized testing programs. Some employers choose to incorporate an instructor with virtual training so that new hires are receiving training considered vital to the role. Employees have greater control over their own learning and development; they can engage in training at a time and place of their choosing, which can help them manage their work-life balance. Managers are able to track the training through the internet, which can help to reduce redundancy in training and training costs.

FINANCIAL MANAGEMENT

Finance is a field that is concerned with the allocation (investment) of assets and liabilities over space and time, often under conditions of risk or uncertainty. Finance can also be defined as the art of money management. Participants in the market aim to price assets based on their risk level, fundamental value, and their expected rate of return. Finance can be split into three sub-categories: Public finance, corporate finance and personal finance.

Areas of Finance

Personal Finance

Matters in personal finance revolve around:

- Protection against unforeseen personal events, as well as events in the wider economies.
- Transference of family wealth across generations (bequests and inheritance).
- Effects of tax policies (tax subsidies or penalties) management of personal finances.
- Effects of credit on individual financial standing.
- Development of a savings plan or financing for large purchases (auto, education, home).
- Planning a secure financial future in an environment of economic instability.
- Pursuing a checking and a savings account.
- Preparation for retirement/long term expenses.

Personal finance may involve paying for education, financing durable goods such as real estate and cars, buying insurance, e.g. health and property insurance, investing and saving for retirement.

Personal finance may also involve paying for a loan, or debt obligations. The six key areas of personal financial planning, as suggested by the Financial Planning Standards Board, are:

1. Financial position: It is concerned with understanding the personal resources available by examining net worth and household cash flows. Net worth is a

person's balance sheet, calculated by adding up all assets under that person's control, minus all liabilities of the household, at one point in time. Household cash flows total up all from the expected sources of income within a year, minus all expected expenses within the same year. From this analysis, the financial planner can determine to what degree and in what time the personal goals can be accomplished. Ratios are frequently used on the corporate level to measure a companies ability to cover its cost given the assets it has on hand. This can be paralleled to an individual level as well. Maintaining a ratio of 2:1 or greater is seen as healthy in this respect. This means that for every dollar of expenses there is an existing dollar value of assets such as cash to cover that cost.

2. Adequate protection:The analysis of how to protect a household from unforeseen risks. These risks can be divided into the following: liability, property, death, disability, health and long term care. Some of these risks may be self-insurable, while most will require the purchase of an insurance contract. Determining how much insurance to get, at the most cost effective terms requires knowledge of the market for personal insurance. Business owners, professionals, athletes and entertainers require specialized insurance professionals to adequately protect themselves. Since insurance also enjoys some tax benefits, utilizing insurance investment products may be a critical piece of the overall investment planning.

3. Tax planning: Typically the income tax is the single largest expense in a household. Managing taxes is not a question of if you will pay taxes, but when and how much. Governments give many incentives in the form of tax deductions and credits, which can be used to reduce the lifetime tax burden. Most modern governments use a progressive tax. Typically, as one's income grows, a higher marginal rate of tax must be paid. Understanding how to take advantage of the myriad tax breaks when planning one's personal finances can make a significant impact, which can save you money in the long term.

4. Investment and accumulation goals: Planning how to accumulate enough money – for large purchases and life events – is what most people consider to be financial planning. Major reasons to accumulate assets include purchasing a house or car, starting a business, paying for education expenses, and saving for retirement. Achieving these goals requires projecting what they will cost, and when you need to withdraw funds that will be necessary to be able to achieve these goals. A major risk to the household in achieving their accumulation goal is the rate of price increases over time, or inflation. Using net present value calculators, the financial planner will suggest a combination of asset earmarking and regular savings to be invested in a variety of investments. In order to overcome the rate of inflation, the investment portfolio has to get a higher rate of return, which typically will subject the portfolio to a number of risks. Managing these portfolio risks is most often accomplished using asset allocation, which seeks to diversify investment risk and

opportunity. This asset allocation will prescribe a percentage allocation to be invested in stocks (either preferred stock or common stock), bonds (for example mutual bonds or government bonds, or corporate bonds), cash and alternative investments. The allocation should also take into consideration the personal risk profile of every investor, since risk attitudes vary from person to person.

5. Retirement planning is the process of understanding how much it costs to live at retirement, and coming up with a plan to distribute assets to meet any income shortfall. Methods for retirement plans include taking advantage of government allowed structures to manage tax liability including: individual (IRA) structures, or employer sponsored retirement plans, annuities and life insurance products. Oftentimes this field of personal finance is overlooked as many individuals see this being something in their distant future. However, the sooner you start investing the greater likelihood you have for actually being prepared. Accrual compounding from the prime "work years" can create a significant impact down the road as these earlier donation years will have more time to compound on themselves giving the individual more wiggle room in their future for unexpected unforeseen events. With every additional year of missed contributions, this creates more tension on the individual to contribute a greater sum leading up to the maturity date of what they may have always thought would be their retirement age. In the same respect an individual who is able to attain a healthy amount of wealth at a young age may then be able to invest it into a mutual fund or stocks accordingly depending on how much they believe they will need to maintain their standard of living once retirement arrives. Allocating a portfolio according to your goals is crucial and also needs to be continuously adjusted as your personal needs and desires change. Oftentimes, individuals will allocate 80% of their earnings into stocks while there is still room for error (more time away from retirement) with only 20% being distributed to mutual funds as these are considered more 'steady' streams of investment. As an individual begins to get closer to their retirement, oftentimes they will gradually adjust these allocations to have a greater percentage in their mutual fund section to solidify their gains and only leave 20% to still generate higher returns. This allocation is commonly recommended by financial planners as it allows the individual to build capital in their work years and keep their gains safe in the long run, leaving less room for volatility.

6. Estate planning involves planning for the disposition of one's assets after death. Typically, there is a tax due to the state or federal government at one's death. Avoiding these taxes means that more of one's assets will be distributed to one's heirs. One can leave one's assets to family, friends or charitable groups.

Corporate Finance

Corporate finance deals with the sources of funding and the capital structure of corporations, the actions that managers take to increase the value of the firm to the shareholders, and the tools and analysis used to allocate financial resources. Although it is in principle different from managerial finance which studies the financial management of all firms, rather than corporations alone, the main concepts in the study of corporate finance are applicable to the financial problems of all kinds of firms. Corporate finance generally involves balancing risk and profitability, while attempting to maximize an entity's assets, net incoming cash flow and the value of its stock, and generically entails three primary areas of capital resource allocation. In the first, "capital budgeting", management must choose which "projects" (if any) to undertake. The discipline of capital budgeting may employ standard business valuation techniques or even extend to real options valuation. The second, "sources of capital" relates to how these investments are to be funded: investment capital can be provided through different sources, such as by shareholders, in the form of equity (privately or via an initial public offering), creditors, often in the form of bonds, and the firm's operations (cash flow). Short-term funding or working capital is mostly provided by banks extending a line of credit. The balance between these elements forms the company's capital structure. The third, "the dividend policy", requires management to determine whether any unappropriated profit (excess cash) is to be retained for future investment/operational requirements, or instead to be distributed to shareholders, and if so, in what form. Short term financial management is often termed "working capital management", and relates to cash-, inventory- and debtors management.

Corporate finance also includes within its scope business valuation, stock investing, or investment management. An investment is an acquisition of an asset in the hope that it will maintain or increase its value over time that will in hope give back a higher rate of return when it comes to disbursing dividends. In investment management – in choosing a portfolio – one has to use financial analysis to determine what, how much and when to invest. To do this, a company must:

- Identify relevant objectives and constraints: institution or individual goals, time horizon, risk aversion and tax consideration.
- Identify the appropriate strategy: active versus passive hedging strategy.
- Measure the portfolio performance.

Financial management overlaps with the financial function of the accounting profession. However, financial accounting is the reporting of historical financial information, while financial management is concerned with the allocation of capital resources to increase a firm's value to the shareholders and increase their rate of return on the investments.

Financial risk management, an element of corporate finance, is the practice of creating and protecting economic value in a firm by using financial instruments to manage exposure to risk, particularly credit risk and market risk. (Other risk types include foreign exchange, shape, volatility, sector, liquidity, inflation risks, etc.). It focuses on when and how to hedge using financial instruments; in this sense it overlaps with financial engineering. Similar to general risk management, financial risk management requires identifying its sources, measuring it, and formulating plans to address these, and can be qualitative and quantitative. In the banking sector worldwide, the Basel Accords are generally adopted by internationally active banks for tracking, reporting and exposing operational, credit and market risks.

Financial Services

An entity whose income exceeds its expenditure can lend or invest the excess income to help that excess income produce more income in the future. Though on the other hand, an entity whose income is less than its expenditure can raise capital by borrowing or selling equity claims, decreasing its expenses, or increasing its income. The lender can find a borrower—a financial intermediary such as a bank—or buy notes or bonds (corporate bonds, government bonds, or mutual bonds) in the bond market. The lender receives interest, the borrower pays a higher interest than the lender receives, and the financial intermediary earns the difference for arranging the loan.

A bank aggregates the activities of many borrowers and lenders. A bank accepts deposits from lenders, on which it pays interest. The bank then lends these deposits to borrowers. Banks allow borrowers and lenders, of different sizes, to coordinate their activity.

Finance is used by individuals (personal finance), by governments (public finance), by businesses (corporate finance) and by a wide variety of other organizations such as schools and non-profit organizations. In general, the goals of each of the above activities are achieved through the use of appropriate financial instruments and methodologies, with consideration to their institutional setting.

Finance is one of the most important aspects of business management and includes analysis related to the use and acquisition of funds for the enterprise.

In corporate finance, a company's capital structure is the total mix of financing methods it uses to raise funds. One method is *debt financing*, which includes bank loans and bond sales. Another method is equity financing – the sale of stock by a company to investors, the original shareholders (they own a portion of the business) of a share. Ownership of a share gives the shareholder certain contractual rights and powers, which typically include the right to receive declared dividends and to vote the proxy on important matters (e.g., board elections). The owners of both bonds (either government bonds or corporate bonds) and stock (whether its preferred stock or common stock), may be institutional investors – financial institutions such as investment banks and pension funds or private individuals, called private investors or retail investors.

Public Finance

Public finance describes finance as related to sovereign states and sub-national entities (states/provinces, counties, municipalities, etc.) and related public entities (e.g. school districts) or agencies. It usually encompasses a long-term strategic perspective regarding investment decisions that affect public entities. These long-term strategic periods usually encompass five or more years. Public finance is primarily concerned with:

- Identification of required expenditure of a public sector entity.
- Source(s) of that entity's revenue.
- The budgeting process.
- Debt issuance (municipal bonds) for public works projects.

Central banks, such as the Federal Reserve System banks in the United States and Bank of England in the United Kingdom, are strong players in public finance, acting as lenders of last resort as well as strong influences on monetary and credit conditions in the economy.

Capital

Capital, in the financial sense, is the money that gives the business the power to buy goods to be used in the production of other goods or the offering of a service. (Capital has two types of sources, equity and debt).

The deployment of capital is decided by the budget. This may include the objective of business, targets set, and results in financial terms, e.g., the target set for sale, resulting cost, growth, required investment to achieve the planned sales, and financing source for the investment.

A budget may be long term or short term. Long term budgets have a time horizon of 5–10 years giving a vision to the company; short term is an annual budget which is drawn to control and operate in that particular year.

Budgets will include proposed fixed asset requirements and how these expenditures will be financed. Capital budgets are often adjusted annually (done every year) and should be part of a longer-term Capital Improvements Plan.

A cash budget is also required. The working capital requirements of a business are monitored at all times to ensure that there are sufficient funds available to meet short-term expenses.

The cash budget is basically a detailed plan that shows all expected sources and uses of cash when it comes to spending it appropriately. The cash budget has the following six main sections:

1. Beginning cash balance contains the last period's closing cash balance, in other words, the remaining cash of the last year.

2. Cash collections includes all expected cash receipts (all sources of cash for the period considered, mainly sales).
3. Cash disbursements lists all planned cash outflows for the period such as dividend, excluding interest payments on short-term loans, which appear in the financing section. All expenses that do not affect cash flow are excluded from this list (e.g. depreciation, amortization, etc.)
4. Cash excess or deficiency: A function of the cash needs and cash available. Cash needs are determined by the total cash disbursements plus the minimum cash balance required by company policy. If total cash available is less than cash needs, a deficiency exists.
5. Financing discloses the planned borrowings and repayments of those planned borrowings, including interest.

Financial Theory

Financial Economics

Financial economics is the branch of economics studying the interrelation of financial variables, such as prices, interest rates and shares, as opposed to goods and services. Financial economics concentrates on influences of real economic variables on financial ones, in contrast to pure finance. It centres on managing risk in the context of the financial markets, and the resultant economic and financial models.

It essentially explores how rational investors would apply risk and return to the problem of an investment policy. Here, the twin assumptions of rationality and market efficiency lead to modern portfolio theory (the CAPM), and to the Black–Scholes theory for option valuation; it further studies phenomena and models where these assumptions do not hold, or are extended.

"Financial economics", at least formally, also considers investment under "certainty" (Fisher separation theorem, "theory of investment value", Modigliani–Miller theorem) and hence also contributes to corporate finance theory.

Financial econometrics is the branch of financial economics that uses econometric techniques to parameterize the relationships suggested.

Although they are closely related, the disciplines of economics and finance are distinct. The "economy" is a social institution that organizes a society's production, distribution, and consumption of goods and services, all of which must be financed.

Financial Mathematics

Financial mathematics is a field of applied mathematics, concerned with financial markets. The subject has a close relationship with the discipline of financial economics, which is concerned with much of the underlying theory that is involved in financial mathematics. Generally, mathematical finance will derive, and extend, the mathematical or numerical models suggested by financial economics. In terms of practice, mathematical finance also overlaps heavily with the field of computational finance (also known as financial engineering). Arguably, these are largely synonymous, although the latter focuses on application, while the former focuses on modelling and derivation . The field is largely focused on the modelling of derivatives, although other important subfields include insurance mathematics and quantitative portfolio problems.

Experimental Finance

Experimental finance aims to establish different market settings and environments to observe experimentally and provide a lens through which science can analyze agents' behavior and the resulting characteristics of trading flows, information diffusion and aggregation, price setting mechanisms, and returns processes. Researchers in experimental finance can study to what extent existing financial economics theory makes valid predictions and therefore prove them, and attempt to discover new principles on which such theory can be extended and be applied to future financial decisions. Research may proceed by conducting trading simulations or by establishing and studying the behavior, and the way that these people act or react, of people in artificial competitive market-like settings.

Behavioral Finance

Behavioral finance studies how the psychology of investors or managers affects financial decisions and markets when making a decision that can impact either negatively or positively on one of their areas. Behavioral finance has grown over the last few decades to become central and very important to finance.

Behavioral finance includes such topics as:

1. Empirical studies that demonstrate significant deviations from classical theories.
2. Models of how psychology affects and impacts trading and prices.
3. Forecasting based on these methods.
4. Studies of experimental asset markets and use of models to forecast experiments.

A strand of behavioral finance has been dubbed quantitative behavioral finance, which uses mathematical and statistical methodology to understand behavioral biases in conjunction with valuation. Some of these endeavors has been led by Gunduz Caginalp and collaborators including Vernon Smith, David Porter, Don Balenovich, Vladimira Ilieva, Ahmet Duran. Studies by Jeff Madura, Ray Sturm and others have demonstrated significant behavioral effects in stocks and exchange traded funds. Among other topics, quantitative behavioral finance studies behavioral effects together with the non-classical assumption of the finiteness of assets.

MARKETING MANAGEMENT

Marketing management is the organizational discipline which focuses on the practical application of marketing orientation, techniques and methods inside enterprises and organizations and on the management of a firm's marketing resources and activities.

Structure

Marketing management employs tools from economics and competitive strategy to analyze the industry context in which the firm operates. These include Porter's five forces, analysis of strategic groups of competitors, value chain analysis and others.

In competitor analysis, marketers build detailed profiles of each competitor in the market, focusing on their relative competitive strengths and weaknesses using SWOT analysis. Marketing managers will examine each competitor's cost structure, sources of profits, resources and competencies, competitive positioning and product differentiation, degree of vertical integration, historical responses to industry developments, and other factors.

Marketing management often conduct market research and marketing research to perform marketing analysis. Marketers employ a variety of techniques to conduct market research, but some of the more common include:

- Qualitative marketing research, such as focus groups and various types of interviews.
- Quantitative marketing research, such as statistical surveys.
- Experimental techniques such as test markets.
- Observational techniques such as ethnographic (on-site) observation.

Marketing managers may also design and oversee various environmental scanning and competitive intelligence processes to help identify trends and inform the company's marketing analysis.

Brand Audit

A brand audit is a thorough examination of a brand's current position in an industry compared to its competitors and the examination of its effectiveness. When it comes to brand auditing, six questions should be carefully examined and assessed:

1. How well the business' current brand strategy is working?

2. What the company's established resource strengths and weaknesses are?
3. What its external opportunities and threats are?
4. How competitive the business' prices and costs are?
5. How strong the business' competitive position in comparison to its competitors is?
6. What strategic issues are facing the business?

When a business is conducting a brand audit, the goal is to uncover business' resource strengths, deficiencies, best market opportunities, outside threats, future profitability, and its competitive standing in comparison to existing competitors. A brand audit establishes the strategic elements needed to improve brand position and competitive capabilities within the industry. Once a brand is audited, any business that ends up with a strong financial performance and market position is more likely than not to have a properly conceived and effectively executed brand strategy.

A brand audit examines whether a business' share of the market is increasing, decreasing, or stable. It determines if the company's margin of profit is improving, decreasing, and how much it is in comparison to the profit margin of established competitors. Additionally, a brand audit investigates trends in a business' net profits, the return on existing investments, and its established economic value. It determines whether or not the business' entire financial strength and credit rating is improving or getting worse. This kind of audit also assesses a business' image and reputation with its customers. Furthermore, a brand audit seeks to determine whether or not a business is perceived as an industry leader in technology, offering product or service innovations, along with exceptional customer service, among other relevant issues that customers use to decide on a brand of preference.

A brand audit usually focuses on a business' strengths and resource capabilities because these are the elements that enhance its competitiveness. A business' competitive strengths can exist in several forms. Some of these forms include skilled or pertinent expertise, valuable physical assets, valuable human assets, valuable organizational assets, valuable intangible assets, competitive capabilities, achievements and attributes that position the business into a competitive advantage, and alliances or cooperative ventures.

The basic concept of a brand audit is to determine whether a business' resource strengths are competitive assets or competitive liabilities. This type of audit seeks to ensure that a business maintains a distinctive competence that allows it to build and reinforce its competitive advantage. What's more, a successful brand audit seeks to establish what a business capitalizes on best, its level of expertise, resource strengths, and strongest competitive capabilities, while aiming to identify a business' position and future performance.

Implementation Planning

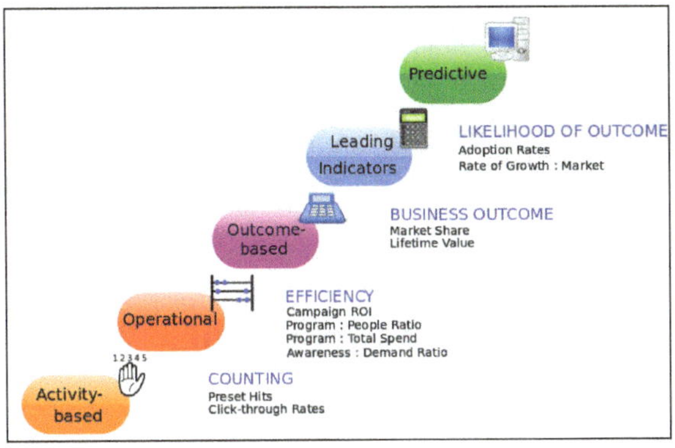

The Marketing Metrics Continuum provides a framework for how to categorize metrics from the tactical to strategic.

If the company has obtained an adequate understanding of the customer base and its own competitive position in the industry, marketing managers are able to make their own key strategic decisions and develop a marketing strategy designed to maximize the revenues and profits of the firm. The selected strategy may aim for any of a variety of specific objectives, including optimizing short-term unit margins, revenue growth, market share, long-term profitability, or other goals.

After the firm's strategic objectives have been identified, the target market selected, and the desired positioning for the company, product or brand has been determined, marketing managers focus on how to best implement the chosen strategy. Traditionally, this has involved implementation planning across the "4 Ps": product management, pricing (at what price slot does a producer position a product, e.g. low, medium or high price), place (the place or area where the products are going to be sold, which could be local, regional, countrywide or international) (i.e. sales and distribution channels), and promotion.

Taken together, the company's implementation choices across the 4 P's are often described as the marketing mix, meaning the mix of elements the business will employ to "go to market" and execute the marketing strategy. The overall goal for the marketing mix is to consistently deliver a compelling value proposition that reinforces the firm's chosen positioning, builds customer loyalty and brand equity among target customers, and achieves the firm's marketing and financial objectives.

In many cases, marketing management will develop a marketing plan to specify how the company will execute the chosen strategy and achieve the business' objectives. The content of marketing plans varies for each firm, but commonly includes:

- An executive summary.
- Situation analysis to summarize facts and insights gained from market research and marketing analysis.

- The company's mission statement or long-term strategic vision.
- A statement of the company's key objectives, often subdivided into marketing objectives and financial objectives.
- The marketing strategy the business has chosen, specifying the target segments to be pursued and the competitive positioning to be achieved.
- Implementation choices for each element of the marketing mix (the 4 P's).

Project, Process and Vendor Management

More broadly, marketing managers work to design and improve the effectiveness of core marketing processes, such as new product development, brand management, marketing communications, and pricing. Marketers may employ the tools of business process reengineering to ensure these processes are properly designed, and use a variety of process management techniques to keep them operating smoothly.

Effective execution may require management of both internal resources and a variety of external vendors and service providers, such as the firm's advertising agency. Marketers may therefore coordinate with the company's Purchasing department on the procurement of these services. Under the area of marketing agency management (i.e. working with external marketing agencies and suppliers) are techniques such as agency performance evaluation, scope of work, incentive compensation, RFx's and storage of agency information in a supplier database.

Reporting, Measurement, Feedback and Control Systems

Marketing management employs a variety of metrics to measure progress against objectives. It is the responsibility of marketing managers to ensure that the execution of marketing programs achieves the desired objectives and does so in a cost-efficient manner.

Marketing management therefore often makes use of various organizational control systems, such as sales forecasts, and sales force and reseller incentive programs, sales force management systems, and customer relationship management tools (CRM). Some software vendors have begun using the term marketing operations management or marketing resource management to describe systems that facilitate an integrated approach for controlling marketing resources. In some cases, these efforts may be linked to various supply chain management systems, such as enterprise resource planning (ERP), material requirements planning (MRP), efficient consumer response (ECR), and inventory management systems.

International Marketing Management

Globalization has led some firms to market beyond the borders of their home countries, making international marketing a part of those firms' marketing strategy. Marketing managers are often responsible for influencing the level, timing, and composition of customer demand. In part, this is because the role of a marketing manager (or sometimes called managing marketer in small- and medium-sized enterprises) can vary significantly based on a business's size, corporate culture, and industry context. For example, in a small- and medium-sized enterprises, the managing marketer may contribute in both managerial and marketing operations roles for the company brands. In a large consumer products company, the marketing manager may act as the overall general manager of his or her assigned product. To create an effective, cost-efficient marketing management strategy, firms must possess a detailed, objective understanding of their own business and the market in which they operate. In analyzing these issues, the discipline of marketing management often overlaps with the related discipline of strategic planning.

Marketing Strategy

Marketing strategy is a long-term, forward-looking approach to planning with the fundamental goal of achieving a sustainable competitive advantage.

Scholars continue to debate the precise meaning of marketing strategy. Consequently, the literature offers many different definitions. On close examination, however, these definitions appear to centre around the notion that strategy refers to a broad statement of what is to be achieved.

Strategic planning involves an analysis of the company's strategic initial situation prior to the formulation, evaluation and selection of market-oriented competitive position that contributes to the company's goals and marketing objectives.

Strategic marketing, as a distinct field of study emerged in the 1970s, and built on strategic management that preceded it. Marketing strategy highlights the role of marketing as a link between the organization and its customers.

- The marketing strategy lays out target markets and the value proposition that will be offered based on an analysis of the best market opportunities.
- An over-riding directional concept that sets out the planned path.
- Essentially a formula for how a business is going to compete, what its goals should be and what policies will be needed to carry out these goals.
- The pattern of major objectives, purposes and goals and essential policies and plans for achieving those goals, stated in such a way as to define what business the company is in or is to be in.
- Strategy is "reserved for actions aimed directly at altering the strengths of the enterprise relative to that of its competitors. Perfect strategies are not called for. What counts is performance relative to competitors.

- Strategy formulation is built on the match between organisational resources and skills and environmental opportunities and risks it faces and the purposes it wishes to accomplish.

Marketing Management vs Marketing Strategy

The distinction between "strategic" and "managerial" marketing is used to distinguish "two phases having different goals and based on different conceptual tools. Strategic marketing concerns the choice of policies aiming at improving the competitive position of the firm, taking account of challenges and opportunities proposed by the competitive environment. On the other hand, managerial marketing is focused on the implementation of specific targets." Marketing strategy is about "lofty visions translated into less lofty and practical goals while marketing management is where we start to get our hands dirty and make plans for things to happen." Marketing strategy is sometimes called higher order planning because it sets out the broad direction and provides guidance and structure for the marketing program.

Strategic Marketing Planning

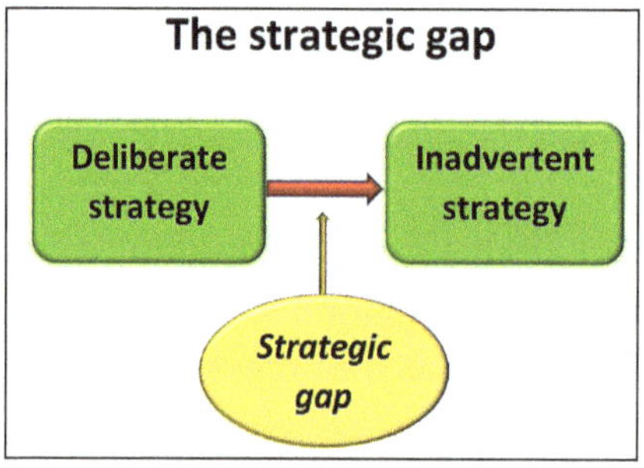

The strategic gap.

Marketing strategy involves mapping out the company's direction for the forthcoming planning period, whether that be three, five or ten years. It involves undertaking a 360° review of the firm and its operating environment with a view to identifying new business opportunities that the firm could potentially leverage for competitive advantage. Strategic planning may also reveal market threats that the firm may need to consider for long-term sustainability. Strategic planning makes no assumptions about the firm continuing to offer the same products to the same customers into the future. Instead, it is concerned with identifying the business opportunities that are likely to be successful and evaluates the firm's capacity to leverage such opportunities. It seeks to identify the strategic gap; that is the difference between where a firm is currently situated (the strategic reality or inadvertent strategy) and where it should be situated for sustainable, long-term growth (the strategic intent or deliberate strategy).

Strategic planning seeks to address three deceptively simple questions, specifically:

- Where are we now? (Situation analysis)?

- What business should we be in? (Vision and mission)?
- How should we get there? (Strategies, plans, goals and objectives)?

A fourth question may be added to the list, namely 'How do we know when we got there?' Due to increasing need for accountability, many marketing organisations use a variety of marketing metrics to track strategic performance, allowing for corrective action to be taken as required. On the surface, strategic planning seeks to address three simple questions, however, the research and analysis involved in strategic planning is very sophisticated and requires a great deal of skill and judgement.

Strategic Analysis: Tools and Techniques

Strategic analysis is designed to address the first strategic question, "Where are we now?" Traditional market research is less useful for strategic marketing because the analyst is not seeking insights about customer attitudes and preferences. Instead strategic analysts are seeking insights about the firm's operating environment with a view to identifying possible future scenarios, opportunities and threats.

Strategic planning focuses on the 3C's, namely: Customer, Corporation and Competitors. A detailed analysis of each factor is key to the success of strategy formulation. The 'competitors' element refers to an analysis of the strengths of the business relative to close rivals, and a consideration of competitive threats that might impinge on the business' ability to move in certain directions. The 'customer' element refers to an analysis of any possible changes in customer preferences that potentially give rise to new business opportunities. The 'corporation' element refers to a detailed analysis of the company's internal capabilities and its readiness to leverage market-based opportunities or its vulnerability to external threats.

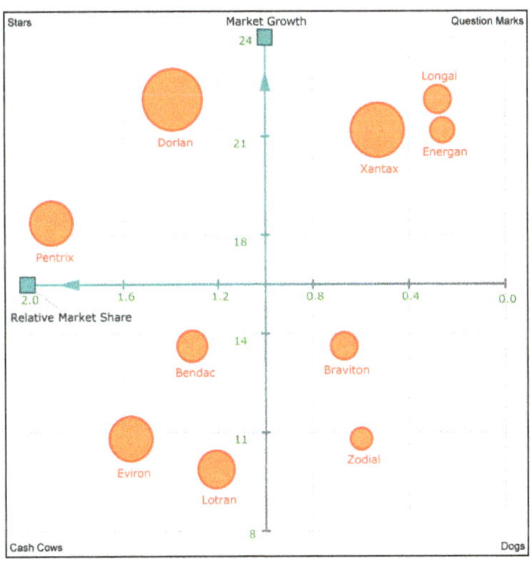

The BCG Matrix is just one of the many analytical techniques used by strategic analysts as a means of evaluating the performance of the firm's current stable of brands.

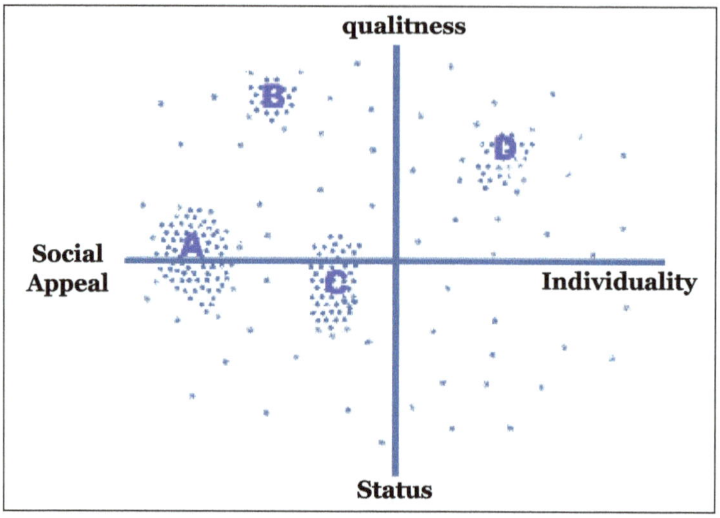

Perceptual mapping assists analysts to evaluate the competitive performance of brands.

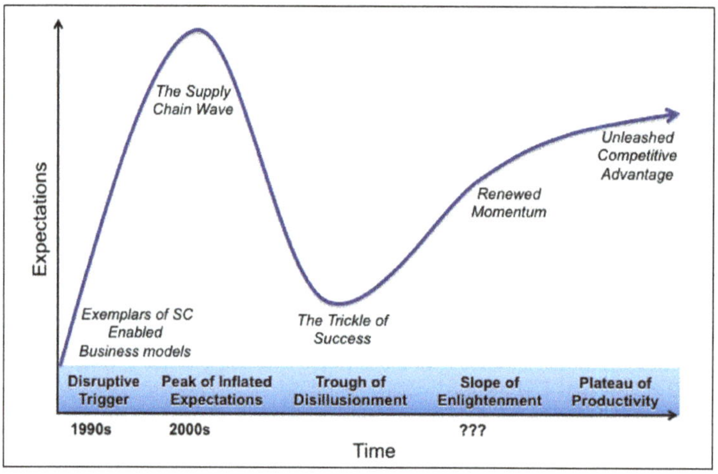

A product evolutionary cycle helps to envision future directions for product development.

Mintzberg suggests that the top planners spend most of their time engaged in analysis and are concerned with industry or competitive analyses as well as internal studies, including the use of computer models to analyze trends in the organization. Strategic planners use a variety of research tools and analytical techniques, depending on the environment complexity and the firm's goals. Fleitcher and Bensoussan, for instance, have identified some 200 qualitative and quantitative analytical techniques regularly used by strategic analysts, while a recent publication suggests that 72 techniques are essential. No optimal technique can be identified as useful across all situations or problems. Determining which technique to use in any given situation rests with the skill of the analyst. The choice of tool depends on a variety of factors including: data availability; the nature of the marketing problem; the objective or purpose, the analyst's skill level as well as other constraints such as time or motivation.

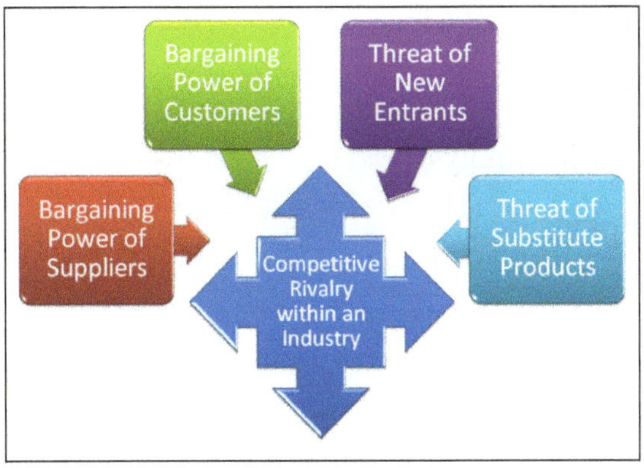

Porter's five forces.

The most commonly used tools and techniques include:

Research Methods

- Environmental scanning
- Marketing intelligence
- Futures research

Analytical Techniques

- Brand Development Index (BDI)/Category development index (CDI)
- Brand/Category penetration
- Benchmarking
- Blindspots analysis
- Functional capability and resource analysis
- Impact analysis
- Demand analysis
- Emerging Issues Analysis
- Experience curve analysis
- Gap analysis
- Impact analysis
- Industry Analysis
- Management profiling

- Market segmentation analysis
- Market share analysis
- Market Segmentation analysis
- Perceptual mapping
- Portfolio analysis
- Precursor Analysis or Evolutionary analysis
- Situation analysis
- Strategic Group Analysis
- SWOT analysis
- Trend Analysis
- Value chain analysis

Gap Analysis

Gap analysis is a type of higher order analysis that seeks to identify the difference between the organisation's current strategy and its desired strategy. This difference is sometimes known as the strategic gap. Mintzberg identifies two types of strategy namely deliberate strategy and inadvertent strategy. The deliberate strategy represents the firm's strategic intent or its desired path while the inadvertent strategy represents the path that the firm may have followed as it adjusted to environmental, competitive and market changes. Other scholars use the terms realized strategy versus intended strategy to refer to the same concepts. This type of analysis indicates whether an organisation has strayed from its desired path during the planning period. The presence of a large gap may indicate the organisation has become stuck in the middle; a recipe for strategic mediocrity and potential failure.

Category or Brand Development Index

The category/brand development index is a method used to assess the sales potential for a region or market and identify market segments that can be developed (i.e. high CDI and high BDI). In addition, it may be used to identify markets where the category or brand is under-performing and may signal underlying marketing problems such as poor distribution (i.e. high CDI and low BDI).

BDI and CDI are calculated as follows:

- BDI = (Brand Sales (%) in Market A/Population (%) in Market A) X 100
- CDI = (Category Sales (%) in Market/Population (%) in Market A) X 100

PEST Analysis

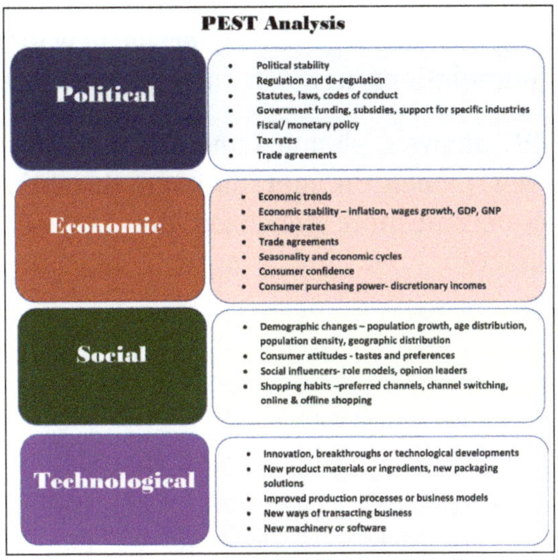

PEST analysis: variables that may be considered in the environmental scan.

Strategic planning typically begins with a scan of the business environment, both internal and external, this includes understanding strategic constraints. An understanding of the external operating environment, including political, economic, social and technological which includes demographic and cultural aspects, is necessary for the identification of business opportunities and threats. This analysis is called PEST; an acronym for Political, Economic, Social and Technological. A number of variants of the PEST analysis can be identified in literature, including: PESTLE analysis (Political, Economic, Social, Technological, Legal and Environmental); STEEPLE (adds ethics); STEEPLED (adds demographics) and STEER (adds regulatory).

The aim of the PEST analysis is to identify opportunities and threats in the wider operating environment. Firms try to leverage opportunities while trying to buffer themselves against potential threats. Basically, the PEST analysis guides strategic decision-making. The main elements of the PEST analysis are:

- Political: Political interventions with the potential to disrupt or enhance trading conditions e.g. government statutes, policies, funding or subsidies, support for specific industries, trade agreements, tax rates and fiscal policy.
- Economic: Economic factors with the potential to affect profitability and the prices that can be charged, such as, economic trends, inflation, exchange rates, seasonality and economic cycles, consumer confidence, consumer purchasing power and discretionary incomes.
- Social: Social factors that affect demand for products and services, consumer attitudes, tastes and preferences like demographics, social influencers, role models, shopping habits.

- Technological: Innovation, technological developments or breakthroughs that create opportunities for new products, improved production processes or new ways of transacting business e.g. new materials, new ingredients, new machinery, new packaging solutions, new software and new intermediaries.

When carrying out a PEST analysis, planners and analysts may consider the operating environment at three levels, namely the supranational; the national and subnational or local level. As businesses become more globalized, they may need to pay greater attention to the supranational level.

SWOT Analysis

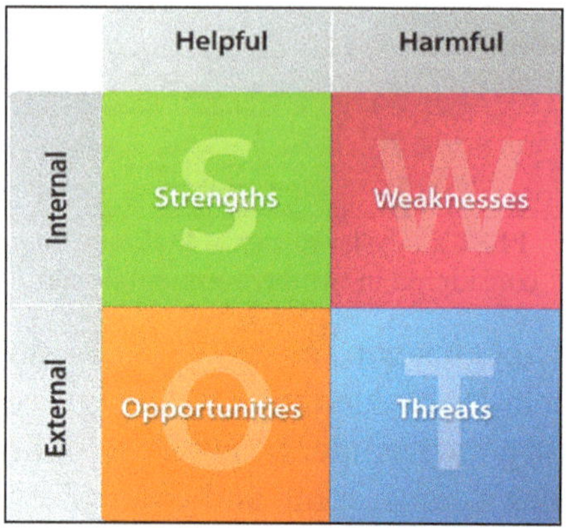

A SWOT analysis, with its four elements in a 2×2 matrix.

In addition to the PEST analysis, firms carry out a Strengths, Weakness, Opportunities and Threats (SWOT) analysis. A SWOT analysis identifies:

- Strengths: Distinctive capabilities, competencies, skills or assets that provide a business or project with an advantage over potential rivals; internal factors that are favourable to achieving company objectives.

- Weaknesses: Internal deficiencies that place the business or project at a disadvantage relative to rivals; or deficiencies that prevent an entity from moving in a new direction or acting on opportunities. internal factors that are unfavourable to achieving company objectives.

- Opportunities: Elements in the environment that the business or project could exploit to its advantage external factors of the organization including: new products, new markets, new demand, foreign market barriers, competitors' mistakes, etc.

- Threats: elements in the environment that could erode the firm's market position; external factors that prevent or hinder an entity from moving in a desired direction or achieving its goals.

Typically the firm will attempt to leverage those opportunities that can be matched with internal strengths; that is to say the firm has a capability in any area where strengths are matched with external opportunities. It may need to build capability if it wishes to leverage opportunities in areas of weakness. An area of weakness that is matched with an external threat represents vulnerability, and the firm may need to develop contingency plans.

Developing the Vision and Mission

The vision and mission address the second central question, 'Where are we going?' At the conclusion of the research and analysis stage, the firm will typically review its vision statement, mission statement and, if necessary, devise a new vision and mission for the outlook period. At this stage, the firm will also devise a generic competitive strategy as the basis for maintaining a sustainable competitive advantage for the forthcoming planning period.

A vision statement is a realistic, long term future scenario for the organisation. (Vision statements should not be confused with slogans or mottos.) A vision statement is designed to present a realistic long-term future scenario for the organisation. It is a "clearly articulated statement of the business scope." A strong vision statement typically includes the following:

- Competitive scope.
- Market scope.
- Geographic scope.
- Vertical scope.

Some scholars point out the market visioning is a skill or competency that encapsulates the planners' capacity "to link advanced technologies to market opportunities of the future, and to do so through a shared understanding of a given product market.

A mission statement is a clear and concise statement of the organisation's reason for being and its scope of operations, while the generic strategy outlines how the company intends to achieve both its vision and mission.

Mission statements should include detailed information and must be more than a simple motherhood statement. A mission statement typically includes the following:

- Specification of target customers.
- Identification of principal products or services offered.
- Specification of the geographic scope of operations.

- Identification of core technologies and core capabilities.
- An outline of the firm's commitment to long-term survival, growth and profitability.
- An outline of the key elements in the company's philosophy and core values.
- Identification of the company's desired public image.

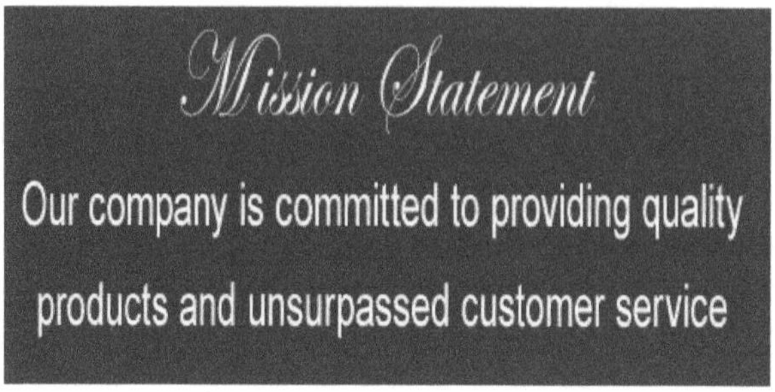

This mission statement might be described as a "motherhood statement" because it lacks sufficient detail to be meaningful.

Developing the Generic Competitive Strategy

The generic competitive strategy outlines the fundamental basis for obtaining a sustainable competitive advantage within a category. Firms can normally trace their competitive position to one of three factors:

- Superior skills (e.g. coordination of individual specialists, created through the interplay of investment in training and professional development, work and learning).
- Superior resources (e.g. patents, trade-mark protection, specialized physical assets and relationships with suppliers and distribution infrastructure).
- Superior position (the products or services offered, the market segments served, and the extent to which the product-market can be isolated from direct competition).

It is essential that the internal analysis provide a frank and open evaluation of the firm's superiority in terms of skills, resources or market position since this will provide the basis for competing over the forthcoming planning period. For this reason, some companies engage external consultants, often advertising or marketing agencies, to provide an independent assessment of the firms capabilities and resources.

Approach to Strategy Formulation

In 1980, Michael Porter developed an approach to strategy formulation that proved to be extremely popular with both scholars and practitioners. The approach became known as the positioning school because of its emphasis on locating a defensible competitive position within an industry or sector. In this approach, strategy formulation consists of three key strands of thinking: analysis of the five forces to determine the sources of competitive advantage; the selection of one of three possible positions which leverage the advantage and the value chain to implement the strategy. In this approach, the strategic choices involve decisions about whether to compete for a share of the total market or for a specific target group (competitive scope) and whether to compete on costs or product differences (competitive advantage). This type of thinking leads to three generic strategies:

- Cost leadership - The firm targets the mass market and attempts to be the lowest cost producer in the market.
- Differentiation - The firm targets the mass market and tries to maintain unique points of product difference perceived as desirable by customers and for which they are prepared to pay premium prices.
- Focus - The firm does not compete head to head, but instead selects a narrow target market and focuses its efforts on satisfying the needs of that segment.

Target Scope	*Advantage*	
	Low cost	Product uniqueness
Broad (Industry Wide)	**Cost Leadership Strategy**	**Differentiation Strategy**
Narrow (Market Segment)	**Focus Strategy** (low cost)	**Focus Strategy** (differentiation)

According to Porter, these strategies are mutually exclusive and the firm must select one approach to the exclusion of all others. Firms that try to be all things to all people can present a confused market position which ultimately leads to below average returns. Any ambiguity about the firm's approach is a recipe for "strategic mediocrity" and any firm that tries to pursue two approaches simultaneously is said to be "stuck in the middle" and destined for failure.

Porter's approach was the dominant paradigm throughout the 1980s. However, the approach has attracted considerable criticism. One important criticism is that it is possible to identify successful companies that pursue a hybrid strategy - such as low cost position and a differentiated position simultaneously. Toyota is a classic example of this hybrid approach. Other scholars point to the simplistic nature of the analysis and the overly prescriptive nature of the strategic choices which limits strategies to just three options. Yet others point to research showing that many practitioners find the approach to be overly theoretical and not applicable to their business.

Resource-based View (RBV)

During the 1990s, the resource-based view (also known as the resource-advantage theory) of the firm became the dominant paradigm. It is an inter-disciplinary approach that represents a substantial shift in thinking. It focuses attention on an organisation's internal resources as a means of organising processes and obtaining a competitive advantage. The resource-based view suggests that organisations must develop unique, firm-specific core competencies that will allow them to outperform competitors by doing things differently and in a superior manner.

Barney stated that for resources to hold potential as sources of sustainable competitive advantage, they should be valuable, rare and imperfectly imitable. A key insight arising from the resource-based view is that not all resources are of equal importance nor possess the potential to become a source of sustainable competitive advantage. The sustainability of any competitive advantage depends on the extent to which resources can be imitated or substituted. Barney and others point out that understanding the causal relationship between the sources of advantage and successful strategies can be very difficult in practice. Barney uses the term "causally ambiguous" which he describes as a situation when "the link between the resources controlled by the firm and the firm's sustained competitive advantage is not understood or understood only very imperfectly". Thus, a great deal of managerial effort must be invested in identifying, understanding and classifying core competencies. In addition, management must invest in organisational learning to develop and maintain key resources and competencies.

Market Based Resources include:

- Organisational culture e.g. market orientation, research orientation, culture of innovation, etc.
- Assets e.g. brands, Mktg IS, databases, etc.
- Capabilities (or competencies) e.g. market sensing, marketing research, relationships, know-how, tacit knowledge, etc.

In the resource-based view, strategists select the strategy or competitive position that best exploits the internal resources and capabilities relative to external opportunities. Given that strategic resources represent a complex network of inter-related assets and capabilities, organisations can adopt many possible competitive positions. Although scholars debate the precise categories of competitive positions that are used, there is general agreement, within the literature, that the resource-based view is much more flexible than Porter's prescriptive approach to strategy formulation.

Hooley et al., suggest the following classification of competitive positions:

- Price positioning.

- Quality positioning.
- Innovation positioning.
- Service positioning.
- Benefit positioning.
- Tailored positioning (one-to-one marketing).

Other Approaches

The choice of competitive strategy often depends on a variety of factors including: the firm's market position relative to rival firms, the stage of the product life cycle. A well-established firm in a mature market will likely have a different strategy than a start-up.

Growth Strategies

Growth of a business is critical for business success. A firm may grow by developing the market or by developing new products. The Ansoff product and market growth matrix illustrates the two broad dimensions for achieving growth. The Ansoff matrix identifies four specific growth strategies: market penetration, product development, market development and diversification.

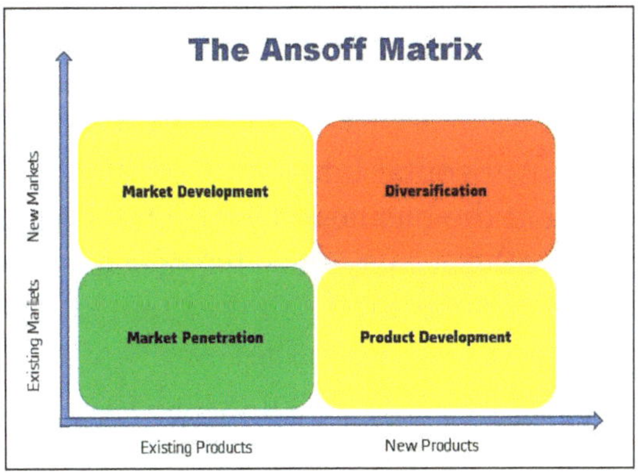

The Ansoff Product/market Growth Matrix.

- Market penetration involves selling existing products to existing consumers. This is a conservative, low risk approach since the product is already on the established market.
- Product development is the introduction of a new product to existing customers. This can include modifications to an already existing market which can create a product that has more appeal.
- Market development involves the selling of existing products to new customers

in order to identify and build a new clientele base. This can include new geographical markets, new distribution channels, and different pricing policies that bring the product price within the competence of new market segments.

- Diversification is the riskiest area for a business. This is where a new product is sold to a new market. There are two type of Diversification; horizontal and vertical. 'Horizontal diversification focuses more on product(s) where the business is knowledgeable, whereas vertical diversification focuses more on the introduction of new product into new markets, where the business could have less knowledge of the new market.

Horizontal Integration

A horizontal integration strategy may be indicated in fast changing work environments as well as providing a broad knowledge base for the business and employees. A benefit of horizontal diversification is that it is an open platform for a business to expand and build away from the already existing market.

High levels of horizontal integration lead to high levels of communication within the business. Another benefit of using this strategy is that it leads to a larger market for merged businesses, and it is easier to build good reputations for a business when using this strategy. A disadvantage of using a diversification strategy is that the benefits could take a while to start showing, which could lead the business to believe that the strategy in ineffective. Another disadvantage or risk is, it has been shown that using the horizontal diversification method has become harmful for stock value, but using the vertical diversification had the best effects.

A disadvantage of using the horizontal integration strategy is that this limits and restricts the field of interest that the business. Horizontal integration can affect a business's reputation, especially after a merge has happened between two or more businesses. There are three main benefits to a business's reputation after a merge. A larger business helps the reputation and increases the severity of the punishment. As well as the merge of information after a merge has happened, this increases the knowledge of the business and marketing area they are focused on. The last benefit is more opportunities for deviation to occur in merged businesses rather than independent businesses.

Vertical Integration

Vertical integration is when business is expanded through the vertical production line on one business. An example of a vertically integrated business could be Apple. Apple owns all their own software, hardware, designs and operating systems instead of relying on other businesses to supply these. By having a highly vertically integrated business this creates different economies therefore creating a positive performance for the business. Vertical integration is seen as a business controlling the inputs of supplies and outputs of products as well as the distribution of the final product. Some benefits of using a Vertical integration strategy is that costs may be reduced because of the reducing transaction costs which include finding, selling, monitoring, contracting and negotiating with other firms. Also by decreasing outside businesses input it will increase the efficient use of inputs into the business. Another benefit of vertical integration is that it improves the exchange of information through the different stages of the production line. Some competitive advantages could include; avoiding foreclosures, improving the business marketing intelligence, and opens up opportunities to create different products for the market. Some disadvantages of using a Vertical Integration Strategy include the internal costs for the business and the need for overhead costs. Also if the business is not well organised and fully equipped and prepared the business will struggle using this strategy. There are also competitive disadvantages as well, which include; creates barriers for the business, and loses access to information from suppliers and distributors.

Market Position and Strategy

In terms of market position, firms may be classified as market leaders, market challengers, market followers or market nichers.

Market position and strategic implications.				
Market Position (Rank by market share)	Strategy	Internal Requirements	Market Share	
			Concentrated market	Fragmented market
Market leader (Top 1 or 2)	Price leader	Simple business model, large capital reserves, growth through acquisitions, superior technology or organization, 'first mover' advantage	20-60%	15-25%
Market challenger (3rd-6th)	Quality leader	Superior R & D, strong market execution capabilities, strong management	15-25%	10-15%
Middle rung (4th-8th)	Customisation/ Personalised service	Organic growth, modest capital, good price, rapid response to market changes, flexible service, loyal customers, not overly R & D oriented	10-15 %	5-8%
Minor player (Below 8th place)	Market nicher (i.e., occupy niche too small or difficult for major competitors)	Rich understanding of a specific market	<10%	< 5%

- Market leader: The market leader dominates the market by objective measure of market share. Their overall posture is defensive because they have more to lose. Their objectives are to reinforce their prominent position through the use of PR to develop corporate image and to block competitors brand for brand, matching distribution through tactics such as the use of "fighting" brands, pre-emptive strikes, use of regulation to block competitors and even to spread rumours about competitors. Market leaders may adopt unconventional or unexpected approaches to building growth and their tactical responses are likely to include: product proliferation; diversification; multi-branding; erecting barriers to entry; vertical and horizontal integration and corporate acquisitions.

- Market challenger: The market challenger holds the second highest market share in the category, following closely behind the dominant player. Their market posture is generally offensive because they have less to lose and more to gain by taking risks. They will compete head to head with the market leader in an effort to grow market share. Their overall strategy is to gain market share through product, packaging and service innovations; new market development and redefinition of the to broaden its scope and their position within it.

- Market follower: Followers are generally content to play second fiddle. They rarely invest in R & D and tend to wait for market leaders to develop innovative products and subsequently adopt a "me-too" approach. Their market posture is typically neutral. Their strategy is to maintain their market position by maintaining existing customers and capturing a fair share of any new segments. They tend to maintain profits by controlling costs.

- Market nicher: The market nicher occupies a small niche in the market in order to avoid head to head competition. Their objective is to build strong ties with the customer base and develop strong loyalty with existing customers. Their market posture is generally neutral. Their strategy is to develop and build the segment and protect it from erosion. Tactically, nichers are likely to improve the product or service offering, leverage cross-selling opportunities, offer value for money and build relationships through superior after sales service, service quality and other related value adding activities.

As the speed of change in the marketing environment quickens, time horizons are becoming shorter. Nevertheless, most firms carry out strategic planning every 3– 5 years and treat the process as a means of checking whether the company is on track to achieve its vision and mission. Ideally, strategies are both dynamic and interactive, partially planned and partially unplanned. Strategies are broad in their scope in order to enable a firm to react to unforeseen developments while trying to keep focused on a specific pathway. A key aspect of marketing strategy is to keep marketing consistent with a company's overarching mission statement.

Strategies often specify how to adjust the marketing mix; firms can use tools such as Marketing Mix Modeling to help them decide how to allocate scarce resources, as well as how to allocate funds across a portfolio of brands. In addition, firms can conduct analyses of performance, customer analysis, competitor analysis, and target market analysis.

Entry Strategies

Marketing strategies may differ depending on the unique situation of the individual business. According to Lieberman and Montgomery, every entrant into a market – whether it is new or not – is classified under a Market Pioneer, Close Follower or a Late follower.

Pioneers

Market pioneers are known to often open a new market to consumers based off a major innovation. They emphasise these product developments, and in a significant number of cases, studies have shown that early entrants – or pioneers – into a market have serious market-share advantages above all those who enter later. Pioneers have the first-mover advantage, and in order to have this advantage, business' must ensure they have at least one or more of three primary sources: Technological Leadership, Preemption of Assets or Buyer Switching Costs. Technological Leadership means gaining an advantage through either Research and Development or the "learning curve". This lets a business use the research and development stage as a key point of selling due to primary research of a new or developed product. Preemption of Assets can help gain an advantage through acquiring scarce assets within a certain market, allowing the first-mover to be able to have control of existing assets rather than those that are created through new technology. Thus allowing pre-existing information to be used and a lower risk when first entering a new market. By being a first entrant, it is easy to avoid higher switching costs compared to later entrants. For example, those who enter later would have to invest more expenditure in order to encourage customers away from early entrants. However, while Market Pioneers may have the "highest probability of engaging in product development" and lower switching costs, to have the first-mover advantage, it can be more expensive due to product innovation being more costly than product imitation. It has been found that while Pioneers in both consumer goods and industrial markets have gained "significant sales advantages", they incur larger disadvantages cost-wise.

Close Followers

Being a Market Pioneer can, more often than not, attract entrepreneurs and investors depending on the benefits of the market. If there is an upside potential and the ability to have a stable market share, many businesses would start to follow in the footsteps of these pioneers. These are more commonly known as Close Followers. These entrants into the market can also be seen as challengers to the Market Pioneers and the Late Followers. This is because early followers are more than likely to invest a significant amount in Product Research and Development than later entrants. By doing this, it allows businesses to find weaknesses in the products produced before, thus leading to improvements and expansion on the aforementioned product. Therefore, it could also lead to customer preference, which is essential in market success. Due to the nature of early followers and the research time being later than Market Pioneers, different development strategies are used as opposed to those who entered the market in the beginning, and the same is applied to those who are Late Followers in the market. By having a different strategy, it allows the followers to create their own unique selling point and perhaps target a different audience in comparison to that of the Market Pioneers. Early following into a market can often be encouraged by an established business' product that is "threatened or has industry-specific supporting assets".

Late Entrants

Those who follow after the Close Followers are known as the Late Entrants. While being a Late Entrant can seem very daunting, there are some perks to being a latecomer. For example, Late Entrants have the ability to learn from those who are already in the market or have previously entered. Late Followers have the advantage of learning from their early competitors and improving the benefits or reducing the total costs. This allows them to create a strategy that could essentially mean gaining market share and most importantly, staying in the market. In addition to this, markets evolve, leading to consumers wanting improvements and advancements on products. Late Followers have the advantage of catching the shifts in customer needs and wants towards the products. When bearing in mind customer preference, customer value has a significant influence. Customer value means taking into account the investment of customers as well as the brand or product. It is created through the "perceptions of benefits" and the "total cost of ownership". On the other hand, if the needs and wants of consumers have only slightly altered, Late Followers could have a cost advantage over early entrants due to the use of product imitation. However, if a business is switching markets, this could take the cost advantage away due to the expense of changing markets for the business. Late Entry into a market does not necessarily mean there is a disadvantage when it comes to market share, it depends on how the marketing mix is adopted and the performance of the business. If the marketing mix is not used correctly – despite the entrant time – the business will gain little to no advantages, potentially missing out on a significant opportunity.

- The requirements of individual customer markets are unique, and their purchases sufficient to make viable the design of a new marketing mix for each customer.
- If a company adopts this type of market strategy, a separate marketing mix is to be designed for each customer.
- Specific marketing mixes can be developed to appeal to most of the segments when market segmentation reveals several potential targets.

Developing Marketing Goals and Objectives

Whereas the vision and mission provide the framework, the "goals define targets within the mission, which, when achieved, should move the organization toward the performance of that mission." Goals are broad primary outcomes whereas, objectives are measurable steps taken to achieve a goal or strategy. In strategic planning, it is important for managers to translate the overall strategy into goals and objectives. Goals are designed to inspire action and focus attention on specific desired outcomes. Objectives, on the other hand, are used to measure an organisation's performance on specific dimensions, thereby providing the organisation with feedback on how well it is achieving its goals and strategies.

Managers typically establish objectives using the balanced scorecard approach. This means that objectives do not include desired financial outcomes exclusively, but also specify measures of performance for customers (e.g. satisfaction, loyalty, repeat patronage), internal processes (e.g., employee satisfaction, productivity) and innovation and improvement activities.

After setting the goals marketing strategy or marketing plan should be developed. The marketing strategy plan provides an outline of the specific actions to be taken over time to achieve the objectives. Plans can be extended to cover many years, with sub-plans for each year. Plans usually involve monitoring, to assess progress, and prepare for contingencies if problems arise. Simultaneous such as customer lifetime value models can be used to help marketers conduct "what-if" analyses to forecast what potential scenarios arising from possible actions, and to gauge how specific actions might affect such variables as the revenue-per-customer and the churn rate.

Strategy Typologies

Developing competitive strategy requires significant judgement and is based on a deep understanding of the firm's current situation, its past history and its operating environment. No heuristics have yet been developed to assist strategists choose the optimal strategic direction. Nevertheless, some researchers and scholars have sought to classify broad groups of strategy approaches that might serve as broad frameworks for thinking about suitable choices.

Raymond Miles' Strategy Categories

In 2003, Raymond Miles proposed a detailed scheme using the categories:

- Prospectors: proactively seek to locate and exploit new market opportunities.
- Analyzers: are very innovative in their product-market choices; tend to follow prospectors into new markets; often introduce new or improved product designs.
- Defenders: are relatively cautious in their initiatives; seek to seal off a portion of the market which they can defend against competitive incursions; often market highest quality offerings and position as a quality leader.

- Reactors: tend to vacillate in their responses to environmental changes and are generally the least profitable organisations.

Marketing Warfare

Marketing warfare strategies are competitor-centered strategies drawn from analogies with the field of military science. Warfare strategies were popular in the 1980s, but interest in this approach has waned in the new era of relationship marketing. An increased awareness of the distinctions between business and military cultures also raises questions about the extent to which this type of analogy is useful. In spite of its limitations, the typology of marketing warfare strategies is useful for predicting and understanding competitor responses.

In the 1980s, Kotler and Singh developed a typology of marketing warfare strategies:

- Frontal attack: Where an aggressor goes head to head for the same market segments on an offer by offer, price by price basis; normally used by a market challenger against a more dominant player.
- Flanking attack: Attacking an organisation on its weakest front; used by market challengers.
- Bypass attack: Bypassing the market leader by attacking smaller, more vulnerable target organisations in order to broaden the aggressor's resource base.
- Encirclement attack: Attacking a dominant player on all fronts.
- Guerilla warfare: Sporadic, unexpected attacks using both conventional and unconventional means to attack a rival; normally practiced by smaller players against the market leader.

Relationship between the Marketing Strategy and the Marketing Mix:

Marketing strategy and marketing mix are related elements of a comprehensive marketing plan. While marketing strategy is aligned with setting the direction of a company or product/service line, the marketing mix is majorly tactical in nature and is employed to carry out the overall marketing strategy. The 4P's of the marketing mix (Price, Product, Place and Promotion) represent the tools that marketers can leverage while defining their marketing strategy to create a marketing plan.

OPERATIONS MANAGEMENT

Operations management is an area of management concerned with designing and controlling the process of production and redesigning business operations in the production of goods or services. It involves the responsibility of ensuring that business operations are efficient in terms of using as few resources as needed and effective in terms of meeting customer requirements. Operations management is primarily concerned with planning, organizing and supervising in the contexts of production, manufacturing or the provision of services.

It is concerned with managing an entire production system which is the process that converts inputs (in the forms of raw materials, labor, and energy) into outputs (in the form of goods and services), or delivers a product or services. Operations produce products, manage quality and creates service. Operation management covers sectors like banking systems, hospitals, companies, working with suppliers, customers, and using technology. Operations is one of the major functions in an organization along with supply chains, marketing, finance and human resources. The operations function requires management of both the strategic and day-to-day production of goods and services.

Ford Motor car assembly line.

In managing manufacturing or service operations several types of decisions are made including operations strategy, product design, process design, quality management, capacity, facilities planning, production planning and inventory control. Each of these requires an ability to analyze the current situation and find better solutions to improve the effectiveness and efficiency of manufacturing or service operations.

The history of production and operation systems began around 5000 B.C. when Sumerian priests developed the ancient system of recording inventories, loans, taxes, and business transactions. The next major historical application of operation systems occurred in 4000 B.C. It was during this time that the Egyptians started using planning, organization, and control in large projects such as the construction of the pyramids. By 1100 B.C., labor was being specialized in China; by about 370 B.C., Xenophon described the advantages of dividing the various operations necessary for the production of shoes among different individuals in ancient Greece.

In large cities, on the other hand, inasmuch as many people have demands to make upon each branch of industry, one trade alone, and very often even less than a whole trade, is enough to support a man: one man, for instance, makes shoes for men, and another for women; and there are places even where one man earns a living by only stitching shoes, another by cutting them out, another by sewing the uppers together, while there is another who performs none of these operations but only assembles the parts. It follows, therefore, as a matter of course, that he who devotes himself to a very highly specialized line of work is bound to do it in the best possible manner.

Shoemakers.

In the Middle Ages, kings and queens ruled over large areas of land. Loyal noblemen maintained large sections of the monarch's territory. This hierarchical organization in which people were divided into classes based on social position and wealth became known as the feudal system. In the feudal system, vassals and serfs produced for themselves and people of higher classes by using the ruler's land and resources. Although a large part of labor was employed in agriculture, artisans contributed to economic output and formed guilds. The guild system, operating mainly between 1100 and 1500, consisted of two types: merchant guilds, who bought and sold goods, and craft guilds, which made goods. Although guilds were regulated as to the quality of work performed, the resulting system was rather rigid, shoemakers, for example, were prohibited from tanning hides.

Services were also performed in the Middle Ages by servants. They provided service to the nobility for cooking, cleaning and entertainment. Court jesters were service providers. The medieval army could also be considered a service since they defended the nobility.

The industrial revolution was facilitated by two elements: interchangeability of parts and division of labor. Division of labor has always been a feature from the beginning of civilization, the extent to which the division is carried out varied considerably depending on period and location. Compared to the Middle Ages, the Renaissance and the Age of Discovery were characterized by a greater specialization in labor, one of the characteristics of growing European cities and trade. It was in the late eighteenth century that Eli Whitney popularized the concept of interchangeability of parts when he manufactured 10,000 muskets. Up to this point in the history of manufacturing, each product (e.g. each musket) was considered a special order, meaning that parts of a given musket were fitted only for that particular musket and could not be used in other muskets. Interchangeability of parts allowed the mass production of parts independent of the final products in which they would be used.

In 1883, Frederick Winslow Taylor introduced the stopwatch method for accurately measuring the time to perform each single task of a complicated job. He developed the scientific study of productivity and identifying how to coordinate different tasks to eliminate wasting of time and increase the quality of work. The next generation of scientific study occurred with the development of work sampling and predetermined motion time systems (PMTS). Work sampling is used to measure the random variable associated with the time of each task. PMTS allows the use of standard predetermined tables of the smallest body movements (e.g. turning the left wrist by 90°), and integrating them to predict the time needed to perform a simple task. PMTS has gained substantial importance due to the fact that it can predict work measurements without observing the actual work. The foundation of PMTS was laid out by the research and development of Frank B. and Lillian M. Gilbreth around 1912. The Gilbreths took advantage of taking motion pictures at known time intervals while operators were performing the given task.

Service Industries: At the turn of the twentieth century, the services industries were already developed, but largely fragmented. In 1900 the U.S. service industry consisted of banks, professional services, schools, general stores, railroads and telegraph. Services were largely local in nature (except for railroads and telegraph) and owned by entrepreneurs and families. The U.S. in 1900 had 31% employment in services, 31% in manufacturing and 38% in agriculture.

The idea of the production line has been used multiple times in history prior to Henry Ford: the Venetian Arsenal; Smith's pin manufacturing, in the Wealth of Nations or Brunel's Portsmouth Block Mills. Ransom Olds was the first to manufacture cars using the assembly line system, but Henry Ford developed the first auto assembly system where a car chassis was moved through the assembly line by a conveyor belt while workers added components to it until the car was completed. During World War II, the growth of computing power led to further development of efficient manufacturing methods and the use of advanced mathematical and statistical tools. This was supported by the development of academic programs in industrial and systems engineering disciplines, as well as fields of operations research and management science (as multi-disciplinary fields of problem solving). While systems engineering concentrated on the broad characteristics of the relationships between inputs and outputs of generic systems, operations researchers concentrated on solving specific and focused problems. The synergy of operations research and systems engineering allowed for the realization of solving large scale and complex problems in the modern era. Recently, the development of faster and smaller computers, intelligent systems, and the World Wide Web has opened new opportunities for operations, manufacturing, production, and service systems.

Industrial Revolution

Before the First industrial revolution work was mainly done through two systems: domestic system and craft guilds. In the domestic system merchants took materials to homes where artisans performed the necessary work, craft guilds on the other hand were associations of artisans which passed work from one shop to another, for example: leather was tanned by a tanner, passed to curriers, and finally arrived at shoemakers and saddlers.

The beginning of the industrial revolution is usually associated with 18th century English textile industry, with the invention of flying shuttle by John Kay in 1733, the spinning jenny by James Hargreaves in 1765, the water frame by Richard Arkwright in 1769 and the steam engine by James Watt in 1765. In 1851 at the Crystal Palace Exhibition the term American system of manufacturing was used to describe the new approach that was evolving in the United States of America which was based on two central features: interchangeable parts and extensive use of mechanization to produce them.

Second Industrial Revolution and Post-industrial Society

Henry Ford was 39 years old when he founded the Ford Motor Company in 1903, with $28,000 capital from twelve investors. The model T car was introduced in 1908, however it was not until Ford implemented the assembly line concept, that his vision of making a popular car affordable by every middle-class American citizen would be realized. The first factory in which Henry Ford used the concept of the assembly line was Highland Park, he characterized the system as follows:

- "The thing is to keep everything in motion and take the work to the man and not the man to the work. That is the real principle of our production, and conveyors are only one of many means to an end".

- This became one the central ideas that led to mass production, one of the main elements of the Second Industrial Revolution, along with emergence of the electrical industry and petroleum industry.
- The post-industrial economy was noted in 1973 by Daniel Bell. He stated that the future economy would provide more GDP and employment from services than from manufacturing and have a great effect on society. Since all sectors are highly interconnected, this did not reflect less importance for manufacturing, agriculture, and mining but just a shift in the type of economic activity.

Although productivity benefited considerably from technological inventions and division of labor, the problem of systematic measurement of performances and the calculation of these by the use of formulas remained somewhat unexplored until Frederick Taylor, whose early work focused on developing what he called a "differential piece-rate system" and a series of experiments, measurements and formulas dealing with cutting metals and manual labor. The differential piece-rate system consisted in offering two different pay rates for doing a job: a higher rate for workers with high productivity (efficiency) and who produced high quality goods (effectiveness) and a lower rate for those who fail to achieve the standard. One of the problems Taylor believed could be solved with this system, was the problem of soldiering: Faster workers reducing their production rate to that of the slowest worker. In 1911 Taylor published his "The Principles of Scientific Management", in which he characterized scientific management (also known as Taylorism) as:

1. The development of a true science.
2. The scientific selection of the worker.
3. The scientific education and development of the worker.
4. Intimate friendly cooperation between the management and the workers.

Taylor is also credited for developing stopwatch time study, this combined with Frank and Lillian Gilbreth motion study gave way to time and motion study which is centered on the concepts of standard method and standard time. Frank Gilbreth is also responsible for introducing the flow process chart in 1921. Other contemporaries of Taylor worth remembering are Morris Cooke (rural electrification in the 1920s and implementer of Taylor's principles of scientific management in the Philadelphia's Department of Public Works), Carl Barth (speed-and-feed-calculating slide rules) and Henry Gantt (Gantt chart).

In 1913 Ford Whitman Harris published his "How many parts to make at once" in which he presented the idea of the economic order quantity model. He described the problem as follows:

- "Interest on capital tied up in wages, material and overhead sets a maximum limit to the quantity of parts which can be profitably manufactured at one time; "setup costs" on the job fix the minimum. Experience has shown one manager a way to determine the economical size of lots".

- This paper inspired a large body of mathematical literature focusing on the problem of production planning and inventory control.

In 1924 Walter Shewhart introduced the control chart through a technical memorandum while working at Bell Labs, central to his method was the distinction between common cause and special cause of variation.

In the 1940s methods-time measurement (MTM) was developed by H.B. Maynard, JL Schwab and GJ Stegemerten. MTM was the first of a series of predetermined motion time systems, predetermined in the sense that estimates of time are not determined in loco but are derived from an industry standard. This was explained by its originators in a book they published in 1948 called "Method-Time Measurement".

Up to this point in history, optimization techniques were known for a very long time, from the simple methods employed by F.W.Harris to the more elaborate techniques of the calculus of variations developed by Euler in 1733 or the multipliers employed by Lagrange in 1811, and computers were slowly being developed, first as analog computers by Sir William Thomson and James Thomson moving to the eletromechanical computers of Konrad Zuse. During World War II however, the development of mathematical optimization went through a major boost with the development of the Colossus computer, the first electronic digital computer that was all programmable, and the possibility to computationally solve large linear programming problems, first by Kantorovich in 1939 working for the Soviet government and latter on in 1947 with the simplex method of Dantzig. These methods are known today as belonging to the field of operations research.

From this point on a curious development took place: while in the United States the possibility of applying the computer to business operations led to the development of management software architecture such as MRP and successive modifications, and ever more sophisticated optimization techniques and manufacturing simulation software, in post-war Japan a series of events at Toyota Motor led to the development of the Toyota Production System (TPS) and Lean Manufacturing.

In 1943, in Japan, Taiichi Ohno arrived at Toyota Motor company. Toyota evolved a unique manufacturing system centered on two complementary notions: just in time (produce only what is needed) and autonomation (automation with a human touch). Regarding JIT, Ohno was inspired by American supermarkets: workstations functioned like a supermarket shelf where the customer can get products they need, at the time they need and in the amount needed, the workstation (shelf) is then restocked. Autonomation was developed by Toyoda Sakichi in Toyoda Spinning and Weaving: an automatically activated loom that was also foolproof, that is automatically detected problems. In 1983 J.N Edwards, "MRP and Kanban-American style" in which he described JIT goals in terms of seven zeros: zero defects, zero (excess) lot size, zero setups, zero breakdowns, zero handling, zero lead time and zero surging. This period also marks the spread of Total Quality Management (TQM) in Japan, ideas initially developed by American authors such as Deming, Juran and Armand V. Feigenbaum. TQM is a strategy for implementing and managing quality improvement on an organizational basis, this includes: participation, work culture, customer focus, supplier quality improvement and integration of the quality system with business goals. Schnonberger identified seven fundamentals principles essential to the Japanese approach:

1. Process control: SPC and worker responsibility over quality.
2. Easy able -to-see quality: Boards, gauges, meters, etc. and poka-yoke.
3. Insistence on compliance: “Quality first”.
4. Line stop: Stop the line to correct quality problems.
5. Correcting one’s own errors: Worker fixed a defective part if he produced it.
6. The 100% check: Automated inspection techniques and foolproof machines.
7. Continual improvement: Ideally zero defects.

Meanwhile, in the sixties, a different approach was developed by George W. Plossl and Oliver W. Wight, this approach was continued by Joseph Orlicky as a response to the TOYOTA Manufacturing Program which led to Material Requirements Planning (MRP) at IBM, latter gaining momentum in 1972 when the American Production and Inventory Control Society launched the “MRP Crusade”. One of the key insights of this management system was the distinction between dependent demand and independent demand. Independent demand is demand which originates outside of the production system, therefore not directly controllable, and dependent demand is demand for components of final products, therefore subject to being directly controllable by management through the bill of materials, via product design. Orlicky wrote “Materials Requirement Planning” in 1975, the first hard cover book on the subject. MRP II was developed by Gene Thomas at IBM, and expanded the original MRP software to include additional production functions. Enterprise resource planning (ERP) is the modern software architecture, which addresses, besides production operations, distribution, accounting, human resources and procurement.

Dramatic changes were occurring in the service industries, as well. Beginning in 1955 McDonald’s provided one of the first innovations in service operations. McDonald’s is founded on the idea of the production-line approach to service. This requires a standard and limited menu, an assembly-line type of production process in the back-room, high customer service in the front-room with cleanliness, courtesy and fast service. While modeled after manufacturing in the production of the food in the back-room, the service in the front-room was defined and oriented to the customer. It was the McDonald's operations system of both production and service that made the difference. McDonald's also pioneered the idea of franchising this operation system to rapidly spread the business around the country and later the world.

FedEx in 1971 provided the first overnight delivery of packages in the U.S. This was based on the innovative idea of flying all packages into the single airport in Memphis Tenn by midnight each day, resorting the packages for delivery to destinations and then flying them back out the next morning for delivery to numerous locations. This concept of a fast package delivery system created a whole new industry, and eventually allowed fast delivery of online orders by Amazon and other retailers.

Walmart provided the first example of very low cost retailing through design of their stores and efficient management of their entire supply chain. Starting with a single store in Roger's Arkansas in 1962, Walmart has now become the world's largest company. This was accomplished by adhering to their system of delivering the goods and the service to the customers at the lowest possible cost. The operations system included careful selection of merchandise, low cost sourcing, ownership of transportation, cross-docking, efficient location of stores and friendly home-town service to the customer.

In 1987 the International Organization for Standardization (ISO), recognizing the growing importance of quality, issued the ISO 9000, a family of standards related to quality management systems. There standards apply to both manufacturing and service organizations. There has been some controversy regarding the proper procedures to follow and the amount of paperwork involved, but much of that has improved in current ISO 9000 revisions.

With the coming of the Internet, in 1994 Amazon devised a service system of on-line retailing and distribution. With this innovative system customers were able to search for products they might like to buy, enter the order for the product, pay online, and track delivery of the product to their location, all in two days. This required not only very large computer operations, but dispersed warehouses, and an efficient transportation system. Service to customers including a high merchandise assortment, return services of purchases, and fast delivery is at the forefront of this business. It is the customer being in the system during the production and delivery of the service that distinguishes all services from manufacturing.

Recent trends in the field revolve around concepts such as:

- Business Process Re-engineering (launched by Michael Hammer in 1993): A business management strategy focusing on the analysis and design of workflows and business processes within an organization. BPR seeks to help companies radically restructure their organizations by focusing on the ground-up design of their business processes.
- Lean systems is a systemic method for the elimination of waste ("Muda") within

a manufacturing or service process. Lean also takes into account waste created through overburden ("Muri") and waste created through unevenness in work loads ("Mura").

- Six Sigma (an approach to quality developed at Motorola between 1985-1987): Six Sigma refers to control limits placed at six (6) standard deviations from the mean of a normal distribution, this became very famous after Jack Welch of General Electric launched a company-wide initiative in 1995 to adopt this set of methods to all manufacturing, service and administrative processes. More recently, Six Sigma has included DMAIC (for improving processes) and DFSS (for designing new products and new processes).
- Reconfigurable Manufacturing Systems: A production system designed at the outset for rapid change in its structure, as well as its hardware and software components, in order to quickly adjust its production capacity and functionality within a part family in response to sudden market changes or intrinsic system change.
- Project Production Management: The application of the analytical tools and techniques developed for operations management, as described in Factory Physics to the activities within major capital projects such as encountered in oil & gas and civil infrastructure delivery.

Production Systems

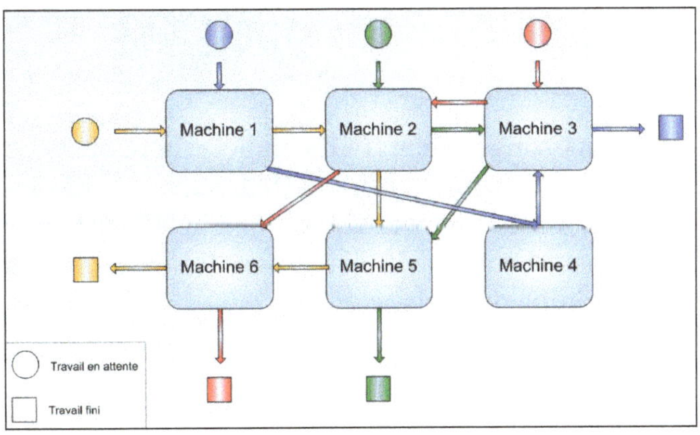

In a job shop machines are grouped by technological similarities regarding transformation processes, therefore a single shop can work very different products. Also notice that in this drawing each shop contains a single machine.

A production system comprises both the technological elements (machines and tools) and organizational behavior (division of labor and information flow). An individual production system is usually analyzed in the literature referring to a single business, therefore it's usually improper to include in a given production system the operations necessary to process goods that are obtained by purchasing or the operations carried by the customer on the sold products, the reason being simply that since businesses need to design their own production systems this then becomes the focus of analysis, modeling and decision making (also called "configuring" a production system).

A first possible distinction in production systems (technological classification) is between continuous process production and discrete part production (manufacturing).

- Process production means that the product undergoes physical-chemical transformations and lacks assembly operations, therefore the original raw materials can't easily be obtained from the final product, examples include: paper, cement, nylon and petroleum products.
- Part production (ex: cars and ovens) comprises both fabrication systems and assembly systems. In the first category we find job shops, manufacturing cells, flexible manufacturing systems and transfer lines, in the assembly category we have fixed position systems, assembly lines and assembly shops (both manual and/or automated operations).

In figure, flexible Manufacturing System: In the middle there are two rails for the shuttle to move pallets between machining centers (there are also FMS which use AGVs), in front of each machining center there is a buffer and in left we have a shelf for storing pallets. Usually in the back there is a similar system for managing the set of tools required for different machining operations.

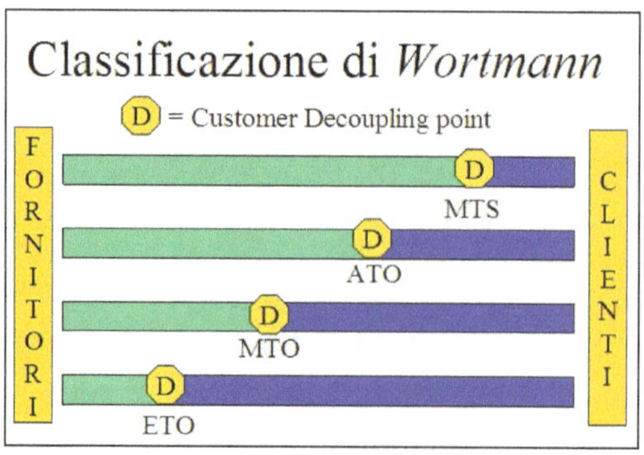

Delivery lead time is the blue bar, manufacturing time is the whole bar, the green bar is the difference between the two.

Another possible classification is one based on Lead Time (manufacturing lead time vs delivery lead time): Engineer to order (ETO), purchase to order (PTO), make to order (MTO), assemble to order (ATO) and make to stock (MTS). According to this classification different kinds of systems will have different customer order decoupling points (CODP), meaning that work in progress (WIP) cycle stock levels are practically nonexistent regarding operations located after the CODP (except for WIP due to queues).

The concept of production systems can be expanded to the service sector world keeping in mind that services have some fundamental differences in respect to material goods: intangibility, client always present during transformation processes, no stocks for "finished goods". Services can be classified according to a service process matrix: degree of labor intensity (volume) vs degree of customization (variety). With a high degree of labor intensity there are Mass Services (e.g., commercial banking bill payments and state schools) and Professional Services (e.g., personal physicians and lawyers), while with a low degree of labor intensity there are Service Factories (e.g., airlines and hotels) and Service Shops (e.g., hospitals and auto mechanics).

The systems described above are ideal types: real systems may present themselves as hybrids of those categories. Consider, for example, that the production of jeans involves initially carding, spinning, dyeing and weaving, then cutting the fabric in different shapes and assembling the parts in pants or jackets by combining the fabric with thread, zippers and buttons, finally finishing and distressing the pants/jackets before being shipped to stores. The beginning can be seen as process production, the middle as part production and the end again as process production: it's unlikely that a single company will keep all the stages of production under a single roof, therefore the problem of vertical integration and outsourcing arises. Most products require, from a supply chain perspective, both process production and part production.

Metrics: Efficiency and Effectiveness

Operations strategy concerns policies and plans of use of the firm productive resources with the aim of supporting long term competitive strategy. Metrics in operations management can be broadly classified into efficiency metrics and effectiveness metrics. Effectiveness metrics involve:

1. Price (actually fixed by marketing, but lower bounded by production cost): purchase price, use costs, maintenance costs, upgrade costs, disposal costs.
2. Quality: specification and compliance.
3. Time: productive lead time, information lead time, punctuality.
4. Flexibility: mix, volume, gamma.

5. Stock availability.
6. Ecological Soundness: biological and environmental impacts of the system under study.

A more recent approach, introduced by Terry Hill, involves distinguishing competitive variables in order winner and order qualifiers when defining operations strategy. Order winners are variables which permit differentiating the company from competitors, while order qualifiers are prerequisites for engaging in a transaction. This view can be seen as a unifying approach between operations management and marketing.

Productivity is a standard efficiency metric for evaluation of production systems, broadly speaking a ratio between outputs and inputs, and can assume many specific forms, for example: machine productivity, workforce productivity, raw material productivity, warehouse productivity (inventory turnover). It is also useful to break up productivity in use U (productive percentage of total time) and yield η (ratio between produced volume and productive time) to better evaluate production systems performances. Cycle times can be modeled through manufacturing engineering if the individual operations are heavily automated, if the manual component is the prevalent one, methods used include: Time and motion study, predetermined motion time systems and work sampling.

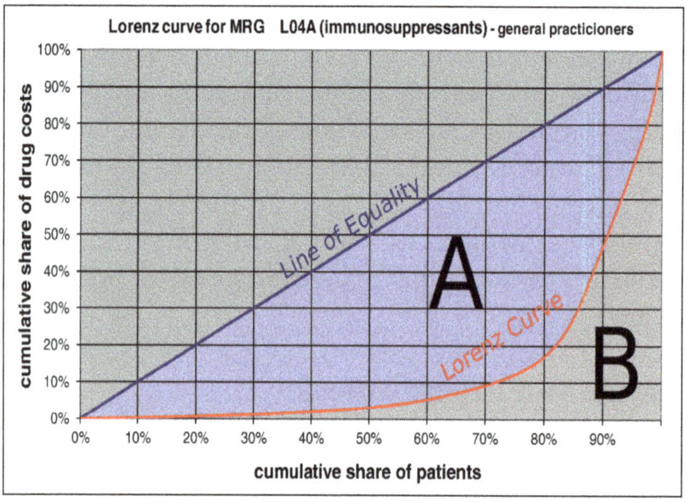

An ABC cumulated curve. Typically one curve is constructed for revenue (consumption) and another for inventory (stock).

ABC analysis is a method for analyzing inventory based on Pareto distribution, it posits that since revenue from items on inventory will be power law distributed then it makes sense to manage items differently based on their position on a revenue-inventory level matrix, 3 classes are constructed (A, B and C) from cumulative item revenues, so in a matrix each item will have a letter (A, B or C) assigned for revenue and inventory. This method posits that items away from the diagonal should be managed differently: items in the upper part are subject to risk of obsolescence, items in the lower part are subject to risk of stockout.

Throughput is a variable which quantifies the number of parts produced in the unit of time. Although estimating throughput for a single process maybe fairly simple, doing so for an entire production system involves an additional difficulty due to the presence of queues which can come from: machine breakdowns, processing time variability, scraps, setups, maintenance time, lack of orders, lack of materials, strikes, bad coordination between resources, mix variability, plus all these inefficiencies tend to compound depending on the nature of the production system. One important example of how system throughput is tied to system design are bottlenecks: in job shops bottlenecks are typically dynamic and dependent on scheduling while on transfer lines it makes sense to speak of "the bottleneck" since it can be univocally associated with a specific station on the line. This leads to the problem of how to define capacity measures, that is an estimation of the maximum output of a given production system, and capacity utilization.

Overall equipment effectiveness (OEE) is defined as the product between system availability, cycle time efficiency and quality rate. OEE is typically used as key performance indicator (KPI) in conjunction with the lean manufacturing approach.

Configuration and Management

Designing the configuration of production systems involves both technological and organizational variables. Choices in production technology involve: dimensioning capacity, fractioning capacity, capacity location, outsourcing processes, process technology, automation of operations, trade-off between volume and variety. Choices in the organizational area involve: defining worker skills and responsibilities, team coordination, worker incentives and information flow.

Regarding production planning, there is a basic distinction between the push approach and the pull approach, with the later including the singular approach of just in time. Pull means that the production system authorizes production based on inventory level; push means that production occurs based on demand (forecasted or present, that is purchase orders). An individual production system can be both push and pull; for example activities before the CODP may work under a pull system, while activities after the CODP may work under a push system.

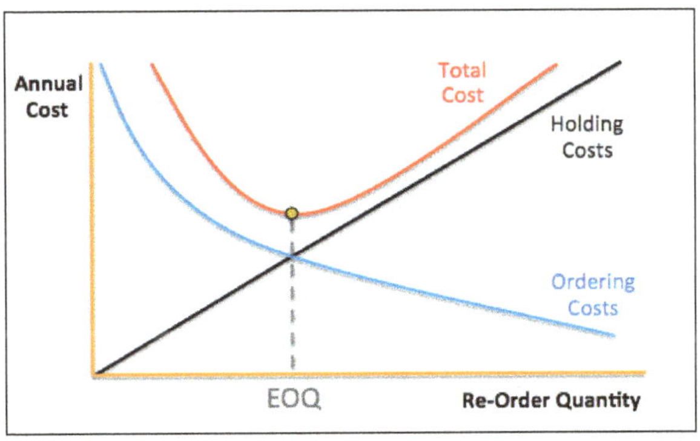

Classic EOQ model

Regarding the traditional pull approach to inventory control, a number of techniques have been developed based on the work of Ford W. Harris, which came to be known as the economic order quantity (EOQ) model. This model marks the beginning of inventory theory, which includes the Wagner-Within procedure, the newsvendor model, base stock model and the Fixed Time Period model. These models usually involve the calculation of cycle stocks and buffer stocks, the latter usually modeled as a function of demand variability. The economic production quantity (EPQ) differs from the EOQ model only in that it assumes a constant fill rate for the part being produced, instead of the instantaneous refilling of the EOQ model.

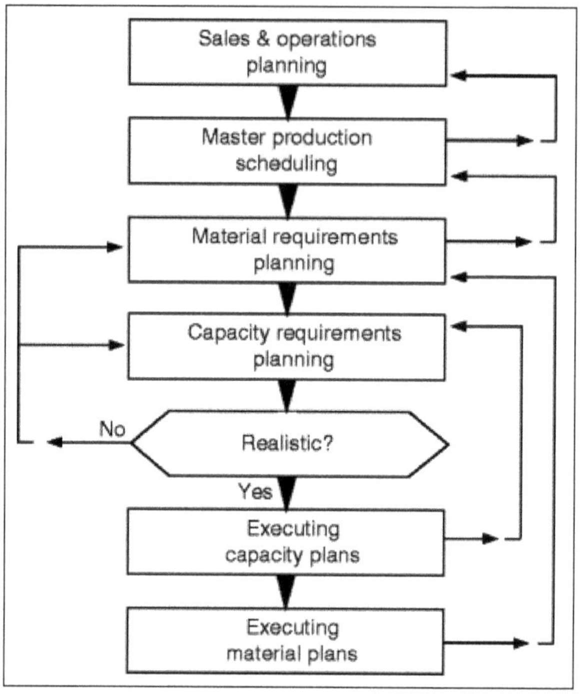

A typical MRPII construct: general planning (top) concerned with forecasts, capacity planning and inventory levels, programming (middle) concerned with calculation of workloads, rough-cut capacity planning, MPS, capacity requirements planning, traditional MRP planning, control (bottom) concerned with scheduling.

Joseph Orlickly and others at IBM developed a push approach to inventory control and production planning, now known as material requirements planning (MRP), which takes as input both the master production schedule (MPS) and the bill of materials (BOM) and gives as output a schedule for the materials (components) needed in the production process. MRP therefore is a planning tool to manage purchase orders and production orders (also called jobs).

The MPS can be seen as a kind of aggregate planning for production coming in two fundamentally opposing varieties: plans which try to chase demand and level plans which try to keep uniform capacity utilization. Many models have been proposed to solve MPS problems:

- Analytical models (e.g. Magee Boodman model).
- Exact optimization algorithmic models (e.g. LP and ILP).
- Heuristic models (e.g. Aucamp model).

MRP can be briefly described as a 3s procedure: sum (different orders), split (in lots), shift (in time according to item lead time). To avoid an "explosion" of data processing in MRP (number of BOMs required in input) planning bills (such as family bills or super bills) can be useful since they allow a rationalization of input data into common codes. MRP had some notorious problems such as infinite capacity and fixed lead times, which influenced successive modifications of the original software architecture in the form of MRP II, enterprise resource planning (ERP) and advanced planning and scheduling (APS).

In this context problems of scheduling (sequencing of production), loading (tools to use), part type selection (parts to work on) and applications of operations research have a significant role to play.

Lean manufacturing is an approach to production which arose in Toyota between the end of World War II and the seventies. It comes mainly from the ideas of Taiichi Ohno and Toyoda Sakichi which are centered on the complementary notions of just in time and autonomation (jidoka), all aimed at reducing waste (usually applied in PDCA style). Some additional elements are also fundamental: production smoothing (Heijunka), capacity buffers, setup reduction, cross-training and plant layout.

- Heijunka: Production smoothing presupposes a level strategy for the MPS and a final assembly schedule developed from the MPS by smoothing aggregate production requirements in smaller time buckets and sequencing final assembly to achieve repetitive manufacturing. If these conditions are met, expected throughput can be equaled to the inverse of takt time. Besides volume, heijunka also means attaining mixed model production, which however may only be feasible through set-up reduction. A standard tool for achieving this is the Heijunka box.
- Capacity buffers: Ideally a JIT system would work with zero breakdowns, this however is very hard to achieve in practice, nonetheless Toyota favors acquiring extra capacity over extra WIP to deal with starvation.
- Set-up reduction: Typically necessary to achieve mixed model production, a key distinction can be made between internal and external setup. Internal setups (e.g. removing a die) refers to tasks when the machine is not working, while external setups can be completed while the machine is running (ex:transporting dies).
- Cross training: Important as an element of Autonomation, Toyota cross trained their employees through rotation, this served as an element of production flexibility, holistic thinking and reducing boredom.

- Layout: U-shaped lines or cells are common in the lean approach since they allow for minimum walking, greater worker efficiency and flexible capacity.

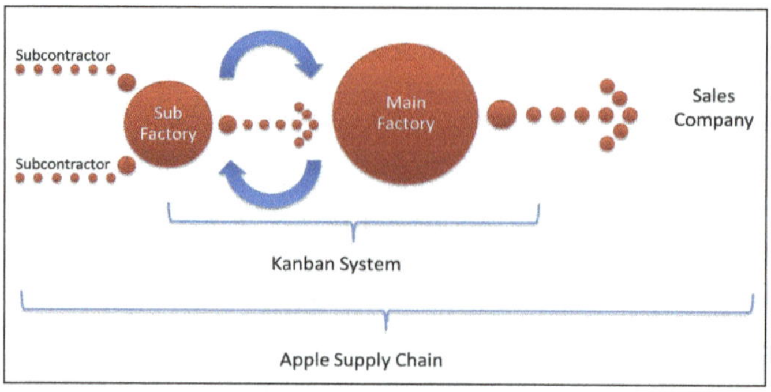

When introducing kanbans in real production systems, attaining unitary lot from the start maybe unfeasible, therefore the kanban will represent a given lot size defined by management.

A series of tools have been developed mainly with the objective of replicating Toyota success: a very common implementation involves small cards known as kanbans; these also come in some varieties: reorder kanbans, alarm kanbans, triangular kanbans, etc. In the classic kanban procedure with one card:

- Parts are kept in containers with their respective kanbans.
- The downstream station moves the kanban to the upstream station and starts producing the part at the downstream station.
- The upstream operator takes the most urgent kanban from his list (compare to queue discipline from queue theory) and produces it and attach its respective kanban.

The two-card kanban procedure differs a bit:

- The downstream operator takes the production kanban from his list.
- If required parts are available he removes the move kanban and places them in another box, otherwise he chooses another production card.
- He produces the part and attach its respective production kanban.
- Periodically a mover picks up the move kanbans in upstream stations and search for the respective parts, when found he exchanges production kanbans for move kanbans and move the parts to downstream stations.

Since the number of kanbans in the production system is set by managers as a constant number, the kanban procedure works as WIP controlling device, which for a given arrival rate, per Little's law, works as a lead time controlling device.

In Toyota the TPS represented more of a philosophy of production than a set of specific lean tools, the latter would include:

- SMED: A method for reducing changeover times.
- Value stream mapping: A graphical method for analyzing the current state and designing a future state.
- Lot-size reduction.
- Elimination of time batching.
- Rank order clustering: An algorithm which groups machines and product families together, used for designing manufacturing cells.
- Single-point scheduling, the opposite of the traditional push approach.
- Multi-process handling: When one operator is responsible for operating several machines or processes.
- Poka-yoke: Any mechanism in lean manufacturing that helps an equipment operator avoid (*yokeru*) mistakes (*poka*).
- 5S: Describes how to organize a work space for efficiency and effectiveness by identifying and storing the items used, maintaining the area and items, and sustaining the new order.
- Backflush accounting: A product costing approach in which costing is delayed until goods are finished.

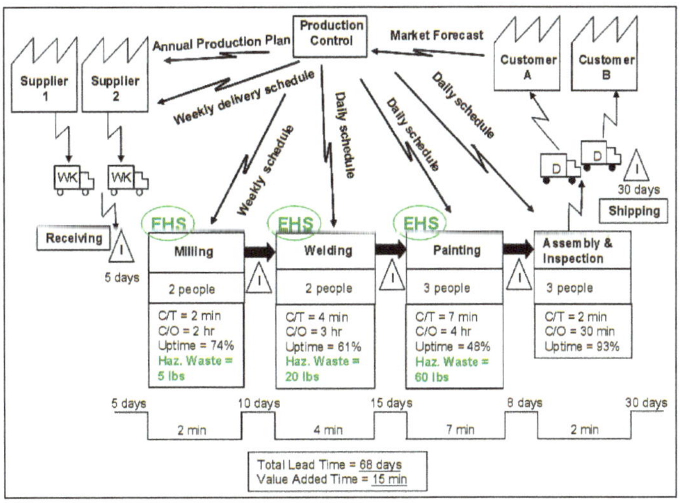

In figure, value stream mapping, a representation of materials and information flows inside a company, mainly used in the lean manufacturing approach. The calculation of the time-line (bottom) usually involves using Little's law to derive lead time from stock levels and takt time.

JIT can include methods such as: Product standardization and modularity, group technology, total productive maintenance, job enlargement, job enrichment, flat organization and vendor rating (JIT production is very sensitive to replenishment conditions).

In heavily automated production systems production planning and information gathering may be executed via the control system, attention should be paid however to avoid problems such as deadlocks, as these can lead to productivity losses.

Project Production Management (PPM) applies the concepts of operations management to the execution of delivery of capital projects by viewing the sequence of activities in a project as a production system. Operations managements principles of variability reduction and management are applied by buffering through a combination of capacity, time and inventory.

Service Operations

Service industries are a major part of economic activity and employment in all industrialized countries comprising 80 percent of employment and GDP in the U.S. Operations management of these services, as distinct from manufacturing, has been developing since the 1970s through publication of unique practices and academic research.

According to Fitzsimmons, Fitzsimmons and Bordoloi differences between manufactured goods and services are as follows:

- Simultaneous production and consumption: High contact services (e.g. health care) must be produced in the presence of the customer, since they are consumed as produced. As a result, services cannot be produced in one location and transported to another, like goods. Service operations are therefore highly dispersed geographically close to the customers. Furthermore, simultaneous production and consumption allows the possibility of self-service involving the customer at the point of consumption (e.g. gas stations). Only low-contact services produced in the "backroom" (e.g., check clearing) can be provided away from the customer.
- Perishable: Since services are perishable, they cannot be stored for later use. In manufacturing companies, inventory can be used to buffer supply and demand. Since buffering is not possible in services, highly variable demand must be met by operations or demand modified to meet supply.
- Ownership: In manufacturing, ownership is transferred to the customer. Ownership is not transferred for service. As a result, services cannot be owned or resold.
- Tangibility: A service is intangible making it difficult for a customer to evaluate the service in advance. In the case of a manufactured good, customers can see it and evaluate it. Assurance of quality service is often done by licensing, government regulation, and branding to assure customers they will receive a quality service.

These four comparisons indicate how management of service operations are quite different from manufacturing regarding such issues as capacity requirements (highly variable), quality assurance (hard to quantify), location of facilities (dispersed), and interaction with the customer during delivery of the service (product and process design).

While there are differences there are also many similarities. For example, quality management approaches used in manufacturing such as the Baldrige Award, and Six Sigma have been widely applied to services. Likewise, lean service principles and practices have also been applied in service operations. The important difference being the customer is in the system while the service is being provided and needs to be considered when applying these practices.

One important difference is service recovery. When an error occurs in service delivery, the recovery must be delivered on the spot by the service provider. If a waiter in a restaurant spills soup on the customer's lap, then the recovery could include a free meal and a promise of free dry cleaning. Another difference is in planning capacity. Since the product cannot be stored, the service facility must be managed to peak demand which requires more flexibility than manufacturing. Location of facilities must be near the customers and scale economics can be lacking. Scheduling must consider the customer can be waiting in line. Queuing theory has been devised to assist in design of service facilities waiting lines. Revenue management is important for service operations, since empty seats on an airplane are lost revenue when the plane departs and cannot be stored for future use.

Mathematical Modeling

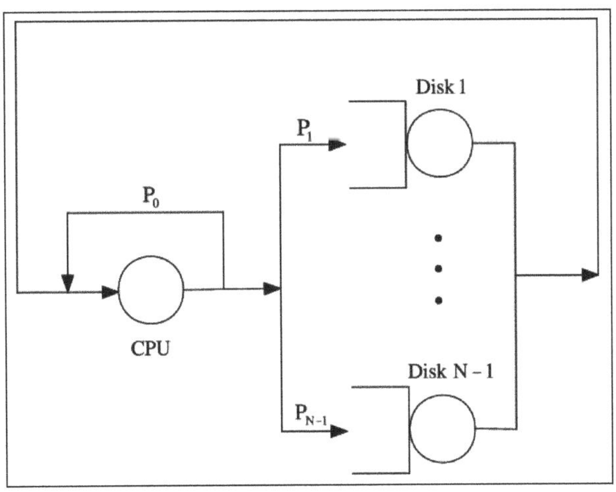

Queue networks are systems in which single queues are connected by a routing network. In this image servers are represented by circles, queues by a series of retangles and the routing network by arrows. In the study of queue networks one typically tries to obtain the equilibrium distribution of the network.

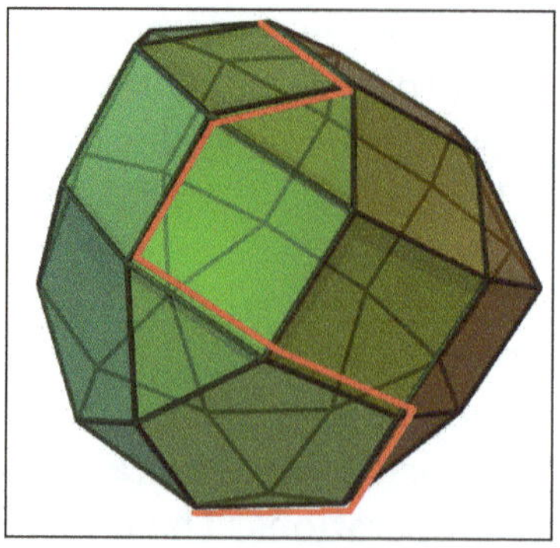

Illustration of the Simplex method, a classical approach to solving LP optimization problems and also integer programming (ex: branch and cut). This technique is mainly used in push approach but also in production system configuration. The interior and surface of the green polytope geometrically represent the feasible region, while the red line indicates the optimally chosen sequence of pivot operations used to reach the optimal solution.

There are also fields of mathematical theory which have found applications in the field of operations management such as operations research: mainly mathematical optimization problems and queue theory. Queue theory is employed in modelling queue and processing times in production systems while mathematical optimization draws heavily from multivariate calculus and linear algebra. Queue theory is based on Markov chains and stochastic processes. Computations of safety stocks are usually based on modeling demand as a normal distribution and MRP and some inventory problems can be formulated using optimal control.

When analytical models are not enough, managers may resort to using simulation. Simulation has been traditionally done through the discrete event simulation paradigm, where the simulation model possesses a state which can only change when a discrete event happens, which consists of a clock and list of events. The more recent transaction-level modeling paradigm consists of a set of resources and a set of transactions: transactions move through a network of resources (nodes) according to a code, called a process.

Since real production processes are always affected by disturbances in both inputs and outputs, many companies implement some form of quality management or quality control. The Seven Basic Tools of Quality designation provides a summary of commonly used tools:

- Check sheets.
- Pareto charts.
- Ishikawa diagrams (Cause-and-effect diagram).
- Control charts.
- Histogram.

- Scatter diagram.
- Stratification.

These are used in approaches like total quality management and Six Sigma. Keeping quality under control is relevant to both increasing customer satisfaction and reducing processing waste.

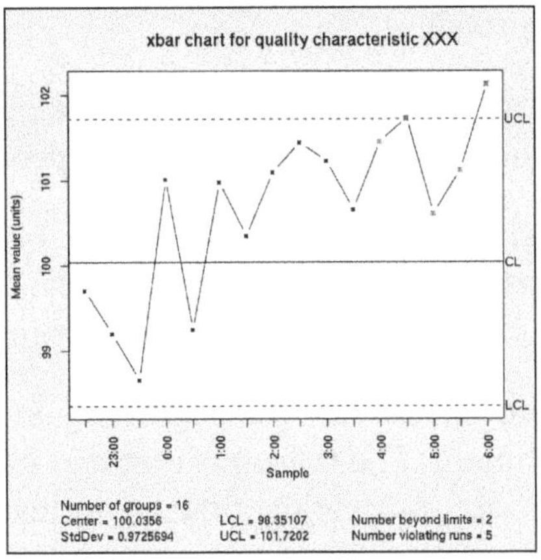

A control chart: process output variable is modeled by a probability density function and for each statistic of the sample an upper control line and lower control line are fixed. When the statistic moves out of bounds, an alarm is given and possible causes are investigated. In this drawing the statistic of choice is the mean and red points represent alarm points.

Operations management textbooks usually cover demand forecasting, even though it is not strictly speaking an operations problem, because demand is related to some production systems variables. For example, a classic approach in dimensioning safety stocks requires calculating the standard deviation of forecast errors. Demand forecasting is also a critical part of push systems, since order releases have to be planned ahead of actual clients' orders. Also, any serious discussion of capacity planning involves adjusting company outputs with market demands.

Safety, Risk and Maintenance

Other important management problems involve maintenance policies, safety management systems, facility management and supply chain integration.

PRODUCTION MANAGEMENT

Production Management refers to the application of management principles to the production function in a factory. In other words, production management involves application of planning, organizing, directing and controlling the production process.

The application of management to the field of production has been the result of at least three developments:

1. First is the development of factory system of production. Until the emergence of the concept of manufacturing, there was no such thing as management as we know it. It is true that people operated business of one type or another, but for the most part, these people were owners of business and did not regard themselves as managers as well.

2. Essentially stems from the first, namely, the development of the large corporation with many owners and the necessity to hire people to operate the business.

3. Stems from the work of many of the pioneers of scientific management who were able to demonstrate the value, from a performance and profit point of view, of some of the techniques they were developing.

It is observed that one cannot demarcate the beginning and end points of Production Management in an establishment. The reason is that it is interrelated with many other functional areas of business, viz., marketing, finance, industrial relation policies etc.

Alternately, Production Management is not independent of marketing, financial and personnel management due to which it is very difficult to formulate some single appropriate definition of Production Management.

The following definitions try to explain main characteristics of production management:

- In the words of Mr, E.L. Brech: "Production Management is the process of effective planning and regulating the operations of that section of an enterprise which is responsible for the actual transformation of materials into finished products." This definition limits the scope of production management to those activities of an enterprise which are associated with the transformation process of inputs into outputs. & the definition does not include the human factors involved in a production process. It lays stress on materialistic features only.

- Production Management deals with decision-making related to production process. So that the resulting goods and services are produced in accordance with the quantitative specifications and demand schedule with minimum cost. According to this definition design and control of the production system are two main functions of production management.

- Production Management is a set of general principles for production economies, facility design, job design, schedule design, quality control, inventory control, work study and cost and budgetary control. This definition explains the main areas of an enterprise where the principles of production management can be applied. This definition clearly points out that production management is not a set of techniques.

It is evident from above definitions that production planning and its control are the main characteristics of production management. In the case of poor planning and control of production activities the organization may not be able to attain its objectives and may result in loss of customer's confidence and retardation in the progress of the establishment.

In short, the main activities of production management can be listed as:

1. Specification and procurement of input resources namely management, material, and land, labour, equipment and capital.
2. Product design and development to determine the production process for transforming the input factors into output of goods and services.
3. Supervision and control of transformation process for efficient production of goods and services.

Functions of Production Management

The definitions clearly shows that the concept of production management is related mainly to the organizations engaged in production of goods and services. Earlier these organizations were mostly in the form of one man shops having insignificant problems of managing the productions.

But with development and expansion of production organizations in the shape of factories more complicated problems like location and lay out, inventory control, quality control, routing and scheduling of the production process etc. came into existence which required more detailed analysis and study of the whole phenomenon.

This resulted in the development of production management in the area of factory management. In the beginning the main function of production management was to control labour costs which at that time constituted the major proportion of costs associated with production.

But with development of factory system towards mechanization and automation the indirect labour costs increased tremendously in comparison to direct labour costs, e.g., designing and packing of the products, production and inventory control, plant layout and location, transportation of raw materials and finished products etc. The planning and control of all these activities required more expertise and special techniques.

In modern times production management has to perform a variety of functions, namely:

1. Design and development of production process.
2. Production planning and control.
3. Implementation of the plan and related activities to produce the desired output.

4. Administration and co-ordination of the activities of various components and departments responsible for producing the necessary goods and services.

However, the responsibility of determining the output characteristics and the distribution strategy followed by an organization including pricing and selling policies are normally outside the scope of Production Management.

Scope of Production Management

The scope of production management is indeed vast. Commencing with the selection of location, production management covers such activities as acquisition of land, constructing building, procuring and installing machinery, purchasing and storing raw materials and converting them into saleable products. Added to the above are other related topics such as quality management, maintenance management, production planning and control, methods improvement and work simplification and other related areas.

References

- Kotler, Philip.; Kevin Lane Keller (2006). Marketing Management, 12th ed. Pearson Prentice Hall. ISBN 0-13-145757-8
- Information-technology-its-uses-business-management-51648: smallbusiness.chron.com, Retrieved 14 March, 2019
- "Financial Planning Curriculum Framework". Financial Planning Standards Board. 2011. Archived from the original on 1 February 2012. Retrieved 7 April, 2012
- Production-management, production-management-its-meaning-definition-function-and-scope-27925: yourarticlelibrary.com, Retrieved 26 July, 2019
- Frates, Janice; Sharp, Seena (2005). "Using Business Intelligence to Discover New Market Opportunities" (PDF). Journal of Competitive Intelligence and Management. 3 (1): 16–28

6

Diverse Aspects of Business Management

There are varied aspects which are studied under business management. Some of these are business operations, business intelligence, business process, asset management, change management, conflict management and constraint management. The topics elaborated in this chapter will help in gaining a better perspective about these aspects of business management.

BUSINESS OPERATIONS

Everything that happens within a company to keep it running and earning money is referred to collectively as business operations. Business plans often include a topic dedicated to operations so that company founders understand the systems, equipment, people, and processes need to make the organization function.

Business Operations Elements

Business operations vary according to business type, industry, size, and so on. Operations for a brick-and-mortar store, for example, will look different from operations for an online retailer. The former will need point of sale terminals to process purchases, for example, while the latter will need e-commerce software that provides electronic shopping cart services.

Business operations for most businesses, though, take into account the following elements:

- Process
- Staffing
- Location
- Equipment or technology

Process is important because of its impact on productivity and efficiency. Processes done manually that can be done quicker with software or that duplicate work done by other departments can cost a business time and money. Business operations processes should be documented department by department so that operations managers can study them to find areas for improvement, consolidation, or cost-savings. Documentation also helps companies train new employees. Staffing is determined by the processes. Who needs to do the work outlined in the work processes and how many of them are needed? A small business might need a few people who are generalists while a large company will need many more people who are specialists.

Location is more important to certain types of businesses than to others – and the reason for the location will vary. A solopreneur consultant might only need room for a desk at home, a pet groomer will need a location with parking, and a software developer will need to be located in a region with access to appropriate talent.

The equipment or technology needed for optimum business operations will often have an impact on location. The pet groomer with a staff and several grooming bays will need more space and different equipment from the mobile groomer who offers services provided at the pet's home. A carpet cleaning business won't need a storefront, but it will need a garage to store its trucks plus office space for business operations management.

Business Operations Analysis

Once a business is established, and particularly after a growth spurt, it's important to periodically assess and analyse business operations to identify inefficiencies and improve communication. Comparisons with industry benchmarks and best practices can help a company make sure its business operations are optimum.

BUSINESS INTELLIGENCE

Business intelligence (BI) comprise the strategies and technologies used by enterprises for the data analysis of business information. BI technologies provide historical, current and predictive views of business operations. Common functions of business intelligence technologies include reporting, online analytical processing, analytics, data mining, process mining, complex event processing, business performance management, benchmarking, text mining, predictive analytics and prescriptive analytics. BI technologies can handle large amounts of structured and sometimes unstructured data to help identify, develop and otherwise create new strategic business opportunities. They aim to allow for the easy interpretation of these big data. Identifying new opportunities and implementing an effective strategy based on insights can provide businesses with a competitive market advantage and long-term stability.

Business intelligence can be used by enterprises to support a wide range of business decisions ranging from operational to strategic. Basic operating decisions include product positioning or pricing. Strategic business decisions involve priorities, goals and directions at the broadest level. In all cases, BI is most effective when it combines data derived from the market in which a company operates (external data) with data from company sources internal to the business such as financial and operations data (internal data). When combined, external and internal data can provide a complete picture which, in effect, creates an "intelligence" that cannot be derived from any singular set of data. Amongst myriad uses, business intelligence tools empower organizations to gain insight into new markets, to assess demand and suitability of products and services for different market segments and to gauge the impact of marketing efforts.

Often BI applications use data gathered from a data warehouse (DW) or from a data mart, and the concepts of BI and DW combine as "BI/DW" or as "BIDW". A data warehouse contains a copy of analytical data that facilitate decision support.

According to Solomon Negash and Paul Gray, we define business intelligence (BI) as systems that combine:

- Data gathering
- Data storage
- Knowledge management

With analysis to evaluate complex corporate and competitive information for presentation to planners and decision maker, with the objective of improving the timeliness and the quality of the input to the decision process."

According to Forrester Research, business intelligence is "a set of methodologies, processes, architectures, and technologies that transform raw data into meaningful and useful information used to enable more effective strategic, tactical, and operational insights and decision-making." Under this definition, business intelligence encompasses information management (data integration, data quality, data warehousing, master-data management, text- and content-analytics, et al.). Therefore, Forrester refers to data preparation and data usage as two separate but closely linked segments of the business-intelligence architectural stack.

Some elements of business intelligence are:

- Multidimensional aggregation and allocation;
- Denormalization, tagging, and standardization;
- Realtime reporting with analytical alert;
- A method of interfacing with unstructured data sources;
- Group consolidation, budgeting and rolling forecasts;

- Statistical inference and probabilistic simulation;
- Key performance indicators optimization;
- Version control and process management;
- Open item management.

Forrester distinguishes this from the business-intelligence market, which is "just the top layers of the BI architectural stack, such as reporting, analytics, and dashboards."

Compared with Competitive Intelligence

Though the term business intelligence is sometimes a synonym for competitive intelligence (because they both support decision making), BI uses technologies, processes, and applications to analyze mostly internal, structured data and business processes while competitive intelligence gathers, analyzes and disseminates information with a topical focus on company competitors. If understood broadly, business intelligence can include the subset of competitive intelligence.

Compared with Business Analytics

Business intelligence and business analytics are sometimes used interchangeably, but there are alternate definitions. Thomas Davenport, professor of information technology and management at Babson College argues that business intelligence should be divided into querying, reporting, Online analytical processing (OLAP), an "alerts" tool, and business analytics. In this definition, business analytics is the subset of BI focusing on statistics, prediction, and optimization, rather than the reporting functionality.

Data

Business operations can generate a very large amount of information in the form of e-mails, memos, notes from call-centers, news, user groups, chats, reports, web-pages, presentations, image-files, video-files, and marketing material. According to Merrill Lynch, more than 85% of all business information exists in these forms; a company might only use such a document a single time. Because of the way it is produced and stored, this information is either unstructured or semi-structured.

The management of semi-structured data is an unsolved problem in the information technology industry. According to projections from Gartner, white collar workers spend 30–40% of their time searching, finding, and assessing unstructured data. BI uses both structured and unstructured data. The former is easy to search, and the latter contains a large quantity of the information needed for analysis and decision making. Because of the difficulty of properly searching, finding and assessing unstructured or semi-structured data, organizations may not draw upon these vast reservoirs of information, which could influence a particular decision, task or project. This can ultimately lead to poorly informed decision making.

Therefore, when designing a business intelligence/DW-solution, the specific problems associated with semi-structured and unstructured data must be accommodated for as well as those for the structured data.

Unstructured Data vs. Semi-structured Data

Unstructured and semi-structured data have different meanings depending on their context. In the context of relational database systems, unstructured data cannot be stored in predictably ordered columns and rows. One type of unstructured data is typically stored in a BLOB (binary large object), a catch-all data type available in most relational database management systems. Unstructured data may also refer to irregularly or randomly repeated column patterns that vary from row to row or files of natural language that do not have detailed metadata.

Many of these data types, however, like e-mails; word processing text files, PPTs, image-files, and video-files conform to a standard that offers the possibility of metadata. Metadata can include information such as author and time of creation, and this can be stored in a relational database. Therefore, it may be more accurate to talk about this as semi-structured documents or data, but no specific consensus seems to have been reached.

Unstructured data can also simply be the knowledge that business users have about future business trends. Business forecasting naturally aligns with the BI system because business users think of their business in aggregate terms. Capturing the business knowledge that may only exist in the minds of business users provides some of the most important data points for a complete BI solution.

Limitations of Semi-structured and Unstructured Data

There are several challenges to developing BI with semi-structured data. According to Inmon & Nesavich, some of those are:

- Physically accessing unstructured textual data – unstructured data is stored in a huge variety of formats.
- Terminology – Among researchers and analysts, there is a need to develop a standardized terminology.
- Volume of data – As stated earlier, up to 85% of all data exists as semi-structured data. Couple that with the need for word-to-word and semantic analysis.
- Searchability of unstructured textual data – A simple search on some data, e.g. apple, results in links where there is a reference to that precise search term. gives an example: “a search is made on the term felony. In a simple search, the

term felony is used, and everywhere there is a reference to felony, a hit to an unstructured document is made. But a simple search is crude. It does not find references to crime, arson, murder, embezzlement, vehicular homicide, and such, even though these crimes are types of felonies."

Metadata

To solve problems with searchability and assessment of data, it is necessary to know something about the content. This can be done by adding context through the use of metadata. Many systems already capture some metadata (e.g. filename, author, size, etc.), but more useful would be metadata about the actual content – e.g. summaries, topics, people or companies mentioned. Two technologies designed for generating metadata about content are automatic categorization and information extraction.

Applications

Business intelligence can be applied to the following business purposes:

- Performance metrics and benchmarking inform business leaders of progress towards business goals (business process management).
- Analytics quantify processes for a business to arrive at optimal decisions, and to perform business knowledge discovery. Analytics may variously involve data mining, process mining, statistical analysis, predictive analytics, predictive modeling, business process modeling, data lineage, complex event processing and prescriptive analytics.
- Business reporting can use BI data to inform strategy. Business reporting may involve data visualization, executive information system, and/or OLAP.
- BI can facilitate collaboration both inside and outside the business by enabling data sharing and electronic data interchange.
- Knowledge management is concerned with the creation, distribution, use, and management of business intelligence, and of business knowledge in general. Knowledge management leads to learning management and regulatory compliance.

ASSET MANAGEMENT

Asset management refers to the management of investments on behalf of others. The process essentially has a dual mandate - appreciation of a client's assets over time while mitigating risk. There are investment minimums, which mean that this service is generally available to high net-worth individuals, government entities, corporations and financial intermediaries.

The role of an asset manager consists of determining what investments to make, or avoid, that will grow a client's portfolio. Rigorous research is conducted utilizing both macro and micro analytical tools. This includes statistical analysis of the prevailing market trends, interviews with company officials, and anything else that would aid in achieving the stated goal of client asset appreciation. Most commonly, the advisor will invest in products such as equity, fixed income, real estate, commodities, alternative investments and mutual funds.

Accounts held by financial institutions often include check writing privileges, credit cards, debit cards, margin loans, the automatic sweep of cash balances into a money market fund and brokerage services. When individuals deposit money into the account, it is typically placed into a money market fund that offers a greater return that can be found in regular savings and checking accounts. Account holders can choose between Federal Deposit Insurance Company-backed (FDIC) funds and non-FDIC funds. The added benefit to account holders is all of their banking and investing needs can be serviced by the same institution rather than having separate brokerage account and banking options.

These types of accounts resulted from the passing of the Gramm-Leach-Bliley Act in 1999, which replaced the Glass-Steagall Act. The Glass-Steagall Act of 1933 was created during the Great Depression and did not allow financial institutions to offer both banking and security services.

CHANGE MANAGEMENT

Change management is the discipline that guides how we prepare, equip and support individuals to successfully adopt change in order to drive organizational success and outcomes. While all changes are unique and all individuals are unique, decades of research shows there are actions we can take to influence people in their individual transitions. Change management provides a structured approach for supporting the individuals in your organization to move from their own current states to their own future states.

Three Levels of Change Management

Individual Change Management

While it is the natural psychological and physiological reaction of humans to resist change, we are actually quite resilient creatures. When supported through times of change, we can be wonderfully adaptive and successful.

Individual change management requires understanding how people experience change and what they need to change successfully. It also requires knowing what will help people make a successful transition: what messages do people need to hear when and from whom, when the optimal time to teach someone a new skill is, how to coach people to demonstrate new behaviors, and what makes changes "stick" in someone's work. Individual change management draws on disciplines like psychology and neuroscience to apply actionable frameworks to individual change.

Organizational or Initiative Change Management

While change happens at the individual level, it is often impossible for a project team to manage change on a person-by-person basis. Organizational or initiative change management provides us with the steps and actions to take at the project level to support the hundreds or thousands of individuals who are impacted by a project.

Organizational change management involves first identifying the groups and people who will need to change as the result of the project, and in what ways they will need to change. Organizational change management then involves creating a customized plan for ensuring impacted employees receive the awareness, leadership, coaching, and training they need in order to change successfully. Driving successful individual transitions should be the central focus of the activities in organizational change management. Organizational change management is complementary to your project management. Project management ensures your project's solution is designed, developed and delivered, while change management ensures your project's solution is effectively embraced, adopted and used.

Enterprise Change Management Capability

Enterprise change management is an organizational core competency that provides competitive differentiation and the ability to effectively adapt to the ever-changing world. An enterprise change management capability means effective change management is embedded into your organization's roles, structures, processes, projects and leadership competencies. Change management processes are consistently and effectively applied to initiatives, leaders have the skills to guide their teams through change, and employees know what to ask for in order to be successful.

The end result of an enterprise change management capability is that individuals embrace change more quickly and effectively, and organizations are able to respond quickly to market changes, embrace strategic initiatives, and adopt new technology more quickly and with less productivity impact. This capability does not happen by chance, however, and requires a strategic approach to embed change management across an organization.

Benefits of Change Management

Change management reduces the risk that a new system or other change will be rejected by the enterprise. By itself OCM does not reduce costs or increase sales. Instead, it increases the teamwork required for the enterprise accept the change and operate more efficiently.

When is Organizational Change Management Needed?

OCM is needed whenever the enterprise undertakes a program or event that interrupts day-to-day operations. Such an undertaking will impact:

1. The work content of individual jobs: Many jobs require individuals or groups to perform tasks repeatedly. An accounting department has daily, weekly, monthly, and annual activities. Over time, most people become comfortable with the tools provided and the rhythm of the work calendar. Even simple changes may disrupt the workflow and be disconcerting for the staff.
2. The roles of individual employees: Many people view their value to the organization as being a good technical architect, programmer, or security specialist. When asked to take on a different role, they may become very uncomfortable. People with excellent technical skills often struggle when asked to become managers. Rather than performing all of the tasks, they have to learn to work through other people. Once they are no longer rewarded for the skills that made them successful, employees may question their purpose.
3. For a deeper look at how: The organization itself. Executive team debate major changes for months before making final decisions, enabling each member to gain a deeper understanding of the effects the change will have on the enterprise. Even if they don't agree with the final decision, they have time to determine whether to accept the new direction or to depart gracefully. Individuals lower in the hierarchy rarely have time to process major changes. Executives do not want employees to worry about events that may never happen until it is clear the change will take place. In addition, tighter insider trading enforcement prohibits executives from sharing information about upcoming mergers, acquisitions, or divestitures. As such, individuals who are not part of the executive team have much less time to prepare for the planned change and may decide to leave while the change is undertaken, making change management more difficult.

What are the Requirements for Change Management Success?

Organization change management programs require several things to be successful:

1. The right executive sponsor: Sponsorship is critical. The OCM sponsor is responsible for developing the case for change and obtaining the necessary OCM resources. For this, the sponsor needs the support of the CEO to make it clear that the effort is important. The sponsor must understand the case for change clearly enough have a detailed discussion about the challenges that created the need for a different way of operating. She should be confident enough to confront skeptics and close enough to the details to justify the approach selected and the reasons the alternatives were rejected.

2. The sponsor needs to understand the impact on the staff: Good sponsors are concerned about the people who will be affected by the change. These sponsors communicate honestly while treating everyone fairly and respectfully. Rather than merely relating the facts, they take the time to listen to people and to empathize with the individuals who dislike the new way of operating. If people are to be terminated or reassigned, sponsors should know when it will happen and how everyone will be treated. They explain why the change was necessary, and do what they can to smooth the transition for individuals whose jobs are transformed. The best sponsors help everyone losing a job find the next opportunity.
3. Cultural willingness to adapt and change: All organizations resist change to some degree, but ones that follow the dictum "if it isn't broke don't fix it" often need a major wake-up call to behave differently. The public revelation of sexual misconduct allegations against Harvey Weinstein provides a dramatic example of a call to address a long standing problem. A number of enterprises that had done little to stop sexual harassment suddenly took action.
4. Skilled change management teams embrace the organization's emotional energy: They use company stories, language, and behavior to emphasize those parts of the current culture that are aligned with the planned change. These teams celebrate behaviors they wish to encourage by publicly recognizing individuals exhibiting these behaviors. Change management teams use every opportunity to reinforce the way the change helps the enterprise.
5. Individual willingness to change: Individuals must be willing to examine new information and adopt new behaviors and approaches. Since most people prefer the status quo, this can be difficult. Typically, most people only accept changes that make sense and improve their job content or their work environment.
6. Rewards and consequences: Major changes need to be reinforced by rewards and consequences. Individual performance plans with specific, measurable results need to reinforce the desired future state. Individuals who meet their objectives need to be rewarded appropriately and those that do not need to face consequences.

A consulting firm, wanting broader market recognition, encouraged all partners to speak at industry conferences and to write for industry publications. Several partners became very successful at both. While their articles and talks generated new business, the client revenue each partner managed actually decreased. When the compensation plan did not reward them sufficiently for the additional firm revenue to offset their decreased client revenue, they were very unhappy. The firm's leadership team had to adjust the compensation plan quickly in order to prevent the partners from leaving.

Why is Change Management Difficult?

It takes a great deal of time to change attitudes and behaviors. Application implementations, even large ones, are easier to plan and manage; project managers know when a module is tested or server installed. OCM managers have a much harder time measuring progress; gauging support can be tricky. Just when it appears that a key individual supports the change, the person raises another objection and returns to old behaviors. Executives, often assume that everyone impacted will find the business case so compelling they will automatically accept the new way of operating. But most people resist change or are unpredictable.

This creates several difficulties for the OCM team:

- Change management is not deterministic- Unlike computer programs, people can be unpredictable and illogical. OCM activities that are effective with one group may be ineffective with another. Messages may resonate with some people but not with others.
- Change management is a contact sport- The OCM team needs to interact one on one with individuals who will need to change. Emails, videos, and other mass communication can reinforce a message, but these don't make people feel the enterprise cares about their difficulties. Change is personal; sometimes people whose jobs have been transformed need someone else to listen to their frustrations before they will accept the new reality.
- Midlevel and frontline staff must be engaged- Midlevel and frontline staff can make or break a major program. Since they understand the operational details of the current processes, they can anticipate potential problems and likely customer reactions. Individuals who are not sensitive to the disruption that major change can create often believe it is more efficient to involve fewer people early in the process. While involving more people in the change process creates additional work for the OCM team, it also builds commitment. Midlevel and frontline staffs that see their suggestions accepted are more likely to support the final result.
- Cultural differences can make OCM difficult- Cultural norms are different around the globe. The OCM effort needs to be aware of local customs even with a global system intended to standardize enterprise operations. Care needs to be taken to be sensitive to these and other cultural norms:
  - Communications style- Denmark, Germany, Israel, Netherlands, and U.S. are very direct. India, Japan, Pakistan, and the Philippines tend to be indirect and believe it is very important for both parties to save face. In these cultures, individuals avoid saying no, and frequently mean, "You would understand" rather than "You will agree" when they say "yes."

  - Time orientation- Meetings in Germany, Switzerland, and the U.S. start and end when scheduled. Little time is dedicated to introductions, even when some attendees are meeting each other for the first time. Spain, Thailand, Brazil, and the Caribbean are less concerned about time. Things can wait until later in the day or even tomorrow. In such countries it is impolite to rush into a business discussion; only after the host and the visitor have shared refreshments and pleasantries can business begin.
  - Egalitarianism- Australia, Canada, Israel, New Zealand, U.S. have little hierarchy with almost everyone on a first-name basis. Conversely, hierarchy is very important in India, Iran, Japan, Saudi Arabia and other countries. Junior staff in these countries invariably defer to the senior person.
- Violating cultural norms can cause great resentment- The best OCM teams are very sensitive to local cultural norms even when the people at headquarters demand a standard project rollout and standard OCM program globally.
- Change management may be an afterthought- With major IT efforts, the project team is often consumed by business process changes, interfaces to other systems, data cleanup, etc. If the OCM effort is not started concurrently with the rest of the program, it may only be started when the program team experiences resistance from end users. Even enterprises that assert that OCM is critical sometime reduce or eliminate the OCM budget if the overall program gets too expensive.
- Change management can be started too early- The OCM effort needs to be tightly coupled to the rest of the change program. This is particularly difficult with major IT programs when the OCM efforts begin before new system details have been finalized. In the absence of tangible information about the new system, the OCM team either sounds vague or describes what they hope the new system will do. When the new system fails to materialize quickly or has less functionality than anticipated, supporters often become disillusioned.
- OCM and the change program may be disconnected- The rational and emotional cases for change need to be integrated tightly. Frequently, executives communicate a rational, logical case for change that lacks emotional appeal. People respond to calls to action that make them feel they are part of something that is more important than any single person and are energized by visions that capture their hearts as well as their minds.

CONFLICT MANAGEMENT

Conflict management is the process of limiting the negative aspects of conflict while increasing the positive aspects of conflict. The aim of conflict management is to enhance learning and group outcomes, including effectiveness or performance in an organizational setting. Properly managed conflict can improve group outcomes.

Conflict Resolution

Conflict resolution involves the reduction, elimination, or termination of all forms and types of conflict. Five styles for conflict management, as identified by Thomas and Kilmann, are: competing, compromising, collaborating, avoiding, and accommodating.

- Businesses can benefit from appropriate types and levels of conflict. That is the aim of conflict management, and not the aim of conflict resolution. Conflict management does not imply conflict resolution.
- Conflict management minimizes the negative outcomes of conflict and promotes the positive outcomes of conflict with the goal of improving learning in an organization.
- Properly managed conflict increases organizational learning by increasing the number of questions asked and encourages people to challenge the status quo.

Organizational conflict at the interpersonal level includes disputes between peers as well as supervisor-subordinate conflict. Party-directed mediation (PDM) is a mediation approach particularly suited for disputes between co-workers, colleagues or peers, especially deep-seated interpersonal conflict, multicultural or multiethnic disputes. The mediator listens to each party separately in a pre-caucus or pre-mediation before ever bringing them into a joint session. Part of the pre-caucus also includes coaching and role plays. The idea is that the parties learn how to converse directly with their adversary in the joint session. Some unique challenges arise when organizational disputes involve supervisors and subordinates. The Negotiated Performance Appraisal (NPA) is a tool for improving communication between supervisors and subordinates and is particularly useful as an alternate mediation model because it preserves the hierarchical power of supervisors while encouraging dialogue and dealing with differences in opinion.

Orientations to Conflict

There are three orientations to conflict: lose-lose, win-lose, and win-win. The lose-lose orientation is a type of conflict that tends to end negatively for all parties involved. A win-lose orientation results in one victorious party, usually at the expense of the other. The win-win orientation is one of the most essential concepts to conflict resolution. A win-win solution arrived at by integrative bargaining may be close to optimal for both parties. This approach engages in a cooperative approach rather than a competitive one.

Although the win-win concept is the ideal orientation, the notion that there can only be one winner is constantly being reinforced in American culture: "The win-lose orientation is manufactured in our society in athletic competition, admission to academic programs, industrial promotion systems, and so on. Individuals tend to generalize from their objective win-lose situations and apply these experiences to situations that are not objectively fixed-pies".

This kind of mentality can be destructive when communicating with different cultural groups by creating barriers in negotiation, resolution and compromise; it can also lead the "loser" to feel mediocre. When the win-win orientation is absent in negotiation, different responses to conflict may be observed.

Early Conflict Management Models

Blake and Mouton were among the first to present a conceptual scheme for classifying the modes (styles) for handling interpersonal conflicts in five types: forcing, withdrawing, smoothing, compromising, and problem solving.

In the 1970s and 1980s, researchers began using the intentions of the parties involved to classify the styles of conflict management that they included in their models. Both Thomas and Pruitt put forth a model based on the concerns of the parties involved in the conflict. The combination of the parties' concern for their own interests (i.e. assertiveness) and their concern for the interests of those across the table (i.e. cooperativeness) yielded a particular conflict management style. Pruitt called these styles yielding (low assertiveness/high cooperativeness), problem solving (high assertiveness/high cooperativeness), inaction (low assertiveness/low cooperativeness), and contending (high assertiveness/low cooperativeness). Pruitt argues that problem-solving is the preferred method when seeking mutually beneficial options (win-win).

Khun and Poole's Model

Khun and Poole established a similar system of group conflict management. In their system, they split Kozan's confrontational model into two sub models:

- Distributive – Here conflict is approached as a distribution of a fixed amount of positive outcomes or resources, where one side will end up winning and the other losing, even if they do win some concessions.
- Integrative – Groups utilizing the integrative model see conflict as a chance to integrate the needs and concerns of both groups and make the best outcome possible. This model has a heavier emphasis on compromise than the distributive model. Khun and Poole found that the integrative model resulted in consistently better task related outcomes than those using the distributive model.

DeChurch and Marks's Meta-taxonomy

DeChurch and Marks examined the literature available on conflict management at the time and Ni established what they claimed was a "meta-taxonomy" that encompasses all other models.

They argued that all other styles have inherent in them into two dimensions:

- Activeness ("the extent to which conflict behaviors make a responsive and direct rather than inert and indirect impression"). High activeness is characterized by openly discussing differences of opinion while fully going after their own interest.
- Agreeableness ("the extent to which conflict behaviors make a pleasant and relaxed rather than unpleasant and strainful impression"). High agreeableness is characterized by attempting to satisfy all parties involved.

In the study DeChurch and Marks conducted to validate this division, activeness did not have a significant effect on the effectiveness of conflict resolution, but the agreeableness of the conflict management style, whatever it was, did have a positive impact on how groups felt about the way the conflict was managed, regardless of the outcome.

Rahim's Meta-model

Rahim noted that there is agreement among management scholars that there is no one best approach to how to make decisions, lead or manage conflict.

In a similar vein, rather than creating a very specific model of conflict management, Rahim created a meta-model (in much the same way that DeChurch and Marks, 2001, created a meta-taxonomy) for conflict styles based on two dimensions, concern for self and concern for others.

Within this framework are five management approaches: integrating, obliging, dominating, avoiding, and compromising.

- Integration involves openness exchanging information, looking for alternatives, and examining differences so solve the problem in a manner that is acceptable to both parties.
- Obliging is associated with attempting to minimize the differences and highlight the commonalities to satisfy the concern of the other party.
- Dominating in this style one party goes all out to win his or her objective and, as a result, often ignores the needs and expectations of the other party.
- Avoiding here a party fails to satisfy his or her own concern as well as the concern of the other party.
- Compromising involves give-and-take whereby both parties give up something to make a mutually acceptable decision.

International Conflict Management

Special consideration should be paid to conflict management between two parties from distinct cultures. In addition to the everyday sources of conflict, "misunderstandings, and from this counterproductive, pseudo conflicts, arise when members of one culture are unable to understand culturally determined differences in communication practices, traditions, and thought processing". Indeed, this has already been observed in the business research literature.

Renner recounted several episodes where managers from developed countries moved to less developed countries to resolve conflicts within the company and met with little success due to their failure to adapt to the conflict management styles of the local culture.

As an example, in Kozan's study noted above, he noted that Asian cultures are far more likely to use a harmony model of conflict management. If a party operating from a harmony model comes in conflict with a party using a more confrontational model, misunderstandings above and beyond those generated by the conflict itself will arise.

International conflict management, and the cultural issues associated with it, is one of the primary areas of research in the field at the time, as existing research is insufficient to deal with the ever-increasing contact occurring between international entities.

CONSTRAINT MANAGEMENT

The theory of constraints (TOC) is a management paradigm that views any manageable system as being limited in achieving more of its goals by a very small number of constraints. There is always at least one constraint, and TOC uses a focusing process to identify the constraint and restructure the rest of the organization around it. TOC adopts the common idiom "a chain is no stronger than its weakest link". This means that processes, organizations, etc., are vulnerable because the weakest person or part can always damage or break them or at least adversely affect the outcome.

The theory of constraints (TOC) is an overall management philosophy introduced by Eliyahu M. Goldratt. The Goal, that is geared to help organizations continually achieve their goals. Goldratt adapted the concept to project management in his theory.

An earlier propagator of a similar concept was Wolfgang Mewes in Germany with publications on power-oriented management theory and following with his Energo-Kybernetic System, later renamed Engpasskonzentrierte Strategie (Bottleneck-focused Strategy) as a more advanced theory of bottlenecks. The publications of Wolfgang Mewes are marketed through the FAZ Verlag, publishing house of the German newspaper

Frankfurter Allgemeine Zeitung (Frankfurt General Newspaper). However, the paradigm Theory of constraints was first used by Goldratt.

Key Assumption

The underlying premise of the theory of constraints is that organizations can be measured and controlled by variations on three measures: throughput, operational expense, and inventory. Inventory is all the money that the system has invested in purchasing things which it intends to sell. Operational expense is all the money the system spends in order to turn inventory into throughput. Throughput is the rate at which the system generates money through sales.

Before the goal itself can be reached, necessary conditions must first be met. These typically include safety, quality, legal obligations, etc. For most businesses, the goal itself is to make profit. However, for many organizations and non-profit businesses, making money is a necessary condition for pursuing the goal. Whether it is the goal or a necessary condition, understanding how to make sound financial decisions based on throughput, inventory, and operating expense is a critical requirement.

The Five Focusing Steps

Theory of constraints is based on the premise that the rate of goal achievement by a goal-oriented system (i.e., the system's throughput) is limited by at least one constraint.

The argument by reductio ad absurdum is as follows: If there was nothing preventing a system from achieving higher throughput (i.e., more goal units in a unit of time), its throughput would be infinite — which is impossible in a real-life system. Only by increasing flow through the constraint can overall throughput be increased.

Assuming the goal of a system has been articulated and its measurements defined, the steps are:

1. Identify the system's constraint(s).
2. Decide how to exploit the system's constraint(s).
3. Subordinate everything else to the above decision(s).
4. Alleviate the system's constraint(s).
5. Warning! If in the previous steps a constraint has been broken, go back to step 1, but do not allow inertia to cause a system's constraint.

The goal of a commercial organization is: "Make more money now and in the future", and its measurements are given by throughput accounting as: throughput, inventory, and operating expenses. The five focusing steps aim to ensure ongoing improvement efforts are centered on the organization's constraint(s). In the TOC literature, this is referred to as the process of ongoing improvement (POOGI).

Constraints

A constraint is anything that prevents the system from achieving its goal. There are many ways that constraints can show up, but a core principle within TOC is that there are not tens or hundreds of constraints. There is at least one, but at most only a few in any given system. Constraints can be internal or external to the system. An internal constraint is in evidence when the market demands more from the system than it can deliver. If this is the case, then the focus of the organization should be on discovering that constraint and following the five focusing steps to open it up (and potentially remove it). An external constraint exists when the system can produce more than the market will bear. If this is the case, then the organization should focus on mechanisms to create more demand for its products or services.

Types of (internal) constraints:

- Equipment: The way equipment is currently used limits the ability of the system to produce more salable goods/services.
- People: Lack of skilled people limits the system. Mental models held by people can cause behaviour that becomes a constraint.
- Policy: A written or unwritten policy prevents the system from making more.

The concept of the constraint in Theory of Constraints is analogous to but differs from the constraint that shows up in mathematical optimization. In TOC, the constraint is used as a focusing mechanism for management of the system. In optimization, the constraint is written into the mathematical expressions to limit the scope of the solution (X can be no greater than 5).

Organizations have many problems with equipment, people, policies, etc. (A breakdown is just that – a breakdown – and is not a constraint in the true sense of the TOC concept). The constraint is the limiting factor that is preventing the organization from getting more throughput (typically, revenue through sales) even when nothing goes wrong.

Breaking a Constraint

If a constraint's throughput capacity is elevated to the point where it is no longer the system's limiting factor, this is said to "break" the constraint. The limiting factor is now some other part of the system, or may be external to the system (an external constraint).

Buffers

Buffers are used throughout the theory of constraints. They often result as part of the exploit and subordinate steps of the five focusing steps. Buffers are placed before the governing constraint, thus ensuring that the constraint is never starved. Buffers are also placed behind the constraint to prevent downstream failure from blocking the constraint's output. Buffers used in this way protect the constraint from variations in the rest of the system and should allow for normal variation of processing time and the occasional upset (Murphy) before and behind the constraint.

Buffers can be a bank of physical objects before a work center, waiting to be processed by that work center. Buffers ultimately buy you time, as in the time before work reaches the constraint and are often verbalized as time buffers. There should always be enough (but not excessive) work in the time queue before the constraint and adequate offloading space behind the constraint.

Buffers are *not* the small queue of work that sits before every work center in a Kanban system although it is similar if you regard the assembly line as the governing constraint. A prerequisite in the theory is that with one constraint in the system, all other parts of the system must have sufficient capacity to keep up with the work at the constraint and to catch up if time was lost. In a balanced line, as espoused by Kanban, when one work center goes down for a period longer than the buffer allows, then the entire system must wait until that work center is restored. In a TOC system, the only situation where work is in danger is if the constraint is unable to process (either due to malfunction, sickness or a "hole" in the buffer – if something goes wrong that the time buffer can not protect).

Buffer management, therefore, represents a crucial attribute of the theory of constraints. There are many ways to apply buffers, but the most often used is a visual system of designating the buffer in three colors: green (okay), yellow (caution) and red (action required). Creating this kind of visibility enables the system as a whole to align and thus subordinate to the need of the constraint in a holistic manner. This can also be done daily in a central operations room that is accessible to everybody.

Plant Types

There are four primary types of plants in the TOC lexicon. Draw the flow of material from the bottom of a page to the top, and you get the four types. They specify the general flow of materials through a system, and also provide some hints about where to look for typical problems. This type of analysis is known as VATI analysis as it uses the bottom-up shapes of the letters V, A, T, and I to describe the types of plants. The four types can be combined in many ways in larger facilities, e.g. "an A plant feeding a V plant".

- V-plant: The general flow of material is one-to-many, such as a plant that takes one raw material and can make many final products. Classic examples are meat rendering plants or a steel manufacturer. The primary problem in V-plants is "robbing," where one operation (A) immediately after a diverging point "steals" materials meant for the other operation (B). Once the material has been processed by A, it cannot come back and be run through B without significant rework.

- A-plant: The general flow of material is many-to-one, such as in a plant where many sub-assemblies converge for a final assembly. The primary problem in A-plants is in synchronizing the converging lines so that each supplies the final assembly point at the right time.
- T-plant: The general flow is that of an I-plant (or has multiple lines), which then splits into many assemblies (many-to-many). Most manufactured parts are used in multiple assemblies and nearly all assemblies use multiple parts. Customized devices, such as computers, are good examples. T-plants suffer from both synchronization problems of A-plants (parts aren't all available for an assembly) and the robbing problems of V-plants (one assembly steals parts that could have been used in another).
- I-plant: Material flows in a sequence, such as in an assembly line. The primary work is done in a straight sequence of events (one-to-one). The constraint is the slowest operation.

From the above list, one can deduce that for non-material systems one could draw the flow of work or the flow of processes, instead of physical flows, and arrive at similar basic V, A, T, or I structures. A project, for example, is an A-shaped sequence of work, culminating in a delivered product (i.e., the intended outcome of the project).

Applications

The focusing steps, this process of ongoing improvement, have been applied to manufacturing, project management, supply chain/distribution generated specific solutions. Other tools (mainly the "thinking process") also led to TOC applications in the fields of marketing and sales, and finance. The solution as applied to each of these areas is listed below.

Operations

Within manufacturing operations and operations management, the solution seeks to pull materials through the system, rather than push them into the system. The primary methodology used is drum-buffer-rope (DBR) and a variation called simplified drum-buffer-rope (S-DBR).

Drum-buffer-rope is a manufacturing execution methodology based on the fact the output of a system can only be the same as the output at the constraint of the system. Any attempt to produce more than what the constraint can process just leads to excess inventory piling up. The method is named for its three components. The drum is the rate at which the physical constraint of the plant can work: the work center or machine or operation that limits the ability of the entire system to produce more. The rest of the plant follows the beat of the drum. Schedule at the drum decides what the system should produce, in what sequence to produce and how much to produce. They make sure the drum has work and that anything the drum has processed does not get wasted.

The buffer protects the drum, so that it always has work flowing to it. Buffers in DBR provide the additional lead time beyond the required set up and process times, for materials in the product flow. Since these buffers have time as their unit of measure, rather than quantity of material, this makes the priority system operate strictly based on the time an order is expected to be at the drum. Each work order will have a remaining buffer status that can be calculated. Based on this buffer status, work orders can be color coded into Red, Yellow and Green. The red orders have the highest priority and must be worked on first, since they have penetrated most into their buffers followed by yellow and green. As time evolves, this buffer status might change and the color assigned to the particular work order change with it.

Traditional DBR usually calls for buffers at several points in the system: the constraint, synchronization points and at shipping. S-DBR has a buffer at shipping and manages the flow of work across the drum through a load planning mechanism.

The rope is the work release mechanism for the plant. Orders are released to the shop floor at one "buffer time" before they are due to be processed by the constraint. In other words, if the buffer is 5 days, the order is released 5 days before it is due at the constraint. Putting work into the system earlier than this buffer time is likely to generate too-high work-in-process and slow down the entire system.

High-speed Automated Production Lines

Automated production lines that are used in the beverage industry to fill containers usually have several machines executing parts of the complete process, from filling primary containers to secondary packaging and palletisation. These machines operate at different speeds and capacities and have varying efficiency levels.

To be able to maximize the throughput, the production line usually has a designed constraint. This constraint is typically the slowest and often the most expensive machine on the line. The overall throughput of the line is determined by this machine. All other machines can operate faster and are connected by conveyors.

The conveyors usually have the ability to buffer product. In the event of a stoppage at a machine other than the constraint, the conveyor can buffer the product enabling the constraint machine to keep on running.

A typical line setup is such that in normal operation the upstream conveyors from the constraint machine are always run full to prevent starvation at the constraint and the downstream conveyors are run empty to prevent a back-up at the constraint. The overall aim is to prevent minor stoppages at the machines from impacting the constraint.

For this reason as the machines get further from the constraint, they have the ability to run faster than the previous machine and this creates a V curve.

Supply Chain and Logistics

In general, the solution for supply chains is to create flow of inventory so as to ensure greater availability and to eliminate surpluses. The TOC distribution solution is effective when used to address a single link in the supply chain and more so across the entire system, even if that system comprises many different companies. The purpose of the TOC distribution solution is to establish a competitive advantage based on extraordinary availability by reducing the damages caused when the flow of goods is interrupted by shortages and surpluses.

This approach uses several new rules to protect availability with fewer inventories than is conventionally required:

1. Inventory is held at an aggregation point(s) as close as possible to the source. This approach ensures smoothed demand at the aggregation point, requiring proportionally less inventory. The distribution centers holding the aggregated stock are able to ship goods downstream to the next link in the supply chain much more quickly than a make-to-order manufacturer can.

2. Following this rule may result in a make-to-order manufacturer converting to make-to-stock. The inventory added at the aggregation point is significantly less than the inventory reduction downstream.

3. In all stocking locations, initial inventory buffers are set which effectively create an upper limit of the inventory at that location. The buffer size is equal to the maximum expected consumption within the average RT, plus additional stock to protect in case a delivery is late. In other words, there is no advantage in holding more inventory in a location than the amount that might be consumed before more could be ordered and received. Typically, the sum of the on hand value of such buffers are 25–75% less than currently observed average inventory levels.

4. Once buffers have been established, no replenishment orders are placed as long as the quantity inbound (already ordered but not yet received) plus the quantity on hand are equal to or greater than the buffer size. Following this rule causes surplus inventory to be bled off as it is consumed.

5. For any reason, when on hand plus inbound inventory is less than the buffer, orders are placed as soon as practical to increase the inbound inventory so that the relationship Onhand + Inbound = Buffer is maintained.

6. To ensure buffers remain correctly sized even with changes in the rates of demand and replenishment, a simple recursive algorithm called Buffer Management is used. When the on hand inventory level is in the upper third of the buffer for a full RT, the buffer is reduced by one third. Alternatively, when the on hand inventory is in the bottom one third of the buffer for too long, the buffer is increased by one third (and don't forget rule 4). The definition of "too long"

may be changed depending on required service levels, however, a rule of thumb is 20% of the RT. Moving buffers up more readily than down is supported by the usually greater damage caused by shortages as compared to the damage caused by surpluses.

7. Replenishment Time (RT) is the sum of the delay, after the first consumption following a delivery, before an order is placed plus the delay after the order is placed until the ordered goods arrive at the ordering location.

Once inventory is managed as described above, continuous efforts should be undertaken to reduce RT, late deliveries, supplier minimum order quantities (both per SKU and per order) and customer order batching. Any improvements in these areas will automatically improve both availability and inventory turns, thanks to the adaptive nature of Buffer Management.

A stocking location that manages inventory according to the TOC should help a non-TOC customer (downstream link in a supply chain, whether internal or external) manage their inventory according to the TOC process. This type of help can take the form of a vendor managed inventory (VMI). The TOC distribution link simply extends its buffer sizing and management techniques to its customers' inventories. Doing so has the effect of smoothing the demand from the customer and reducing order sizes per SKU. VMI results in better availability and inventory turns for both supplier and customer. The benefits to the non-TOC customers are sufficient to meet the purpose of capitalizing on the competitive edge by giving the customer a reason to be more loyal and give more business to the upstream link. When the end consumers buy more, the whole supply chain sells more.

One caveat should be considered. Initially and only temporarily, the supply chain or a specific link may sell less as the surplus inventory in the system is sold. However, the sales lift due to improved availability is a countervailing factor. The current levels of surpluses and shortages make each case different.

Finance and Accounting

Holistic thinking applied to the finance application has been termed throughput accounting. Throughput accounting suggests that one examine the impact of investments and operational changes in terms of the impact on the throughput of the business. It is an alternative to cost accounting.

The primary measures for a TOC view of finance and accounting are: throughput, operating expense and investment. Throughput is calculated from sales minus "totally variable cost", where totally variable cost is usually calculated as the cost of raw materials that go into creating the item sold.

Project Management

Critical Chain Project Management (CCPM) are utilized in this area. CCPM is based on the idea that all projects look like A-plants: all activities converge to a final deliverable. As such, to protect the project, there must be internal buffers to protect synchronization points and a final project buffer to protect the overall project.

Marketing and Sales

While originally focused on manufacturing and logistics, TOC has expanded into sales management and marketing. Its role is explicitly acknowledged in the field of sales process engineering. For effective sales management one can apply Drum Buffer Rope to the sales process similar to the way it is applied to operations. This technique is appropriate when your constraint is in the sales process itself, or if you just want an effective sales management technique which includes the topics of funnel management and conversion rates.

Thinking Processes

The thinking processes are a set of tools to help managers walk through the steps of initiating and implementing a project. When used in a logical flow, they help walk through a buy-in process:

1. Gain agreement on the problem.
2. Gain agreement on the direction for a solution.
3. Gain agreement that the solution solves the problem.
4. Agree to overcome any potential negative ramifications.
5. Agree to overcome any obstacles to implementation.

TOC practitioners sometimes refer to these in the negative as working through layers of resistance to a change. Recently, the current reality tree (CRT) and future reality tree (FRT) have been applied to an argumentative academic paper.

Despite its origins as a manufacturing approach, Goldratt's Theory of Constraints (TOC) methodology is now regarded as a systems methodology with strong foundations in the hard sciences. Through its tools for convergent thinking and synthesis, the "Thinking processes", which underpin the entire TOC methodology, help identify and manage constraints and guide continuous improvement and change in organizations.

The process of change requires the identification and acceptance of core issues; the goal and the means to the goal. This comprehensive set of logical tools can be used for exploration, solution development and solution implementation for individuals, groups or organizations. Each tool has a purpose and nearly all tools can be used independent. Since these thinking tools are designed to address successive "layers of resistance" and enable communication, it expedites securing "buy in" of groups. While CRT (current reality tree) represents the undesirable effects of the current situation, the FRT (the future reality tree), NBR (negative branch) help people plan and understand the possible results of their actions. The PRT (prerequisite tree) and TRT (transition tree) are designed to build collective buy in and aid in the Implementation phase. The logical constructs of these tools or diagrams are the necessary condition logic, the sufficient cause logic and the strict logic rules that are used to validate cause-effect relationships which are modelled with these tools.

The associated logical constructs used is presented in the table below:

	Sufficient thinking "If then"	Necessary Thinking "In order to we must"
What to change?	Current Reality Tree	
What to change to?	Future Reality Tree Negative Branch Reservations	Evaporating cloud
How to change?	Transition Tree	Prerequisite Tree

TOC Thinking Process Tools

Use of these tools are based on the fundamental beliefs of TOC that organizations a) are inherently simple (interdependencies exist in organizations) b) desire inherent harmony (win – win solutions are possible) c) are inherently good (people are good) and have inherent potential (people and organizations have potential to do better). the major areas for application of TP tools as:

- To create and enhance thinking and learning skills.
- To make better decisions.
- To develop responsibility for one's own actions through understanding their consequences.
- To handle conflicts with more confidence and win-win outcomes.
- To correct behavior with undesirable consequences.
- Assist in evaluating conditions for achieving a desired outcome.
- To assist in peer mediation.
- To assist in relationship between subordinates and bosses.

Development and Practice

TOC was initiated by Goldratt, who until his recent death was still the main driving force behind the development and practice of TOC. There is a network of individuals and small companies loosely coupled as practitioners around the world. TOC is sometimes referred to as "constraint management". TOC is a large body of knowledge with a strong guiding philosophy of growth.

Criticisms that have been leveled against TOC include:

Claimed Suboptimality of Drum-buffer-rope

While TOC has been compared favorably to linear programming techniques, D. Trietsch from University of Auckland argues that DBR methodology is inferior to competing methodologies. Linhares, from the Getulio Vargas Foundation, has shown that the TOC approach to establishing an optimal product mix is unlikely to yield optimum results, as it would imply that P=NP.

Unacknowledged Debt

Duncan (as cited by Steyn) says that TOC borrows heavily from systems dynamics developed by Forrester in the 1950s and from statistical process control which dates back to World War II. And Noreen Smith and Mackey, in their independent report on TOC, point out that several key concepts in TOC "have been topics in management accounting textbooks for decades."

People claim Goldratt's books fail to acknowledge that TOC borrows from more than 40 years of previous management science research and practice, particularly from program evaluation and review technique/critical path method (PERT/CPM) and the just in time strategy. A rebuttal to these criticisms is offered in Goldratt's "What is the Theory of Constraints and How Should it be Implemented?", and in his audio program, "Beyond The Goal". In these, Goldratt discusses the history of disciplinary sciences, compares the strengths and weaknesses of the various disciplines, and acknowledges the sources of information and inspiration for the thinking processes and critical chain methodologies.

Goldratt has been criticized on lack of openness in his theories, an example being him not releasing the algorithm he used for the Optimum Performance Training system. Some view him as unscientific with many of his theories, tools and techniques not being a part of the public domain, rather a part of his own framework of profiting on his ideas. According to Gupta and Snyder, despite being recognized as a genuine management philosophy nowadays, TOC has yet failed to demonstrate its effectiveness in the academic literature and as such, cannot be considered academically worthy to be called a widely recognized theory. TOC needs more case studies that prove a connection between implementation and improved financial performance. Nave argues that TOC does not take employees into account and fails to empower them in the production process. He also states that TOC fails to address unsuccessful policies as constraints. In contrast, Mukherjee and Chatterjee state that much of the criticism of Goldratt's work has been focused on the lack of rigour in his work, but not of the bottleneck approach, which are two different aspects of the issue.

CORPORATE GOVERNANCE

Corporate governance is the system of rules, practices, and processes by which a firm is directed and controlled. Corporate governance essentially involves balancing the interests of a company's many stakeholders, such as shareholders, senior management executives, customers, suppliers, financiers, the government, and the community. Since corporate governance also provides the framework for attaining a company's objectives, it encompasses practically every sphere of management, from action plans and internal controls to performance measurement and corporate disclosure.

Governance refers specifically to the set of rules, controls, policies, and resolutions put in place to dictate corporate behavior. Proxy advisors and shareholders are important stakeholders who indirectly affect governance, but these are not examples of governance itself. The board of directors is pivotal in governance, and it can have major ramifications for equity valuation.

Communicating a firm's corporate governance is a key component of community and investor relations. On Apple investor relations site, for example, the firm outlines its corporate leadership—its executive team, its board of directors—and its corporate governance, including its committee charters and governance documents, such as bylaws, stock ownership guidelines and articles of incorporation.

Most companies strive to have a high level of corporate governance. For many shareholders, it is not enough for a company to merely be profitable; it also needs to demonstrate good corporate citizenship through environmental awareness, ethical behavior, and sound corporate governance practices. Good corporate governance creates a transparent set of rules and controls in which shareholders, directors, and officers have aligned incentives.

Corporate Governance and the Board of Directors

The board of directors is the primary direct stakeholder influencing corporate governance. Directors are elected by shareholders or appointed by other board members, and they represent shareholders of the company. The board is tasked with making important decisions, such as corporate officer appointments, executive compensation, and dividend policy. In some instances, board obligations stretch beyond financial optimization, as when shareholder resolutions call for certain social or environmental concerns to be prioritized.

Boards are often made up of inside and independent members. Insiders are major shareholders, founders and executives. Independent directors do not share the ties of the insiders, but they are chosen because of their experience managing or directing other large companies. Independents are considered helpful for governance because they dilute the concentration of power and help align shareholder interest with those of the insiders.

Bad Corporate Governance

Bad corporate governance can cast doubt on a company's reliability, integrity or obligation to shareholders—all of which can have implications on the firm's financial health. Tolerance or support of illegal activities can create scandals like the one that rocked Volkswagen AG starting in September 2015. The development of the details of "Dieselgate" (as the affair came to be known) revealed that for years, the automaker had deliberately and systematically rigged engine emission equipment in its cars in order to manipulate pollution test results, in America and Europe. Volkswagen saw its stock shed nearly half its value in the days following the start of the scandal, and its global sales in the first full month following the news fell 4.5%.

Public and government concern about corporate governance tends to wax and wane. Often, however, highly publicized revelations of corporate malfeasance revive interest in the subject. For example, corporate governance became a pressing issue in the United States at the turn of the 21st century, after fraudulent practices bankrupted high-profile companies such as Enron and WorldCom. It resulted in the 2002 passage of the Sarbanes-Oxley Act, which imposed more stringent recordkeeping requirements on companies, along with stiff criminal penalties for violating them and other securities laws. The aim was to restore public confidence in public companies and how they operate.

Other types of bad governance practices include:

- Companies do not cooperate sufficiently with auditors or do not select auditors with the appropriate scale, resulting in the publication of spurious or noncompliant financial documents.
- Bad executive compensation packages fail to create an optimal incentive for corporate officers.
- Poorly structured boards make it too difficult for shareholders to oust ineffective incumbents.

DESIGN MANAGEMENT

Design management is a complex field; it doesn't relate to a single design discipline and the exact responsibilities attached to a design manager will depend on the organization they work for, the size of that organization (and the tier in the hierarchy at which the manager operates), the industry they work in, the current market position and to a large extent the perceived importance of design to the business.

That means that defining "design management" becomes a near impossible task.

However, it is fair to say that design management in general works to support design within a business, the business and its objectives and the business's interface with the market it operates in.

This leads to three general roles that design managers will fulfill:

- Ensuring that design strategy and activities are in keeping with the larger business strategy.
- Ensuring the quality of the outcomes of design activities within their remit.
- Ensuring that user experience is prioritized and ensuring that it is user needs that create new products and differentiation from the competition.

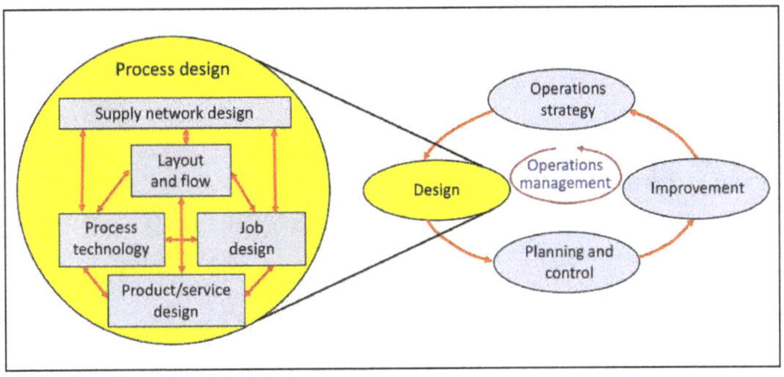

Design and Management

We take design at its most simple definition that of a practical approach to problem solving. This remains true from industrial design to service design – designers build products and/or services to solve user and customer problems. Management, in any business activity, is the act of working with people and processes to reach organization objectives in the most efficient manner possible. It can include planning, organizing, controlling, staffing and directing people and processes.

What it does not include is leadership. While some managers are leaders many are not and leadership is effectively bestowed upon a person by those who follow a leader and cannot be dictated by corporate position. Leadership is a proactive pursuit and leadership may change within a group dynamic depending on the situation currently being faced – management on the other hand is constant and more reactive.

The Evolution of Design Management

Design management has only been formalized as an individual discipline quite recently (in the latter half of the 20th century) however; the tasks of design management have been taking place since the earliest corporations began to invest in design:

- Before the 1960s design management was mainly concerned with managing the aesthetic components of design in terms of products and the corporate brand.

- In the 1960s and 1970s design management became concerned with systemizing the design function so that output became more reliable – checklists and tools for quality control became more widely used.
- Then in the 1980s and 1990s design managers became more high profile as their contributions to a business's success became better understood and the focus of design management became more strategic with the objective being to secure design as a strategic asset. Design began to work alongside production and marketing at the highest levels of organizations.
- In the 2000s (and until now) the focus shifted again. Design started to become a proactive strategic tool and managing design was now all about ensuring the ability to innovate and lead markets rather than to respond to market needs.

Design managers aren't just involved with the needs of design – they're also involved with the larger needs of the business as this cartoon shows.

Areas of Design Management

As we said at the start of this piece; design falls into a large number of disciplines and thus so too does design management. Some of the more common areas in which design management can be found include:

- Product design: The manager here will be looking at managing all functions related to product development and release and securing relationships with other business units to facilitate this. A user-centered (or UX centered) approach is commonly the guiding force for this work.
- Brand design: Responsibilities here are for brand experience, developing touch points, and creating reliable, trustworthy perspectives that are strongly recognizable to clients.
- Service design: The flip side to product design and something that is becoming increasingly importance with the rise of the product-service hybrid. Service design takes a customer experience (CV) or customer-centered approach.

- Business design: Business design is an emerging concept – it's the understanding that businesses can be designed from within to operate more efficiently and at higher levels of effectiveness. Typically, a business design manager will need to be very effective at persuading others of the utility of their designs.
- Engineering design: Engineering design is more concerned with technological outputs than other disciplines of design – be it a technological process (such as manufacturing) or technological artifacts (such as a system).

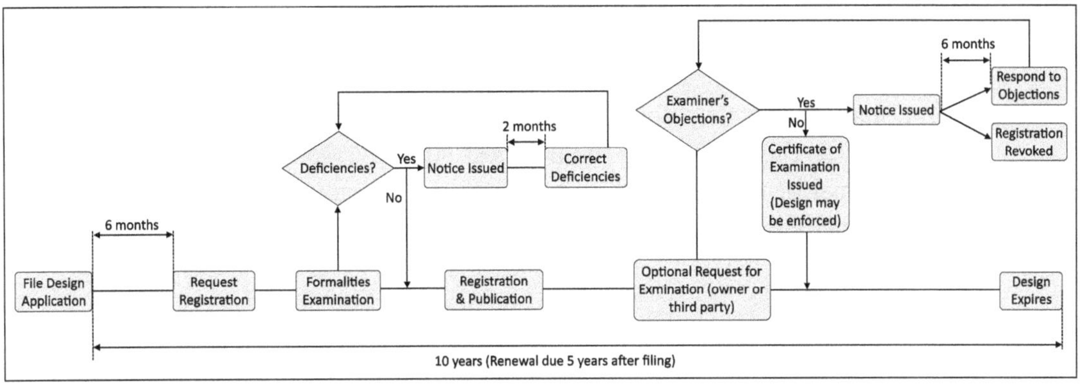

Where design management is best employed often depends on the processes of the business.

Why does Design Management Matter

Design management matters because, for the vast majority of companies not engaged in simple reselling, design offers the only opportunity for a company to innovate and differentiate itself from competitors.

Design management allows companies to better control their design process and enhance:

- Their internal business processes – cutting out waste and inefficiency in processes may not be visible to the company's clients but it will be clearly beneficial to the company in terms of reduced costs.
- Their learning and growth curve – design knowledge can be applied to learning and development too, thus focus is brought to strategic integration and the quality of employees on the ground.
- Customer and brand relationships – design as applied to brand ensures strategic positioning and market differentiation in customer's eyes.
- Finances – design efforts should either increase sales or reduce costs to demonstrate strategic value and measurable value for the business.

Where does Design Management Fall within Businesses?

Design managers will find themselves operating in businesses with one of these strategic orientations:

- Product-driven companies- In this instance it's likely that the majority of design will fall within the company's research and development function.
- Market-driven companies. In these businesses design is likely to belong within the marketing department.
- Brand-driven companies- These companies will often place design within the corporate communications department.

There are also three levels of corporate hierarchy that design managers operate from within:

- Operational- This is the "doing" of design and is concerned with managing projects and teams that deliver on the business strategy. Good managers will be able to measure performance in terms of outcomes. Common job titles for design managers here include: operations design manager, design team lead, senior designer, etc.
- Tactical- This is the "structuring" of design within a business – determining how projects are coordinated to achieve higher objectives, managing the skill and competency frameworks for design in a business, creating high-level systems for cooperation or support of design, etc. Common job titles at this level include: brand design manager, tactical design manager, design director, etc.
- Strategic- This is the "direction" of design within a business – the determination of how design will meet corporate strategy and the development of the individual design strategy. Common job titles at this level include: design director, vice-president for design, chief design officer, etc.

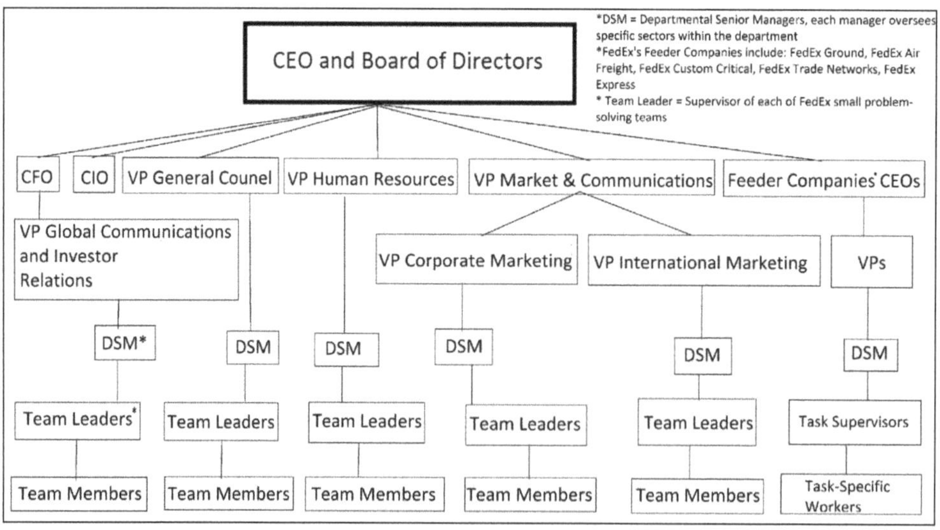

Management structures can vary significantly from one company to another and thus it's hard to say with certainty where design management will be in any given company.

ORGANIZATION DEVELOPMENT

Organization development (OD) is the study of successful organizational change and performance. OD emerged from human relations studies in the 1930s, during which psychologists realized that organizational structures and processes influence worker behavior and motivation. More recently, work on OD has expanded to focus on aligning organizations with their rapidly changing and complex environments through organizational learning, knowledge management and transformation of organizational norms and values. Key concepts of OD theory include: organizational climate (the mood or unique "personality" of an organization, which includes attitudes and beliefs that influence members' collective behavior), organizational culture (the deeply-seated norms, values and behaviors that members share) and organizational strategies (how an organization identifies problems, plans action, negotiates change and evaluates progress).

Organization development as a practice involves an ongoing, systematic process of implementing effective organizational change. OD is both a field of applied science focused on understanding and managing organizational change and a field of scientific study and inquiry. It is interdisciplinary in nature and draws on sociology, psychology, particularly industrial and organizational psychology, and theories of motivation, learning, and personality. Although behavioral science has provided the basic foundation for the study and practice of OD, new and emerging fields of study have made their presence felt. Experts in systems thinking, in organizational learning, in the structure of intuition in decision-making, and in coaching (to name a few) whose perspective is not steeped in just the behavioral sciences, but in a much more multi-disciplinary and inter-disciplinary approach, have emerged as OD catalysts or tools.

Core Values

Underlying Organization Development are humanistic values. Margulies and Raia articulated the humanistic values of OD as follows:

1. Providing opportunities for people to function as human beings rather than as resources in the productive process.
2. Providing opportunities for each organization member, as well as for the organization itself, to develop to their full potential.
3. Seeking to increase the effectiveness of the organization in terms of all of its goals.
4. Attempting to create an environment in which it is possible to find exciting and challenging work.
5. Providing opportunities for people in organizations to influence the way in which they relate to work, the organization, and the environment.

6. Treating each human being as a person with a complex set of needs, all of which are important to their work and their life.

This is a separate concept from change efforts known as:

1. Operation management
2. Training and Development
3. Technological innovations etc.

Objectives

The objectives of OD are:

1. To increase the level of inter-personal trust among employees.
2. To increase employees' level of satisfaction and commitment.
3. To confront problems instead of neglecting them.
4. To effectively manage conflict.
5. To increase cooperation and collaboration among employees.
6. To increase organizational problem-solving.
7. To put in place processes that will help improve the on-going operation of an organization on a continuous basis.

As objectives of organizational development are framed keeping in view specific situations, they vary from one situation to another. In other words, these programs are tailored to meet the requirements of a particular situation. But broadly speaking, all organizational development programs try to achieve the following objectives:

1. Making individuals in the organization aware of the vision of the organization. Organizational development helps in making employees align with the vision of the organization.
2. Encouraging employees to solve problems instead of avoiding them.
3. Strengthening inter-personal trust, cooperation, and communication for the successful achievement of organizational goals.
4. Encouraging every individual to participate in the process of planning, thus making them feel responsible for the implementation of the plan.
5. Creating a work atmosphere in which employees are encouraged To work and participate enthusiastically.

6. Replacing formal lines of authority with personal knowledge and skill.
7. Preparing members to align with changes and to break stereotypes.
8. Creating an environment of trust so that employees willingly accept change.

According to organizational-development thinking, organization development provides managers with a vehicle for introducing change systematically by applying a broad selection of management techniques. This, in turn, leads to greater personal, group, and organizational effectiveness.

Change Agent

A change agent in the sense used here is not a technical expert skilled in such functional areas as accounting, production, or finance. The change agent is a behavioral scientist who knows how to get people in an organization involved in solving their own problems. A change agent's main strength is a comprehensive knowledge of human behavior, supported by a number of intervention techniques. The change agent can be either external or internal to the organization. An internal change agent is usually a staff person who has expertise in the behavioral sciences and in the intervention technology of OD. Beckhard reports several cases in which line people have been trained in OD and have returned to their organizations to engage in successful change-assignments. In the natural evolution of change mechanisms in organizations, this would seem to approach the ideal arrangement.

Researchers at the University of Oxford found that leaders can be effective change-agents within their own organizations if they are strongly committed to "knowledge leadership" targeted towards organizational development. In their three-year study of UK healthcare organizations, the researchers identified three different mechanisms through which knowledge leaders actively "transposed", "appropriated" or "contended" change concepts, effectively translating and embedding these in organizational practice.

The change agent may be a staff or line member of the organization who is schooled in OD theory and technique. In such a case, the "contractual relationship" is an in-house agreement that should probably be explicit with respect to all of the conditions involved except the fee.

Sponsoring Organization

The initiative for OD programs often comes from an organization that has a problem or anticipates facing a problem. This means that top management or someone authorized by top management is aware that a problem exists and has decided to seek help in solving it. There is a direct analogy here to the practice of psychotherapy: The client or patient must actively seek help in finding a solution to his problems. This indicates a willingness on the part of the client organization to accept help and assures the organization that management is actively concerned.

Applied Behavioral Science

One of the outstanding characteristics of OD that distinguishes it from most other improvement programs is that it is based on a "helping relationship". Some believe that the change agent is a physician to the organization's ills; that s/he does not examine the "patient", make a diagnosis, and write a prescription. Nor does s/he try to teach organizational members a new inventory of knowledge which they then transfer to the job situation. Using theory and methods drawn from such behavioral sciences as industrial/organizational psychology, industrial sociology, communication, cultural anthropology, administrative theory, organizational behavior, economics, and political science, the change agent's main function is to help the organization define and solve its own problems. The basic method used is known as action research. This approach, which is described in detail later, consists of a preliminary diagnosis, collecting data, feedback of the data to the client, data exploration by the client group, action planning based on the data, and taking action.

Systems Context

The Holistic and Futuristic View of Organization

OD deals with a total system the organization as a whole, including its relevant environment or with a subsystem or systems departments or work groups in the context of the total system. Parts of systems for example, individuals, cliques, structures, norms, values, and products are not considered in isolation; the principle of interdependency that change in one part of a system affects the other parts is fully recognized. Thus OD interventions focus on the total cultures and cultural processes of organizations. The focus is also on groups, since the relevant behavior of individuals in organizations and groups is generally a product of the influences of groups rather than of personalities.

Improved Organizational Performance

The objective of OD is to improve the organization's capacity to handle its internal and external functioning and relationships. This includes improved interpersonal and group processes, more effective communication, and enhanced ability to cope with organizational problems of all kinds. It also involves more effective decision processes, more appropriate leadership styles, improved skill in dealing with destructive conflict, as well as developing improved levels of trust and cooperation among organizational members. These objectives stem from a value system based on an optimistic view of the nature of man that man in a supportive environment is capable of achieving higher levels of development and accomplishment. Essential to organization development and effectiveness is the scientific method inquiry, a rigorous search for causes, experimental testing of hypotheses, and review of results.

Self-managing work groups allows the members of a work team to manage, control, and monitor all facets of their work, from recruiting, hiring, and new employees to deciding when to take rest breaks. An early analysis of the first-self-managing work groups yielded the following behavioral characteristics:

- Employees assume personal responsibility and accountability for outcomes of their work.
- Employees monitor their own performance and seek feedback on how well they are accomplishing their goals.
- Employees manage their performance and take corrective action when necessary to improve their and the performance of other group members.
- Employees seek guidance, assistance, and resources from the organization when they do not have what they need to do the job.
- Employees help members of their work group and employees in other groups to improve job performance and raise productivity for the organization as a whole.

Organizational Self-renewal

The ultimate aim of OD practitioners is to "work themselves out of a job" by leaving the client organization with a set of tools, behaviors, attitudes, and an action plan with which to monitor its own state of health and to take corrective steps toward its own renewal and development. This is consistent with the systems concept of feedback as a regulatory and corrective mechanism. To this end, OD scholars and practitioners use tools such as simulations with their clients, to be used in workshops and classroom settings. One example of a self-renewal simulation, authored by researchers from Cornell University and Indiana University, can be found here.

Understanding Organizations

Weisbord presents a six-box model for understanding organizations:

1. Purposes: the organization members are clear about the organization's mission and purpose and goal agreements, whether people support the organization's purpose.
2. structure: how is the organization's work divided up? the question is whether there is an adequate fit between the purpose and the internal structure.
3. relationship: between individuals, between units or departments that perform different tasks, and between the people and requirements of their jobs.
4. rewards: the consultant should diagnose the similarities between what the organization formally rewarded or punished members for.
5. leadership: is to watch for blips among the other boxes and maintain balance among them.

6. helpful mechanism: what must the organization attend to in order to survive and thrive - procedures such as planning, control, budgeting, and other information systems.

Modern Development

In recent years, serious questioning has emerged about the relevance of OD to managing change in modern organizations. The need for "reinventing" the field has become a topic that even some of its "founding fathers" are discussing critically.

With this call for reinvention and change, scholars have begun to examine organization development from an emotion-based standpoint. For example, deKlerk writes about how emotional trauma can negatively affect performance. Due to downsizing, outsourcing, mergers, restructuring, continual changes, invasions of privacy, harassment, and abuses of power, many employees experience the emotions of aggression, anxiety, apprehension, cynicism, and fear, which can lead to performance decreases. deKlerk suggests that in order to heal the trauma and increase performance, O.D. practitioners must acknowledge the existence of the trauma, provide a safe place for employees to discuss their feelings, symbolize the trauma and put it into perspective, and then allow for and deal with the emotional responses. One method of achieving this is by having employees draw pictures of what they feel about the situation, and then having them explain their drawings with each other. Drawing pictures is beneficial because it allows employees to express emotions they normally would not be able to put into words. Also, drawings often prompt active participation in the activity, as everyone is required to draw a picture and then discuss its meaning.

The use of new technologies combined with globalization has also shifted the field of organization development. Roland Sullivan defined Organization Development with participants at the 1st Organization Development Conference for Asia in Dubai-2005 as "Organization Development is a transformative leap to a desired vision where strategies and systems align, in the light of local culture with an innovative and authentic leadership style using the support of high tech tools. Bob Aubrey introduced KDIs (Key Development Indicators) to help organisations go beyond performance and align strategy, organisations and individuals and argued that fundamental challenges such as robotics, artificial intelligence and genetics prefigure a regeneration of the field.

BENCHMARKING

Benchmarking is the practice of comparing business processes and performance metrics to industry bests and best practices from other companies. Dimensions typically measured are quality, time and cost. Benchmarking is used to measure performance using a specific indicator (cost per unit of measure, productivity per unit of measure, cycle time of x per unit of measure or defects per unit of measure) resulting in a metric of performance that is then compared to others.

Also referred to as "best practice benchmarking" or "process benchmarking", this process is used in management in which organizations evaluate various aspects of their processes in relation to best-practice companies' processes, usually within a peer group defined for the purposes of comparison. This then allows organizations to develop plans on how to make improvements or adapt specific best practices, usually with the aim of increasing some aspect of performance. Benchmarking may be a one-off event, but is often treated as a continuous process in which organizations continually seek to improve their practices. In project management benchmarking can also support the selection, planning and delivery of projects.

In the process of best practice benchmarking, management identifies the best firms in their industry, or in another industry where similar processes exist, and compares the results and processes of those studied (the "targets") to one's own results and processes. In this way, they learn how well the targets perform and, more importantly, the business processes that explain why these firms are successful. According to National Council on Measurement in Education, benchmark assessments are short assessments used by teachers at various times throughout the school year to monitor student progress in some area of the school curriculum. These also are known as interim assessments.

Procedure

There is no single benchmarking process that has been universally adopted. The wide appeal and acceptance of benchmarking has led to the emergence of benchmarking methodologies. One seminal book is Boxwell's Benchmarking for Competitive Advantage (1994). The first book on benchmarking, written and published by Kaiser Associates, is a practical guide and offers a seven-step approach. Robert Camp (who wrote one of the earliest books on benchmarking in 1989) developed a 12-stage approach to benchmarking.

The 12 stage methodology consists of:

- Select subject
- Define the process
- Identify potential partners
- Identify data sources
- Collect data and select all partners
- Determine the gap

- Establish process differences
- Target future performance
- Communicate
- Adjust goal
- Implement
- Review and recalibrate

The following is an example of a typical benchmarking methodology:

- Identify problem areas: Because benchmarking can be applied to any business process or function, a range of research techniques may be required. They include informal conversations with customers, employees, or suppliers; exploratory research techniques such as focus groups; or in-depth marketing research, quantitative research, surveys, questionnaires, re-engineering analysis, process mapping, quality control variance reports, financial ratio analysis, or simply reviewing cycle times or other performance indicators. Before embarking on comparison with other organizations it is essential to know the organization's function and processes; base lining performance provides a point against which improvement effort can be measured.
- Identify other industries that have similar processes: For instance, if one were interested in improving hand-offs in addiction treatment one would identify other fields that also have hand-off challenges. These could include air traffic control, cell phone switching between towers, transfer of patients from surgery to recovery rooms.
- Identify organizations that are leaders in these areas: Look for the very best in any industry and in any country. Consult customers, suppliers, financial analysts, trade associations, and magazines to determine which companies are worthy of study.
- Survey companies for measures and practices: Companies target specific business processes using detailed surveys of measures and practices used to identify business process alternatives and leading companies. Surveys are typically masked to protect confidential data by neutral associations and consultants.
- Visit the "best practice" companies to identify leading edge practices: Companies typically agree to mutually exchange information beneficial to all parties in a benchmarking group and share the results within the group.
- Implement new and improved business practices: Take the leading edge practices and develop implementation plans which include identification of specific opportunities, funding the project and selling the ideas to the organization for the purpose of gaining demonstrated value from the process.

Costs

The three main types of costs in benchmarking are:

- Visit Costs - This includes hotel rooms, travel costs, meals, a token gift, and lost labor time.
- Time Costs - Members of the benchmarking team will be investing time in researching problems, finding exceptional companies to study, visits, and implementation. This will take them away from their regular tasks for part of each day so additional staff might be required.
- Benchmarking Database Costs - Organizations that institutionalize benchmarking into their daily procedures find it is useful to create and maintain a database of best practices and the companies associated with each best practice now.

The cost of benchmarking can substantially be reduced through utilizing the many internet resources that have sprung up over the last few years. These aim to capture benchmarks and best practices from organizations, business sectors and countries to make the benchmarking process much quicker and cheaper.

Technical and Product Benchmarking

The technique initially used to compare existing corporate strategies with a view to achieving the best possible performance in new situations, has recently been extended to the comparison of technical products. This process is usually referred to as "technical benchmarking" or "product benchmarking". Its use is well-developed within the automotive industry ("automotive benchmarking"), where it is vital to design products that match precise user expectations, at minimal cost, by applying the best technologies available worldwide. Data is obtained by fully disassembling existing cars and their systems. Such analyses were initially carried out in-house by car makers and their suppliers. However, as these analyses are expensive, they are increasingly being outsourced to companies who specialize in this area. Outsourcing has enabled a drastic decrease in costs for each company (by cost sharing) and the development of efficient tools (standards, software).

Types

Benchmarking can be internal (comparing performance between different groups or teams within an organization) or external (comparing performance with companies in a specific industry or across industries). Within these broader categories, there are three specific types of benchmarking: 1) Process benchmarking, 2) Performance benchmarking and 3) Strategic benchmarking.

These can be further detailed as follows:

- Process benchmarking - the initiating firm focuses its observation and investigation of business processes with a goal of identifying and observing the best practices from one or more benchmark firms. Activity analysis will be required where the objective is to benchmark cost and efficiency; increasingly applied to back-office processes where outsourcing may be a consideration. Benchmarking is appropriate in nearly every case where process redesign or improvement is to be undertaking so long as the cost of the study does not exceed the expected benefit.

- Financial benchmarking - performing a financial analysis and comparing the results in an effort to assess your overall competitiveness and productivity.
- Benchmarking from an investor perspective- extending the benchmarking universe to also compare to peer companies that can be considered alternative investment opportunities from the perspective of an investor.
- Benchmarking in the public sector - functions as a tool for improvement and innovation in public administration, where state organizations invest efforts and resources to achieve quality, efficiency and effectiveness of the services they provide.
- Performance benchmarking - allows the initiator firm to assess their competitive position by comparing products and services with those of target firms.
- Product benchmarking - the process of designing new products or upgrades to current ones. This process can sometimes involve reverse engineering which is taking apart competitors' products to find strengths and weaknesses.
- Strategic benchmarking - involves observing how others compete. This type is usually not industry specific, meaning it is best to look at other industries.
- Functional benchmarking - a company will focus its benchmarking on a single function to improve the operation of that particular function. Complex functions such as Human Resources, Finance and Accounting and Information and Communication Technology are unlikely to be directly comparable in cost and efficiency terms and may need to be disaggregated into processes to make valid comparison.
- Best-in-class benchmarking - involves studying the leading competitor or the company that best carries out a specific function.
- Operational benchmarking embraces everything from staffing and productivity to office flow and analysis of procedures performed.
- Energy benchmarking - process of collecting, analysing and relating energy performance data of comparable activities with the purpose of evaluating and comparing performance between or within entities. Entities can include processes, buildings or companies. Benchmarking may be internal between entities within a single organization, or - subject to confidentiality restrictions - external between competing entities.

Tools

Benchmarking software can be used to organize large and complex amounts of information. Software packages can extend the concept of benchmarking and competitive analysis by allowing individuals to handle such large and complex amounts or strategies. Such tools support different types of benchmarking and can reduce the above costs significantly. The emerging technology of benchmarking engines automates the stage of going from data to noteworthy comparative insights, sometimes even expressing the insights in English sentences.

Metric Benchmarking

Another approach to making comparisons involves using more aggregative cost or production information to identify strong and weak performing units. The two most common forms of quantitative analysis used in metric benchmarking are data envelope analysis (DEA) and regression analysis. DEA estimates the cost level an efficient firm should be able to achieve in a particular market. In infrastructure regulation, DEA can be used to reward companies/operators whose costs are near the efficient frontier with additional profits. Regression analysis estimates what the average firm should be able to achieve. With regression analysis, firms that performed better than average can be rewarded while firms that performed worse than average can be penalized. Such benchmarking studies are used to create yardstick comparisons, allowing outsiders to evaluate the performance of operators in an industry. Advanced statistical techniques, including stochastic frontier analysis, have been used to identify high and weak performers in industries, including applications to schools, hospitals, water utilities, and electric utilities.

One of the biggest challenges for metric benchmarking is the variety of metric definitions used among companies or divisions. Definitions may change over time within the same organization due to changes in leadership and priorities. The most useful comparisons can be made when metrics definitions are common between compared units and do not change so improvements can be changed.

LEAN DYNAMICS

Lean dynamics is a business management practice that emphasizes the same primary outcome as lean manufacturing or lean production of eliminating wasteful expenditure of resources. However, it is distinguished by its different focus of creating a structure for accommodating the dynamic business conditions that cause these wastes to accumulate in the first place.

Like lean manufacturing, lean dynamics is a variation on the theme of creating efficiencies and greater value by optimizing flow rather than by maximizing economies of scale.

As such, it represents an important chapter in the broader discussion of Taylorism, Fordisim, Alfred Sloan's standard volume methodology, Peter Drucker's philosophy on the "theory of the business" and Genichi Taguchi's analysis of loss. Its general philosophy has grown in popularity over recent years, in large part because of the increasingly challenging circumstances faced by the global business world.

This need to create greater efficiencies while competing in an environment that demands constant change and innovation seems to be responsible for the emergence of lean dynamics as a recognized business improvement approach.

The term "lean" was first coined by a researcher at MIT and later popularized by the best-selling book, The Machine that Changed the World. Those implementing lean principles generally focus on applying lean tools which have been described in a number of references over the past two decades with the focus of seeking out and directly targeting "waste" (its seven forms described by Taiichi Ohno in Toyota Production System are well known.) This emphasis can result in greater efficiencies that do not necessarily respond well when business conditions shift.

Lean dynamics takes a different approach. It does not directly target the desired *outcome* of waste elimination; instead, it focuses on identifying and addressing sources of "lag", or imbedded disconnects in flowing value through operations, decision-making, information, and innovation that lead to workarounds and amplify disruption when business conditions change. It promotes a different way of structuring the business that creates an inherent "dynamic stability" or greater responsiveness for accommodating shifting business conditions. Companies that are structured in this way show dramatically greater customer value as measured by their quality, innovation, and customer satisfaction; they also sustain greater corporate value as measured by profitability, market capitalization, and growth.

Lean dynamics uses the value curve as a data-driven way of directly comparing companies to distinguish lean firms from other industries. Implementation of lean dynamics focuses on driving down the impact that variation has on loss (based on the loss function from the Taguchi methods often described by the famous business statistician W. Edwards Deming), a concept describing the dramatic reduction of value-creating capabilities that traditional management systems display when subjected to sudden shifts in product demand, energy prices, or other conditions that affect operational stability or predictability.

Lean dynamics is particularly versatile in that it can be applied to a wide range of manufacturing and service industries. Its methods have been studied for Aerospace and Defense (particularly as applied to procuring hard to get spare parts), and medical, and distinguishes the few that stand out during crisis such as airlines, and retail.

Lean dynamics has its roots in a global study of lean manufacturing in the aerospace industry aimed at understanding how to break its cycle of cost escalation that was making new products unaffordable. These results were described in the Shingo Prize winning book, Breaking the Cost Barrier. This study showed that directly targeting "waste" reduction as the focal point for lean programs does not lead to significant cost savings. Instead, it provided strong evidence that emphasis should be placed on applying lean principles to mitigate the amplification of variation that causes workarounds. Addressing this variation was critical to overcoming the disruption that often causes waste to accumulate in the first place. Other sources cited this, identifying occurrences across other industries.

Subsequent research of the aerospace industry showed that firms had accepted these findings, describing this approach of Variation Management as "one of the most prominent approaches to transforming and improving military enterprise performance."

This phenomenon was validated by correlating the disruption caused by variation in flow (measured as cycle time variation) with "loss" as described by the Taguchi Loss Function. Sudden changes in business conditions, such as spikes or decreases in production demand, cause increases in variation from forecasted conditions, causing disruption, and causing waste to accumulate. A lean dynamics approach restructures the way operations, organizations, information, and innovation are structured to overcome this.

One method for companies to deal internally with externally driven variation (such as sudden spikes in demand), a core tenet of lean dynamics, was explored by the Defense Department under the Supplier Utilization through Responsive Grouped Enterprises (SURGE) Program. The SURGE program was partially sponsored by the Joint Strike Fighter Program (JSF)(F-35 Lightning II) This program aimed to reduce factory disruption due to demand variation by grouping parts together that shared similar manufacturing processes. It succeeded in reducing lead time on a number of critical aerospace items by as much as 60%. The SURGE program gained notoriety when it was mentioned on the popular TV Show.

BUSINESS PROCESS MANAGEMENT

Business process management (BPM) is a discipline in operations management in which people use various methods to discover, model, analyze, measure, improve, optimize, and automate business processes. Any combination of methods used to manage a company's business processes is BPM. Processes can be structured and repeatable or unstructured and variable. Though not required, enabling technologies are often used with BPM.

It can be differentiated from program management in that program management is concerned with managing a group of inter-dependent projects. From another view point, process management includes program management. In project management, process management is the use of a repeatable process to improve the outcome of the project.

Key distinctions between process management and project management are repeatability and predictability. If the structure and sequence of work is unique, then it is a project. In business process management, a sequence of work can vary from instance to instance: there are gateways, conditions; business rules etc. The key is predictability: no matter how many forks in the road, we know all of them in advance, and we understand the conditions for the process to take one route or another. If this condition is met, we are dealing with a process.

As an approach, BPM sees processes as important assets of an organization that must be understood, managed, and developed to announce and deliver value-added products and services to clients or customers. This approach closely resembles other total quality management or continual improvement process methodologies.

ISO 9000 promotes the process approach to managing an organization. promotes the adoption of a process approach when developing, implementing and improving the effectiveness of a quality management system, to enhance customer satisfaction by meeting customer requirements. BPM proponents also claim that this approach can be supported, or enabled, through technology.

BPM Institute defined Business process management as the definition, improvement, and management of a firm's end-to-end enterprise business processes in order to achieve three outcomes crucial to a performance-based, customer-driven firm: 1) clarity on strategic direction, 2) alignment of the firm's resources, and 3) increased discipline in daily operations.

The Workflow Management Coalition, Business process management (BPM) is a discipline involving any combination of modeling, automation, execution, control, measurement and optimization of business activity flows, in support of enterprise goals, spanning systems, employees, customers and partners within and beyond the enterprise boundaries.

The Association of Business Process Management Professionals defines BPM as, Business process management (BPM) is a disciplined approach to identify, design, execute, document, measure, monitor, and control both automated and non-automated business processes to achieve consistent, targeted results aligned with an organization's strategic goals. BPM involves the deliberate, collaborative and increasingly technology-aided definition, improvement, innovation, and management of end-to-end business processes that drive business results, create value, and enable an organization to meet its business objectives with more agility.

BPM enables an enterprise to align its business processes to its business strategy, leading to effective overall company performance through improvements of specific work activities either within a specific department, across the enterprise, or between organizations.

Gartner defines business process management as "the discipline of managing processes (rather than tasks) as the means for improving business performance outcomes and operational agility. Processes span organizational boundaries, linking together people, information flows, systems, and other assets to create and deliver value to customers and constituents."

It is common to confuse BPM with a BPM suite (BPMS). BPM is a professional discipline done by people, whereas a BPMS is a technological suite of tools designed to help the BPM professionals accomplish their goals. BPM should also not be confused with an application or solution developed to support a particular process. Suites and solutions represent ways of automating business processes, but automation is only one aspect of BPM.

Changes

The concept of business process may be as traditional as concepts of tasks, department, production, and outputs, arising from job shop scheduling problems in the early 20th Century. The management and improvement approach as of 2010, with formal definitions and technical modeling, has been around since the early 1990s. Note that the term "business process" is sometimes used by IT practitioners as synonymous with the management of middleware processes or with integrating application software tasks.

Although BPM initially focused on the automation of business processes with the use of information technology, it has since been extended to integrate human-driven processes in which human interaction takes place in series or parallel with the use of technology. For example, workflow management systems can assign individual steps requiring deploying human intuition or judgment to relevant humans and other tasks in a workflow to a relevant automated system.

More recent variations such as "human interaction management" are concerned with the interaction between human workers performing a task. As of 2010, technology has allowed the coupling of BPM with other methodologies, such as Six Sigma. Some BPM tools such as SIPOCs, process flows, RACIs, CTQs and histograms allow users to:

- Visualize – functions and processes;
- Measure – determine the appropriate measure to determine success;
- Analyze – compare the various simulations to determine an optimal improvement;
- Improve – select and implement the improvement;
- Control – deploy this implementation and by use of user-defined dashboards monitor the improvement in real time and feed the performance information back into the simulation model in preparation for the next improvement iteration;
- Re-engineer – revamp the processes from scratch for better results.

This brings with it the benefit of being able to simulate changes to business processes based on real-world data (not just on assumed knowledge). Also, the coupling of BPM to industry methodologies allows users to continually streamline and optimize the process to ensure that it is tuned to its market need.

As of 2012 research on BPM has paid increasing attention to the compliance of business processes. Although a key aspect of business processes is flexibility, as business processes continuously need to adapt to changes in the environment, compliance with business strategy, policies, and government regulations should also be ensured. The compliance aspect in BPM is highly important for governmental organizations. As of 2010 BPM approaches in a governmental context largely focus on operational processes and knowledge representation. There have been many technical studies on operational business processes in the public and private sectors, but researchers rarely take legal compliance activities into account—for instance, the legal implementation processes in public-administration bodies.

Life-cycle

Business process management activities can be arbitrarily grouped into categories such as design, modeling, execution, monitoring, and optimization.

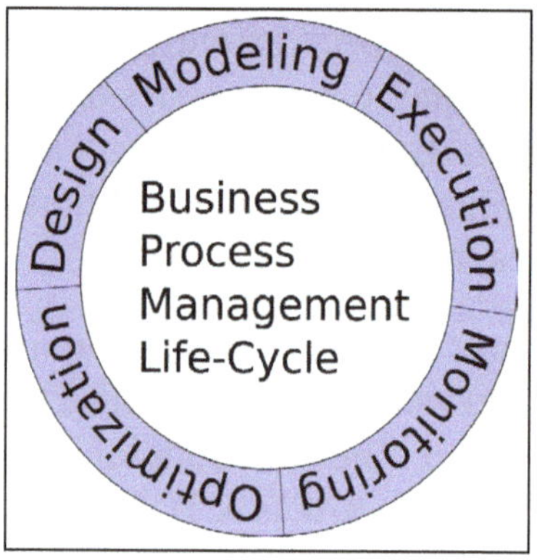

Design

Process design encompasses both the identification of existing processes and the design of "to-be" processes. Areas of focus include representation of the process flow, the factors within it, alerts and notifications, escalations, standard operating procedures, service level agreements, and task hand-over mechanisms. Whether or not existing processes are considered, the aim of this step is to ensure a correct and efficient new design.

The proposed improvement could be in human-to-human, human-to-system or system-to-system workflows, and might target regulatory, market, or competitive challenges faced by the businesses. Existing processes and design of a new process for various applications must synchronize and not cause a major outage or process interruption.

Modeling

Modeling takes the theoretical design and introduces combinations of variables (e.g., changes in rent or materials costs, which determine how the process might operate under different circumstances). It may also involve running "what-if analysis"(Conditions-when, if, else) on the processes: What if you have 75% of resources to do the same task?" "What if you want to do the same job for 80% of the current cost?

Execution

Business process execution is broadly about enacting a discovered and modeled business process. Enacting a business process is done manually or automatically or with a combination of manual and automated business tasks. Manual business processes are human-driven. Automated business processes are software-driven. Business process automation encompasses methods and software deployed for automating business processes.

Business process automation is performed and orchestrated at the business process layer or the consumer presentation layer of SOA Reference Architecture. BPM software suites such as BPMS or iBPMS or low-code platforms are positioned at the business process layer. While the emerging robotic process automation software performs business process automation at the presentation layer, therefore is considered non-invasive to and de-coupled from existing application systems.

One of the ways to automate processes is to develop or purchase an application that executes the required steps of the process; however, in practice, these applications rarely execute all the steps of the process accurately or completely. Another approach is to use a combination of software and human intervention; however this approach is more complex, making the documentation process difficult.

In response to these problems, companies have developed software that defines the full business process (as developed in the process design activity) in a computer language that a computer can directly execute. Process models can be run through execution engines that automate the processes directly from the model (e.g., calculating a repayment plan for a loan) or, when a step is too complex to automate, Business Process Modeling Notation (BPMN) provides front-end capability for human input. Compared to either of the previous approaches, directly executing a process definition can be more straightforward and therefore easier to improve. However, automating a process definition requires flexible and comprehensive infrastructure, which typically rules out implementing these systems in a legacy IT environment.

Business rules have been used by systems to provide definitions for governing behavior, and a business rule engine can be used to drive process execution and resolution.

Monitoring

Monitoring encompasses the tracking of individual processes, so that information on their state can be easily seen, and statistics on the performance of one or more processes can be provided. An example of this tracking is being able to determine the state of a customer order *(e.g.* order arrived, awaiting delivery, invoice paid) so that problems in its operation can be identified and corrected.

In addition, this information can be used to work with customers and suppliers to improve their connected processes. Examples are the generation of measures on how quickly a customer order is processed or how many orders were processed in the last month. These measures tend to fit into three categories: cycle time, defect rate and productivity. The degree of monitoring depends on what information the business wants to evaluate and analyze and how the business wants it monitored, in real-time, near real-time or ad hoc. Here, business activity monitoring (BAM) extends and expands the monitoring tools generally provided by BPMS.

Process mining is a collection of methods and tools related to process monitoring. The aim of process mining is to analyze event logs extracted through process monitoring and to compare them with an a priori process model. Process mining allows process analysts to detect discrepancies between the actual process execution and the a priori model as well as to analyze bottlenecks. Predictive Business Process Monitoring concerns the application of data mining, machine learning, and other forecasting techniques to predict what is going to happen with running instances of a business process, allowing to make forecasts of future cycle time, compliance issues, etc. Techniques for predictive business process monitoring include Support Vector Machines, Deep Learning approaches, and Random Forest.

Optimization

Process optimization includes retrieving process performance information from modeling or monitoring phase; identifying the potential or actual bottlenecks and the potential opportunities for cost savings or other improvements; and then, applying those enhancements in the design of the process. Process mining tools are able to discover critical activities and bottlenecks, creating greater business value.

Re-engineering

When the process becomes too complex or inefficient, and optimization is not fetching the desired output, it is usually recommended by a company steering committee chaired by the president / CEO to re-engineer the entire process cycle. Business process reengineering (BPR) has been used by organizations to attempt to achieve efficiency and productivity at work.

Suites

A market has developed for enterprise software leveraging the business process management concepts to organize and automate processes. The recent convergence of this software from distinct pieces such as business rules engine, business process modelling, business activity monitoring and Human Workflow has given birth to integrated Business Process Management Suites. Forrester Research, Inc recognize the BPM suite space through three different lenses:

- Human-centric BPM
- Integration-centric BPM (Enterprise Service Bus)
- Document-centric BPM (Dynamic Case Management).

However, standalone integration-centric and document-centric offerings have matured into separate, standalone markets.

Rapid application development using no-code/low-code principles is becoming an ever prevalent feature of BPMS platforms. RAD enables businesses to deploy applications more quickly and more cost effectively, while also offering improved change and version management. Gartner notes that as businesses embrace these systems, their budgets rely less on the maintenance of existing systems and show more investment in growing and transforming them.

Practice

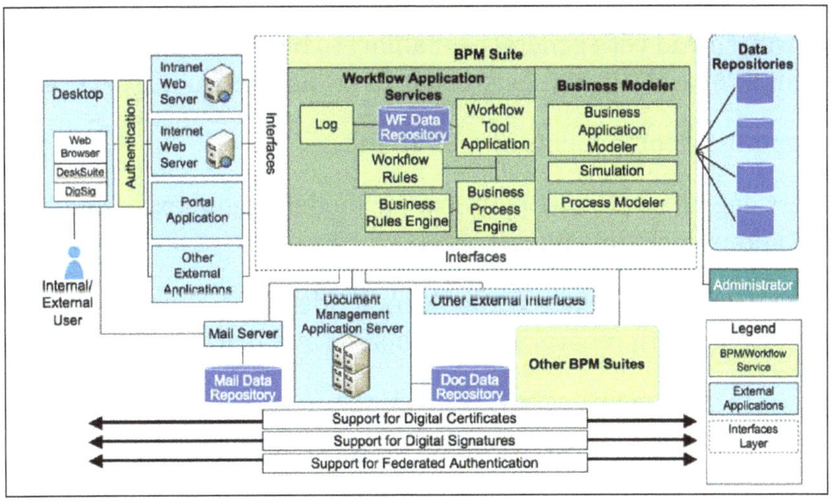

In figure, example of Business Process Management (BPM) Service Pattern: This pattern shows how business process management (BPM) tools can be used to implement business processes through the orchestration of activities between people and systems.

While the steps can be viewed as a cycle, economic or time constraints are likely to limit the process to only a few iterations. This is often the case when an organization uses the approach for short to medium term objectives rather than trying to transform the organizational culture. True iterations are only possible through the collaborative efforts of process participants. In a majority of organizations, complexity requires enabling technology to support the process participants in these daily process management challenges.

To date, many organizations often start a BPM project or program with the objective of optimizing an area that has been identified as an area for improvement.

Currently, the international standards for the task have limited BPM to the application in the IT sector, and ISO/IEC 15944 covers the operational aspects of the business. However, some corporations with the culture of best practices do use standard operating procedures to regulate their operational process. Other standards are currently being worked upon to assist in BPM implementation (BPMN, enterprise architecture, Business Motivation Model).

Technology

BPM is now considered a critical component of operational intelligence (OI) solutions to deliver real-time, actionable information. This real-time information can be acted upon in a variety of ways – alerts can be sent or executive decisions can be made using real-time dashboards. OI solutions use real-time information to take automated action based on pre-defined rules so that security measures and or exception management processes can be initiated. Because "the size and complexity of daily tasks often requires the use of technology to model efficiently" when resources in technology became increasingly widespread with general availability to businesses to provide to their staff, "Many thought BPM as the bridge between Information Technology (IT) and Business."

There are four critical components of a BPM Suite:

- Process engine – a robust platform for modeling and executing process-based applications, including business rules.
- Business analytics – enable managers to identify business issues, trends, and opportunities with reports and dashboards and react accordingly.
- Content management – provides a system for storing and securing electronic documents, images, and other files.
- Collaboration tools – remove intra- and interdepartmental communication barriers through discussion forums, dynamic workspaces, and message boards.

BPM also addresses many of the critical IT issues underpinning these business drivers, including:

- Managing end-to-end, customer-facing processes.
- Consolidating data and increasing visibility into and access to associated data and information.

- Increasing the flexibility and functionality of current infrastructure and data.
- Integrating with existing systems and leveraging service oriented architecture (SOA).
- Establishing a common language for business-IT alignment.

Validation of BPMS is another technical issue that vendors and users must be aware of, if regulatory compliance is mandatory. The validation task could be performed either by an authenticated third party or by the users themselves. Either way, validation documentation must be generated. The validation document usually can either be published officially or retained by users.

Cloud Computing BPM

Cloud computing business process management is the use of (BPM) tools that are delivered as software services (SaaS) over a network. Cloud BPM business logic is deployed on an application server and the business data resides in cloud storage.

Market

According to Gartner, 20% of all the "shadow business processes" are supported by BPM cloud platforms. Gartner refers to all the hidden organizational processes that are supported by IT departments as part of legacy business processes such as Excel spreadsheets, routing of emails using rules, phone calls routing, etc. These can, of course also be replaced by other technologies such as workflow and smart form software.

Benefits

The benefits of using cloud BPM services include removing the need and cost of maintaining specialized technical skill sets in-house and reducing distractions from an enterprise's main focus. It offers controlled IT budgeting and enables geographical mobility.

Internet of Things

The emerging Internet of things poses a significant challenge to control and manage the flow of information through large numbers of devices. To cope with this, a new direction known as BPM Everywhere shows promise as a way of blending traditional process techniques, with additional capabilities to automate the handling of all the independent devices.

Dynamic Business Process Management

Dynamic business process management (dynamic BPM) is a solution which enables enterprises to react to changing conditions of operation (both interior and/or exterior) and cater to the individual needs of their clients in a timely fashion (and even provide a practically instant response in case of critical conditions), in accordance with process adaptations executed in real time by their direct process owners with access to the codified knowledge of their enterprises. The concept of a dynamic BPM is an extension of traditional (static) business process management tailored to learning organizations.

Process Execution should Guarantee Evolutionary Flexibility

Dynamic BPM provides an organizational and technical environment allowing the process owners to modify or transform their processes independent of substantial IT support and a software development or maintenance lifecycle. Processes should be defined and implemented in such a way as to enable supplements to, or even overhauls of, process activities, as authorized by direct process owners (e.g. contract managers or project coordinators). The authority to change executed processes on an ongoing basis should not be limited, as it had been thus far, to process leaders. Instead, it should also be given to the aforementioned groups. Direct process owners should also be allowed access to a process-driven application in order to execute activities, actions and even whole elementary processes not included in the standard process.

Processes are Considered Completed only after having been Documented

The implementation of dynamic BPM should provide the inclusion of process definitions in the executive process-driven application, as well as to ensure that processes are considered completed only after having been documented, without the burden of excess reporting.

Comprehensiveness and Continuity

The implementation of dynamic BPM should include the whole standard process along with vendors and subcontractors, with the aim of minimizing the inclusive costs and total supplies, while simultaneously reducing the total execution time. This approach considerably broadens the range of available options of raising effectiveness, as well as often the time of execution by means of optimization, which takes into account those activities which lie outside the scope of a single enterprise (e.g. deliveries, warranty services) within a single value-adding process.

Implementing Dynamic BPM

Implementing dynamic business process management without the aid of IT solutions is impossible, since it would require a considerably larger amount of work to cope with the ongoing management of executed processes. The rapid evolutionary jump from traditional BPMS solutions to dynamic BPMS solutions enables users to apply process management to those processes which are hard to structure, and therefore necessitate a dynamic approach, usually comprising the majority of an enterprise's processes.

MARKET RESEARCH

Market research is the process of determining the viability of a new service or product through research conducted directly with potential customers. Market research allows a company to discover the target market and get opinions and other feedback from consumers about their interest in the product or service.

This type of research can be conducted in house, by the company itself, or by a third-party company that specializes in market research. It can be done through surveys, product testing, and focus groups. Test subjects are usually compensated with product samples and/or paid a small stipend for their time.

The purpose of market research is to look at the market associated with a particular good or service to ascertain how the audience will receive it. This can include information gathering for the purpose of market segmentation and product differentiation, which can be used to tailor advertising efforts or determine which features are seen as a priority to the consumer. A business must engage in a variety of tasks to complete the market research process. It needs to gather information based on the market sector being examined. The business needs to analyze and interpret the resulting data to determine the presence of any patterns or relevant data points that it can use in the decision-making process.

How Market Research Works

Market research consists of a combination of primary information, or what has been gathered by the company or by a person hired by the company, and secondary information, or what has been gathered by an outside source. Primary information is the data that the company has collected directly or that has been collected by a person or business hired to conduct the research. This type of information generally falls into two categories: exploratory and specific research.

Exploratory research is a less structured option and functions via more open-ended questions, and it results in questions or issues being presented that the company may need to address. Specific research finds answers to previously identified issues that are often brought to attention through exploratory research. Secondary information is data that an outside entity has already gathered. This can include population information from government census data, trade association reports, or presented research from another business operating within the same market sector.

Example of Market Research:

Many companies use market research to test out new products or to get information from consumers about what kinds of products or services they need and don't currently have.

For example, a company that was considering going into business might conduct market research to test the viability of its product or service. If the market research confirms consumer interest, the business can proceed confidently with the business plan. If not, the company should use the results of the market research to make adjustments to the product to bring it in line with customer desires.

Market research was first put into place in the United States in the 1920s and originated during the advertising boom during the Golden Age of Radio. Companies that advertised on the radio began to understand the demographics that were revealed by how different radio shows were sponsored.

From there, companies were developed that would interview people on the street about publications that they read and whether they recognized any ads that were published in the magazines or newspapers the interviewer showed them. Data collected from these interviews were compared to the circulation of the publication in order to see how effective those ads were. Market research and surveys were adapted from these early techniques. Data collection then shifted to the telephone, making face-to-face contact unnecessary. A telephone operator could collect information or organize focus groups – and do so quickly and in a more organized and orderly fashion. This method improved the market research model greatly.

Within the last 10 to 15 years, market research started to make a shift online. While the platform may have changed, data collection is still mainly done in a survey-style form. But instead of companies actively seeking participants by finding them on the street or by cold calling them on the phone, people can choose to sign up and take surveys and offer opinions when they have time. This makes the process far less intrusive and less rushed since people can do so on their own time and by their own volition.

References

- Coker, Frank (2014). Pulse: Understanding the Vital Signs of Your Business. Ambient Light Publishing. pp. 41–42. ISBN 978-0-9893086-0-1
- Business-operations, encyclopedia: shopify.in, Retrieved 17 June, 2019
- Nikolić, B.; Dakić, J.; Ružić-Dimitrijević, L. (2013). "Contemporary management in a higher education institution in Serbia" (PDF). Online Journal of Applied Knowledge Management. 1 (1): 72–81
- What-is-change-management, resources: prosci.com, Retrieved 10 August, 2019
- Design-management-an-introduction-taking-charge-of-processes-and-people, literature: interaction-design.org, Retrieved 20 July, 2019
- Market-research, terms: investopedia.com, Retrieved 14 May, 2019
- De Dreu, C. K. W.; Weingart, L. R. (2003). "Task versus relationship conflict, team performance, and team member satisfaction: A meta-analysis". Journal of Applied Psychology. 88 (4): 741–749. doi:10.1037/0021-9010.88.4.741. PMID 12940412
- Change-management-change-management-definition-and-solutions-2439314: cio.com, Retrieved 10 August, 2019

7

Business Strategy: An Integrated Study

The combination of all the decisions which are taken by a business to achieve their goals is known as business strategy. There are a number of areas which fall under the umbrella of this field such as planning and strategic management analysis. All the diverse concepts related to business strategies have been carefully analyzed in this chapter.

Strategy is an action that managers take to attain one or more of the organization's goals. Strategy can also be defined as "A general direction set for the company and its various components to achieve a desired state in the future. Strategy results from the detailed strategic planning process". A strategy is all about integrating organizational activities and utilizing and allocating the scarce resources within the organizational environment so as to meet the present objectives. While planning a strategy it is essential to consider that decisions are not taken in a vacuum and that any act taken by a firm is likely to be met by a reaction from those affected, competitors, customers, employees or suppliers.

Strategy can also be defined as knowledge of the goals, the uncertainty of events and the need to take into consideration the likely or actual behavior of others. Strategy is the blueprint of decisions in an organization that shows its objectives and goals, reduces the key policies, and plans for achieving these goals, and defines the business the company is to carry on, the type of economic and human organization it wants to be, and the contribution it plans to make to its shareholders, customers and society at large.

Features of Strategy

1. Strategy is Significant because it is not possible to foresee the future. Without a perfect foresight, the firms must be ready to deal with the uncertain events which constitute the business environment.

2. Strategy deals with long term developments rather than routine operations, i.e. it deals with probability of innovations or new products, new methods of productions, or new markets to be developed in future.

3. Strategy is created to take into account the probable behavior of customers and competitors. Strategies dealing with employees will predict the employee behavior.

Strategy is a well-defined roadmap of an organization. It defines the overall mission, vision and direction of an organization. The objective of a strategy is to maximize an organization's strengths and to minimize the strengths of the competitors. Strategy, in short, bridges the gap between "where we are" and "where we want to be".

Strategies at Different Levels of Business

In an organization, strategies can exist at all levels – right from the overall business to the individuals working in it. Here are some common types of strategies:

- Corporate Strategies – These are also explicitly mentioned in the organization's Mission Statement. They involve the overall purpose and scope of the business to help it meet the expectations of stakeholders. These are important strategies due to the heavy influence of investors. Further, corporate strategies act as a guide for strategic decision-making throughout the business.
- Business Unit Strategies – These are more about how a business competes successfully in a particular market. They involve strategic decisions about:
    - Choosing products;
    - Meeting the needs of the consumers;
    - Gaining an advantage over the competitors;
    - Creating new opportunities, etc.
- Operational Strategies – These are about how each part of the business is organized to deliver the corporate and business unit level strategic direction. Therefore, these strategies focus on the issues of resources, people, processes, etc.

BUSINESS STRATEGY

Business strategy can be understood as the course of action or set of decisions which assist the entrepreneurs in achieving specific business objectives. It is nothing but a master plan that the management of a company implements to secure a competitive position in the market, carry on its operations, please customers and achieve the desired ends of the business.

In business, it is the long-range sketch of the desired image, direction and destination of the organisation. It is a scheme of corporate intent and action, which is carefully planned and flexibly designed with the purpose of:

- Achieving effectiveness,
- Perceiving and utilising opportunities,

- Mobilising resources,
- Securing an advantageous position,
- Meeting challenges and threats,
- Directing efforts and behaviour, and
- Gaining command over the situation.

A business strategy is a set of competitive moves and actions that a business uses to attract customers, compete successfully, strengthening performance, and achieve organisational goals. It outlines how business should be carried out to reach the desired ends.

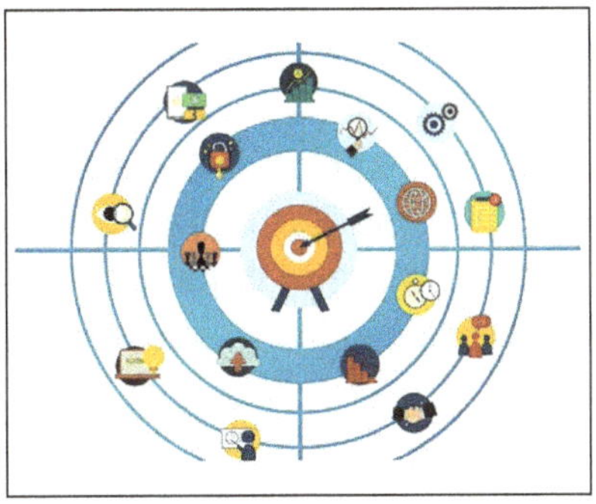

Business strategy equips the top management with an integrated framework, to discover, analyse and exploit beneficial opportunities, to sense and meet potential threats, to make optimum use of resources and strengths, to counterbalance weakness.

Levels of Business Strategy

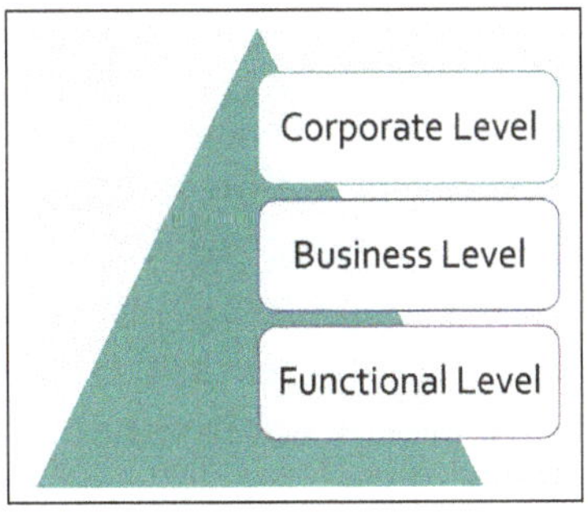

1. Corporate level strategy: Corporate level strategy is long-range, action-oriented, integrated and comprehensive plan formulated by the top management. It is used to ascertain business lines, expansion and growth, takeovers and mergers, diversification, integration, new areas for investment and divestment and so forth.
2. Business level strategy: The strategies that relate to a particular business are known as business level strategies. It is developed by the general managers, who convert mission and vision into concrete strategies. It is like a blueprint of the entire business.

3. Functional level strategy: Developed by the first line managers or supervisors, functional level strategy involves decision making at the operational level concerning particular functional areas like marketing, production, human resource, research and development, finance and so on.

In business, there is always a need for multiple strategies at various levels as a single strategy is not only inadequate but improper too. Therefore, a typical business structure always possesses three levels.

Nature of Business Strategy

A business strategy is a combination of proactive actions on the part of management, for the purpose of enhancing the company's market position and overall performance and reactions to unexpected developments and new market conditions. The maximum part of the company's present strategy is a result of formerly initiated actions and business approaches, but when market conditions take an unanticipated turn, the company requires a strategic reaction to cope with contingencies. Hence, for unforeseen development, a part of the business strategy is formulated as a reasoned response.

STRATEGIC MANAGEMENT

In the field of management, strategic management involves the formulation and implementation of the major goals and initiatives taken by an organization's top managers on behalf of owners, based on consideration of resources and an assessment of the internal and external environments in which the organization operates.

Strategic management provides overall direction to an enterprise and involves specifying the organization's objectives, developing policies and plans to achieve those objectives, and then allocating resources to implement the plans. Academics and practicing managers have developed numerous models and frameworks to assist in strategic decision-making in the context of complex environments and competitive dynamics. Strategic management is not static in nature; the models often include a feedback loop to monitor execution and to inform the next round of planning.

Michael Porter identifies three principles underlying strategy:

- Creating a "unique and valuable [market] position".
- Making trade-offs by choosing "what not to do".
- Creating "fit" by aligning company activities with one another to support the chosen strategy.

Corporate strategy involves answering a key question from a portfolio perspective: "What business should we be in?" Business strategy involves answering the question: "How shall we compete in this business?"

Management theory and practice often make a distinction between strategic management and operational management, with operational management concerned primarily with improving efficiency and controlling costs within the boundaries set by the organization's strategy.

Application

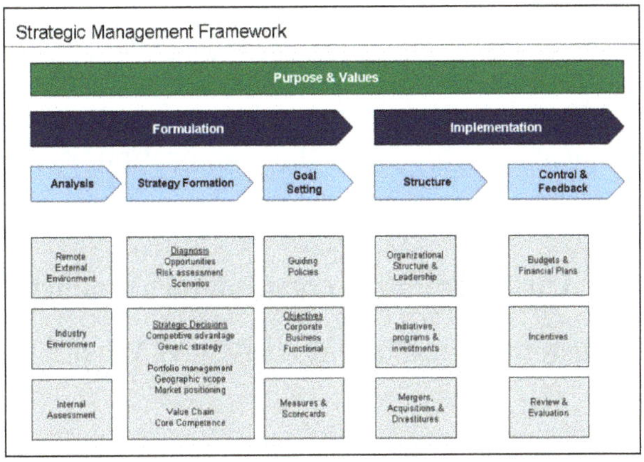

Strategic management processes and activities.

Strategy is defined as "the determination of the basic long-term goals of an enterprise, and the adoption of courses of action and the allocation of resources necessary for carrying out these goals." Strategies are established to set direction, focus effort, define or clarify the organization, and provide consistency or guidance in response to the environment.

Strategic management involves the related concepts of strategic planning and strategic thinking. Strategic planning is analytical in nature and refers to formalized procedures to produce the data and analyses used as inputs for strategic thinking, which synthesizes the data resulting in the strategy. Strategic planning may also refer to control mechanisms used to implement the strategy once it is determined. In other words, strategic planning happens *around* the strategic thinking or strategy making activity.

Strategic management is often described as involving two major processes: formulation and implementation of strategy. While described sequentially below, in practice the two processes are iterative and each provides input for the other.

Formulation

Formulation of strategy involves analyzing the environment in which the organization operates, then making a series of strategic decisions about how the organization will compete. Formulation ends with a series of goals or objectives and measures for the organization to pursue. Environmental analysis includes:

- Remote external environment, including the political, economic, social, technological, legal and environmental landscape (PESTLE);
- Industry environment, such as the competitive behavior of rival organizations, the bargaining power of buyers/customers and suppliers, threats from new entrants to the industry, and the ability of buyers to substitute products (Porter's 5 forces); and
- Internal environment, regarding the strengths and weaknesses of the organization's resources (i.e., its people, processes and IT systems).

Strategic decisions are based on insight from the environmental assessment and are responses to strategic questions about how the organization will compete, such as:

- What is the organization's business?
- Who is the target customer for the organization's products and services?
- Where are the customers and how do they buy? What is considered "value" to the customer?
- Which businesses, products and services should be included or excluded from the portfolio of offerings?
- What is the geographic scope of the business?
- What differentiates the company from its competitors in the eyes of customers and other stakeholders?
- Which skills and capabilities should be developed within the firm?
- What are the important opportunities and risks for the organization?
- How can the firm grow, through both its base business and new business?
- How can the firm generate more value for investors?

The answers to these and many other strategic questions result in the organization's strategy and a series of specific short-term and long-term goals or objectives and related measures.

Implementation

The second major process of strategic management is *implementation*, which involves decisions regarding how the organization's resources (i.e., people, process and IT systems) will be aligned and mobilized towards the objectives. Implementation results in how the organization's resources are structured (such as by product or service or geography), leadership arrangements, communication, incentives, and monitoring mechanisms to track progress towards objectives, among others.

Running the day-to-day operations of the business is often referred to as "operations management" or specific terms for key departments or functions, such as "logistics management" or "marketing management," which take over once strategic management decisions are implemented. Strategy has been practiced whenever an advantage was gained by planning the sequence and timing of the deployment of resources while simultaneously taking into account the probable capabilities and behavior of competition.

In 1988, Henry Mintzberg described the many different definitions and perspectives on strategy reflected in both academic research and in practice. He examined the strategic process and concluded it was much more fluid and unpredictable than people had thought. Because of this, he could not point to one process that could be called strategic planning. Instead Mintzberg concludes that there are five types of strategies:

- Strategy as plan – a directed course of action to achieve an intended set of goals; similar to the strategic planning concept;
- Strategy as pattern – a consistent pattern of past behavior, with a strategy realized over time rather than planned or intended. Where the realized pattern was different from the intent, he referred to the strategy as emergent;
- Strategy as position – locating brands, products, or companies within the market, based on the conceptual framework of consumers or other stakeholders; a strategy determined primarily by factors outside the firm;
- Strategy as ploy – a specific maneuver intended to outwit a competitor; and
- Strategy as perspective – executing strategy based on a "theory of the business" or natural extension of the mindset or ideological perspective of the organization.

In 1998, Mintzberg developed these five types of management strategy into 10 "schools of thought" and grouped them into three categories. The first group is normative. It consists of the schools of informal design and conception, the formal planning, and analytical positioning. The second group, consisting of six schools, is more concerned with how strategic management is actually done, rather than prescribing optimal plans or positions. The six schools are entrepreneurial, visionary, cognitive, learning/adaptive/emergent, negotiation, corporate culture and business environment. The third and final group consists of one school, the configuration or transformation school, a hybrid of the other schools organized into stages, organizational life cycles, or "episodes".

Michael Porter defined strategy in 1980 as the "broad formula for how a business is going to compete, what its goals should be, and what policies will be needed to carry out those goals" and the "combination of the *ends* (goals) for which the firm is striving and the *means* (policies) by which it is seeking to get there." He continued that: "The essence of formulating competitive strategy is relating a company to its environment." Some complexity theorists define strategy as the unfolding of the internal and external aspects of the organization that results in actions in a socio-economic context.

Concepts and Frameworks

The progress of strategy since 1960 can be charted by a variety of frameworks and concepts introduced by management consultants and academics. These reflect an increased focus on cost, competition and customers. These "3 Cs" were illuminated by much more robust empirical analysis at ever-more granular levels of detail, as industries and organizations were disaggregated into business units, activities, processes, and individuals in a search for sources of competitive advantage.

SWOT Analysis

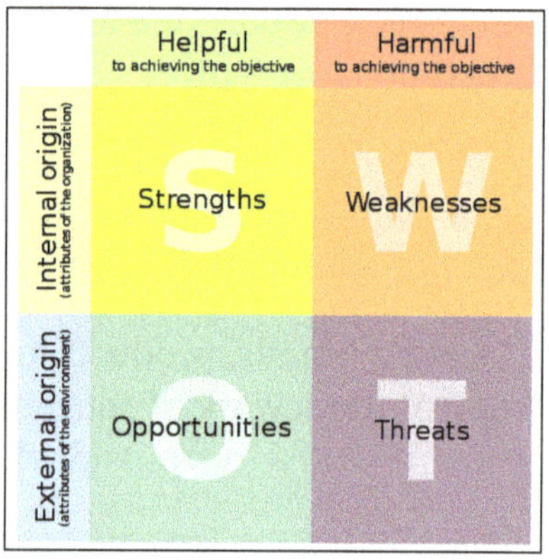

A SWOT analysis, with its four elements in a 2×2 matrix.

By the 1960s, the capstone business policy course at the Harvard Business School included the concept of matching the distinctive competence of a company (its internal strengths and weaknesses) with its environment (external opportunities and threats) in the context of its objectives. This framework came to be known by the acronym SWOT and was "a major step forward in bringing explicitly competitive thinking to bear on questions of strategy". Kenneth R. Andrews helped popularize the framework via a 1963 conference and it remains commonly used in practice.

Experience Curve

The experience curve was developed by the Boston Consulting Group in 1966. It is a hypothesis that total per unit costs decline systematically by as much as 15–25% every time cumulative production (i.e., "experience") doubles. It has been empirically confirmed by some firms at various points in their history. Costs decline due to a variety of factors, such as the learning curve, substitution of labor for capital (automation), and technological sophistication. Author Walter Kiechel wrote that it reflected several insights, including:

- A company can always improve its cost structure;
- Competitors have varying cost positions based on their experience;
- Firms could achieve lower costs through higher market share, attaining a competitive advantage; and
- An increased focus on empirical analysis of costs and processes, a concept which author Kiechel refers to as "Greater Taylorism".

"The experience curve was, simply, the most important concept in launching the strategy revolution with the experience curve, the strategy revolution began to insinuate an acute awareness of competition into the corporate consciousness." Prior to the 1960s, the word competition rarely appeared in the most prominent management literature; U.S. companies then faced considerably less competition and did not focus on performance relative to peers. Further, the experience curve provided a basis for the retail sale of business ideas, helping drive the management consulting industry.

Corporate Strategy and Portfolio Theory

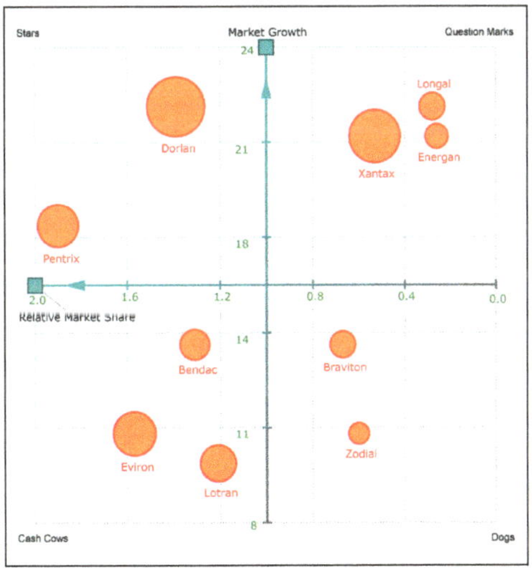

Portfolio growth–share matrix.

The concept of the corporation as a portfolio of business units, with each plotted graphically based on its market share (a measure of its competitive position relative to its peers) and industry growth rate (a measure of industry attractiveness), was summarized in the growth–share matrix developed by the Boston Consulting Group around 1970. By 1979, one study estimated that 45% of the Fortune 500 companies were using some variation of the matrix in their strategic planning. This framework helped companies decide where to invest their resources (i.e., in their high market share, high growth businesses) and which businesses to divest (i.e., low market share, low growth businesses.) C. K. Prahalad and Gary Hamel suggested that companies should build portfolios of businesses around shared technical or operating competencies, and should develop structures and processes to enhance their core competencies.

Porter wrote in 1987 that corporate strategy involves two questions: 1) What business should the corporation be in? and 2) How should the corporate office manage its business units? He mentioned four concepts of corporate strategy; the latter three can be used together:

1. Portfolio theory: A strategy based primarily on diversification through acquisition. The corporation shifts resources among the units and monitors the performance of each business unit and its leaders. Each unit generally runs autonomously, with limited interference from the corporate center provided goals are met.

2. Restructuring: The corporate office acquires then actively intervenes in a business where it detects potential, often by replacing management and implementing a new business strategy.

3. Transferring skills: Important managerial skills and organizational capability are essentially spread to multiple businesses. The skills must be necessary to competitive advantage.

4. Sharing activities: Ability of the combined corporation to leverage centralized functions, such as sales, finance, etc. thereby reducing costs.

Other techniques were developed to analyze the relationships between elements in a portfolio. The growth-share matrix, a part of B.C.G. Analysis, was followed by G.E. multi factoral model, developed by General Electric. Companies continued to diversify as conglomerates until the 1980s, when deregulation and a less restrictive anti-trust environment led to the view that a portfolio of operating divisions in different industries was worth more as many independent companies, leading to the breakup of many conglomerates. While the popularity of portfolio theory has waxed and waned, the key dimensions considered (industry attractiveness and competitive position) remain central to strategy.

Competitive Advantage

In 1980, Porter defined the two types of competitive advantage an organization can achieve relative to its rivals: lower cost or differentiation. This advantage derives from attribute(s) that allow an organization to outperform its competition, such as superior market position, skills, or resources. In Porter's view, strategic management should be concerned with building and sustaining competitive advantage.

Industry Structure and Profitability

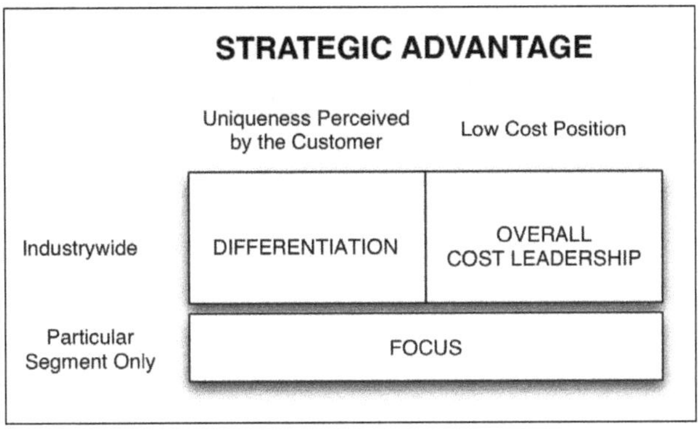

A graphical representation of Porter's Five Forces.

Porter developed a framework for analyzing the profitability of industries and how those profits are divided among the participants in 1980. In five forces analysis he identified the forces that shape the industry structure or environment. The framework involves the bargaining power of buyers and suppliers, the threat of new entrants, the availability of substitute products, and the competitive rivalry of firms in the industry. These forces affect the organization's ability to raise its prices as well as the costs of inputs (such as raw materials) for its processes.

The five forces framework helps describe how a firm can use these forces to obtain a sustainable competitive advantage, either lower cost or differentiation. Companies can maximize their profitability by competing in industries with favorable structure. Competitors can take steps to grow the overall profitability of the industry, or to take profit away from other parts of the industry structure. Porter modified Chandler's dictum about structure following strategy by introducing a second level of structure: while organizational structure follows strategy, it in turn follows industry structure.

Generic Competitive Strategies

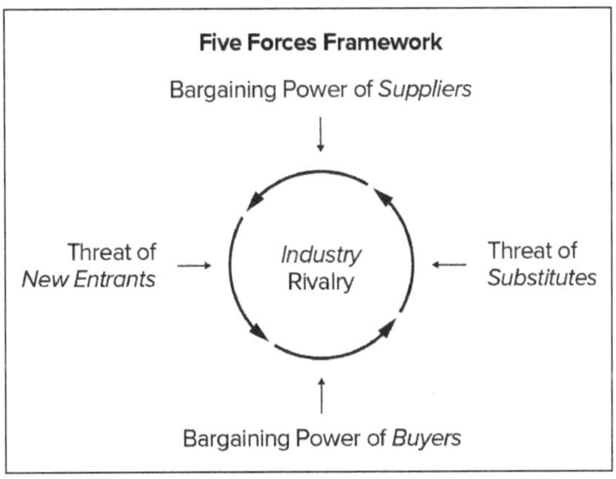

Michael Porter's Three Generic Strategies.

Porter wrote in 1980 that strategy target either cost leadership, differentiation, or focus. These are known as Porter's three generic strategies and can be applied to any size or form of business. Porter claimed that a company must only choose one of the three or risk that the business would waste precious resources. Porter's generic strategies detail the interaction between cost minimization strategies, product differentiation strategies, and market focus strategies.

Porter described an industry as having multiple segments that can be targeted by a firm. The breadth of its targeting refers to the competitive scope of the business. Porter defined two types of competitive advantage: lower cost or differentiation relative to its rivals. Achieving competitive advantage results from a firm's ability to cope with the five forces better than its rivals. Porter wrote: "Achieving competitive advantage requires a firm to make a choice about the type of competitive advantage it seeks to attain and the scope within which it will attain it." He also wrote: "The two basic types of competitive advantage [differentiation and lower cost] combined with the scope of activities for which a firm seeks to achieve them lead to three generic strategies for achieving above average performance in an industry: cost leadership, differentiation and focus. The focus strategy has two variants, cost focus and differentiation focus."

The concept of choice was a different perspective on strategy, as the 1970s paradigm was the pursuit of market share (size and scale) influenced by the experience curve. Companies that pursued the highest market share position to achieve cost advantages fit under Porter's cost leadership generic strategy, but the concept of choice regarding differentiation and focus represented a new perspective.

Value Chain

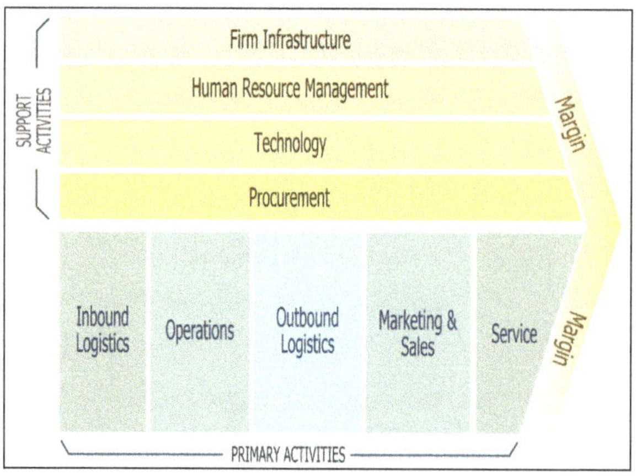

Michael Porter's Value Chain.

Porter's 1985 description of the value chain refers to the chain of activities (processes or collections of processes) that an organization performs in order to deliver a valuable product or service for the market. These include functions such as inbound logistics, operations, outbound logistics, marketing and sales, and service, supported by systems and technology infrastructure. By aligning the various activities in its value chain with the organization's strategy in a coherent way, a firm can achieve a competitive advantage. Porter also wrote that strategy is an internally consistent configuration of activities that differentiates a firm from its rivals. A robust competitive position cumulates from many activities which should fit coherently together.

"Competitive advantage cannot be understood by looking at a firm as a whole. It stems from the many discrete activities a firm performs in designing, producing, marketing, delivering and supporting its product. Each of these activities can contribute to a firm's relative cost position and create a basis for differentiation the value chain disaggregates a firm into its strategically relevant activities in order to understand the behavior of costs and the existing and potential sources of differentiation."

Core Competence

Gary Hamel and C. K. Prahalad described the idea of core competency in 1990, the idea that each organization has some capability in which it excels and that the business should focus on opportunities in that area, letting others go or outsourcing them. Further, core competency is difficult to duplicate, as it involves the skills and coordination of people across a variety of functional areas or processes used to deliver value to customers. By outsourcing, companies expanded the concept of the value chain, with some elements within the entity and others without. Core competency is part of a branch of strategy called the resource-based view of the firm, which postulates that if activities are strategic as indicated by the value chain, then the organization's capabilities and ability to learn or adapt are also strategic.

Theory of the Business

Peter Drucker wrote in 1994 about the "Theory of the Business," which represents the key assumptions underlying a firm's strategy. These assumptions are in three categories: a) the external environment, including society, market, customer, and technology; b) the mission of the organization; and c) the core competencies needed to accomplish the mission. He continued that a valid theory of the business has four specifications: 1) assumptions about the environment, mission, and core competencies must fit reality; 2) the assumptions in all three areas have to fit one another; 3) the theory of the business must be known and understood throughout the organization; and 4) the theory of the business has to be tested constantly.

He wrote that organizations get into trouble when the assumptions representing the theory of the business no longer fit reality. He used an example of retail department stores, where their theory of the business assumed that people who could afford to shop in department stores would do so. However, many shoppers abandoned department stores in favor of specialty retailers (often located outside of malls) when time became the primary factor in the shopping destination rather than income.

Drucker described the theory of the business as a "hypothesis" and a "discipline." He advocated building in systematic diagnostics, monitoring and testing of the assumptions comprising the theory of the business to maintain competitiveness.

Strategic Thinking

Strategic thinking involves the generation and application of unique business insights to opportunities intended to create competitive advantage for a firm or organization. It involves challenging the assumptions underlying the organization's strategy and value proposition. Mintzberg wrote in 1994 that it is more about synthesis (i.e., "connecting the dots") than analysis (i.e., "finding the dots"). It is about "capturing what the manager learns from all sources (both the soft insights from his or her personal experiences and the experiences of others throughout the organization and the hard data from market research and the like) and then synthesizing that learning into a vision of the direction that the business should pursue." Mintzberg argued that strategic thinking is the critical part of formulating strategy, more so than strategic planning exercises.

General Andre Beaufre wrote in 1963 that strategic thinking "is a mental process, at once abstract and rational, which must be capable of synthesizing both psychological and material data. The strategist must have a great capacity for both analysis and synthesis; analysis is necessary to assemble the data on which he makes his diagnosis, synthesis in order to produce from these data the diagnosis itself--and the diagnosis in fact amounts to a choice between alternative courses of action."

Will Mulcaster argued that while much research and creative thought has been devoted to generating alternative strategies, too little work has been done on what influences the quality of strategic decision making and the effectiveness with which strategies are implemented. For instance, in retrospect it can be seen that the financial crisis of 2008–9 could have been avoided if the banks had paid more attention to the risks associated with their investments, but how should banks change the way they make decisions to improve the quality of their decisions in the future? Mulcaster's Managing Forces framework addresses this issue by identifying 11 forces that should be incorporated into the processes of decision making and strategic implementation. The 11 forces are: Time; Opposing forces; Politics; Perception; Holistic effects; Adding value; Incentives; Learning capabilities; Opportunity cost; Risk and Style.

Strategic Planning

Strategic planning is a means of administering the formulation and implementation of strategy. Strategic planning is analytical in nature and refers to formalized procedures to produce the data and analyses used as inputs for strategic thinking, which synthesizes the data resulting in the strategy. Strategic planning may also refer to control mechanisms used to implement the strategy once it is determined. In other words, strategic planning happens around the strategy formation process.

Environmental Analysis

Porter wrote in 1980 that formulation of competitive strategy includes consideration of four key elements:

1. Company strengths and weaknesses;
2. Personal values of the key implementers (i.e., management and the board)
3. Industry opportunities and threats; and
4. Broader societal expectations.

The first two elements relate to factors internal to the company (i.e., the internal environment), while the latter two relate to factors external to the company (i.e., the external environment). There are many analytical frameworks which attempt to organize the strategic planning process. Examples of frameworks that address the four elements described above include:

- External environment: PEST analysis or STEEP analysis is a framework used to examine the remote external environmental factors that can affect the organization, such as political, economic, social/demographic, and technological. Common variations include SLEPT, PESTLE, STEEPLE, and STEER analysis, each of which incorporates slightly different emphases.
- Industry environment: The Porter Five Forces Analysis framework helps to determine the competitive rivalry and therefore attractiveness of a market. It is used to help determine the portfolio of offerings the organization will provide and in which markets.
- Relationship of internal and external environment: SWOT analysis is one of the most basic and widely used frameworks, which examines both internal elements of the organization—Strengths and Weaknesses—and external elements—Opportunities and Threats. It helps examine the organization's resources in the context of its environment.

Scenario Planning

A number of strategists use scenario planning techniques to deal with change. The way Peter Schwartz put it in 1991 is that strategic outcomes cannot be known in advance so the sources of competitive advantage cannot be predetermined. The fast changing business environment is too uncertain for us to find sustainable value in formulas of excellence or competitive advantage. Instead, scenario planning is a technique in which multiple outcomes can be developed, their implications assessed, and their likeliness of occurrence evaluated. According to Pierre Wack, scenario planning is about insight, complexity, and subtlety, not about formal analysis and numbers. The flowchart to the right provides a process for classifying a phenomena as a scenario in the intuitive logics tradition.

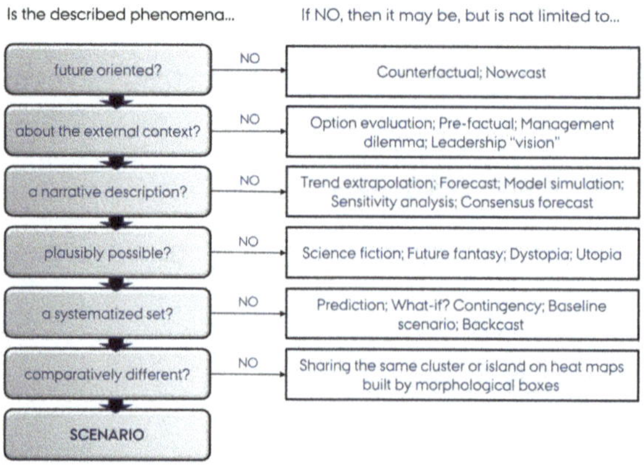

Process for classifying phenomena as a scenario in the Intuitive Logics tradition

Some business planners are starting to use a complexity theory approach to strategy. Complexity can be thought of as chaos with a dash of order. Chaos theory deals with turbulent systems that rapidly become disordered. Complexity is not quite so unpredictable. It involves multiple agents interacting in such a way that a glimpse of structure may appear.

Measuring and Controlling Implementation

Generic Strategy Map illustrating four elements of a balanced scorecard

Once the strategy is determined, various goals and measures may be established to chart a course for the organization, measure performance and control implementation of the strategy. Tools such as the balanced scorecard and strategy maps help crystallize the strategy, by relating key measures of success and performance to the strategy. These tools measure financial, marketing, production, organizational development, and innovation measures to achieve a 'balanced' perspective. Advances in information technology and data availability enable the gathering of more information about performance, allowing managers to take a much more analytical view of their business than before. Strategy may also be organized as a series of "initiatives" or "programs", each of which comprises one or more projects. Various monitoring and feedback mechanisms may also be established, such as regular meetings between divisional and corporate management to control implementation.

Evaluation

A key component to strategic management which is often overlooked when planning is evaluation. There are many ways to evaluate whether or not strategic priorities and plans have been achieved, one such method is Robert Stake's Responsive Evaluation. Responsive evaluation provides a naturalistic and humanistic approach to program evaluation. In expanding beyond the goal-oriented or pre-ordinate evaluation design, responsive evaluation takes into consideration the program's background (history), conditions, and transactions among stakeholders. It is largely emergent, the design unfolds as contact is made with stakeholders.

Limitations

While strategies are established to set direction, focus effort, define or clarify the organization, and provide consistency or guidance in response to the environment, these very elements also mean that certain signals are excluded from consideration or de-emphasized. "Strategy is a categorizing scheme by which incoming stimuli can be ordered and dispatched." Since a strategy orients the organization in a particular manner or direction, that direction may not effectively match the environment, initially (if a bad strategy) or over time as circumstances change. As such, Mintzberg continued, "Strategy once established is a force that resists change, not encourages it."

Therefore, a critique of strategic management is that it can overly constrain managerial discretion in a dynamic environment. "How can individuals, organizations and societies cope as well as possible with issues too complex to be fully understood, given the fact that actions initiated on the basis of inadequate understanding may lead to significant regret?" Some theorists insist on an iterative approach, considering in turn objectives, implementation and resources. i.e., a "repetitive learning cycle [rather than] a linear progression towards a clearly defined final destination." Strategies must be able to adjust during implementation because "humans rarely can proceed satisfactorily except by learning from experience; and modest probes, serially modified on the basis of feedback, usually are the best method for such learning."

In 2000, Gary Hamel coined the term strategic convergence to explain the limited scope of the strategies being used by rivals in greatly differing circumstances. He lamented that successful strategies are imitated by firms that do not understand that for a strategy to work, it must account for the specifics of each situation. Woodhouse and Collingridge claim that the essence of being "strategic" lies in a capacity for "intelligent trial-and error" rather than strict adherence to finely honed strategic plans. Strategy should be seen as laying out the general path rather than precise steps. Means are as likely to determine ends as ends are to determine means. The objectives that an organization might wish to pursue are limited by the range of feasible approaches to implementation. (There will usually be only a small number of approaches that will not only be technically and administratively possible, but also satisfactory to the full range of organizational stakeholders.) In turn, the range of feasible implementation approaches is determined by the availability of resources.

Strategic Themes

Various strategic approaches used across industries (themes) have arisen over the years. These include the shift from product-driven demand to customer- or marketing-driven demand (described above), the increased use of self-service approaches to lower cost, changes in the value chain or corporate structure due to globalization (e.g., off-shoring of production and assembly), and the internet.

Self-service

One theme in strategic competition has been the trend towards self-service, often enabled by technology, where the customer takes on a role previously performed by a worker to lower costs for the firm and perhaps prices.

Examples include:

- Automated teller machine (ATM) to obtain cash rather via a bank teller;
- Self-service at the gas pump rather than with help from an attendant;
- Retail internet orders input by the customer rather than a retail clerk, such as online book sales;
- Mass-produced ready-to-assemble furniture transported by the customer;
- Self-checkout at the grocery store; and
- Online banking and bill payment.

Globalization and the Virtual Firm

One definition of globalization refers to the integration of economies due to technology and supply chain process innovation. Companies are no longer required to be vertically integrated (i.e., designing, producing, assembling, and selling their products). In other words, the value chain for a company's product may no longer be entirely within one firm; several entities comprising a virtual firm may exist to fulfill the customer requirement. For example, some companies have chosen to outsource production to third parties, retaining only design and sales functions inside their organization.

Internet and Information Availability

The internet has dramatically empowered consumers and enabled buyers and sellers to come together with drastically reduced transaction and intermediary costs, creating much more robust marketplaces for the purchase and sale of goods and services. Examples include online auction sites, internet dating services, and internet book sellers. In many industries, the internet has dramatically altered the competitive landscape. Services that used to be provided within one entity (e.g., a car dealership providing financing and pricing information) are now provided by third parties. Further, compared to traditional media like television, the internet has caused a major shift in viewing habits through on demand content which has led to an increasingly fragmented audience.

Author Phillip Evans said in 2013 that networks are challenging traditional hierarchies. Value chains may also be breaking up ("deconstructing") where information aspects can be separated from functional activity. Data that is readily available for free or very low cost makes it harder for information-based, vertically integrated businesses to remain intact. Evans said: "The basic story here is that what used to be vertically integrated, oligopolistic competition among essentially similar kinds of competitors is evolving, by one means or another, from a vertical structure to a horizontal one. Why is that happening? It's happening because transaction costs are plummeting and because scale is polarizing. The plummeting of transaction costs weakens the glue that holds value chains together, and allows them to separate." He used Wikipedia as an example of a network that has challenged the traditional encyclopedia business model. Evans predicts the emergence of a new form of industrial organization called a "stack", analogous to a technology stack, in which competitors rely on a common platform of inputs (services or information), essentially layering the remaining competing parts of their value chains on top of this common platform.

Sustainability

In the recent decade, sustainability—or ability to successfully sustain a company in a context of rapidly changing environmental, social, health, and economic circumstances—has emerged as crucial aspect of any strategy development. Research focusing on corporations and leaders who have integrated sustainability into commercial strategy has led to emergence of the concept of "embedded sustainability" – defined by its authors Chris Laszlo and Nadya Zhexembayeva as "incorporation of environmental, health, and social value into the core business with no trade-off in price or quality—in other words, with no social or green premium." Laszlo and Zhexembayeva's research showed that embedded sustainability offers at least seven distinct opportunities for business value and competitive advantage creation: a) better risk-management, b) increased efficiency through reduced waste and resource use, c) better product differentiation, d) new market entrances, e) enhanced brand and reputation, f) greater opportunity to influence industry standards, and g) greater opportunity for radical innovation. Nadya Zhexembayeva's 2014 research further suggested that innovation driven by resource depletion can result in fundamental competitive advantages for a company's products and services, as well as the company strategy as a whole, when right principles of innovation are applied.

Strategy as Learning

In 1990, Peter Senge, who had collaborated with Arie de Geus at Dutch Shell, popularized de Geus' notion of the "learning organization". The theory is that gathering and analyzing information is a necessary requirement for business success in the information age. To do this, Senge claimed that an organization would need to be structured such that:

- People can continuously expand their capacity to learn and be productive.
- New patterns of thinking are nurtured.
- Collective aspirations are encouraged.
- People are encouraged to see the "whole picture" together.

Senge identified five disciplines of a learning organization. They are:

- Personal responsibility, self-reliance, and mastery – We accept that we are the masters of our own destiny. We make decisions and live with the consequences of them. When a problem needs to be fixed, or an opportunity exploited, we take the initiative to learn the required skills to get it done.
- Mental models – We need to explore our personal mental models to understand the subtle effect they have on our behaviour.
- Shared vision – The vision of where we want to be in the future is discussed and communicated to all. It provides guidance and energy for the journey ahead.
- Team learning – We learn together in teams. This involves a shift from "a spirit of advocacy to a spirit of enquiry".
- Systems thinking – We look at the whole rather than the parts. This is what Senge calls the "Fifth discipline". It is the glue that integrates the other four into a coherent strategy.

Geoffrey Moore and R. Frank and P. Cook also detected a shift in the nature of competition. Markets driven by technical standards or by "network effects" can give the dominant firm a near-monopoly. The same is true of networked industries in which interoperability requires compatibility between users. Examples include Internet Explorer's and Amazon's early dominance of their respective industries. IE's later decline shows that such dominance may be only temporary.

Moore showed how firms could attain this enviable position by using E.M. Rogers' five stage adoption process and focusing on one group of customers at a time, using each group as a base for reaching the next group. The most difficult step is making the transition between introduction and mass acceptance. If successful a firm can create a bandwagon effect in which the momentum builds and its product becomes a de facto standard.

Strategy as Adapting to Change

In 1969, Peter Drucker coined the phrase Age of Discontinuity to describe the way change disrupts lives. In an age of continuity attempts to predict the future by extrapolating from the past can be accurate. But according to Drucker, we are now in an age of discontinuity and extrapolating is ineffective. He identifies four sources of discontinuity: new technologies, globalization, cultural pluralism and knowledge capital.

In 1970, Alvin Toffler in Future Shock described a trend towards accelerating rates of change. He illustrated how social and technical phenomena had shorter lifespans with each generation, and he questioned society's ability to cope with the resulting turmoil and accompanying anxiety. In past eras periods of change were always punctuated with times of stability. This allowed society to assimilate the change before the next change arrived. But these periods of stability had all but disappeared by the late 20th century. In 1980 in The Third Wave, Toffler characterized this shift to relentless change as the defining feature of the third phase of civilization (the first two phases being the agricultural and industrial waves).

In 1978, Derek F. Abell described "strategic windows" and stressed the importance of the timing (both entrance and exit) of any given strategy. This led some strategic planners to build planned obsolescence into their strategies.

In 1983, Noel Tichy wrote that because we are all beings of habit we tend to repeat what we are comfortable with. He wrote that this is a trap that constrains our creativity, prevents us from exploring new ideas, and hampers our dealing with the full complexity of new issues. He developed a systematic method of dealing with change that involved looking at any new issue from three angles: technical and production, political and resource allocation, and corporate culture.

In 1989, Charles Handy identified two types of change. "Strategic drift" is a gradual change that occurs so subtly that it is not noticed until it is too late. By contrast, "transformational change" is sudden and radical. It is typically caused by discontinuities (or exogenous shocks) in the business environment. The point where a new trend is initiated is called a "strategic inflection point" by Andy Grove. Inflection points can be subtle or radical.

In 1990, Richard Pascale wrote that relentless change requires that businesses continuously reinvent themselves. His famous maxim is "Nothing fails like success" by which he means that what was a strength yesterday becomes the root of weakness today, We tend to depend on what worked yesterday and refuse to let go of what worked so well for us in the past. Prevailing strategies become self-confirming. To avoid this trap, businesses must stimulate a spirit of inquiry and healthy debate. They must encourage a creative process of self-renewal based on constructive conflict.

In 1996, Adrian Slywotzky showed how changes in the business environment are reflected in value migrations between industries, between companies, and within companies. He claimed that recognizing the patterns behind these value migrations is necessary if we wish to understand the world of chaotic change. In "Profit Patterns" he described businesses as being in a state of strategic anticipation as they try to spot emerging patterns. Slywotsky and his team identified 30 patterns that have transformed industry after industry.

In 1997, Clayton Christensen took the position that great companies can fail precisely because they do everything right since the capabilities of the organization also define its disabilities. Christensen's thesis is that outstanding companies lose their market leadership when confronted with disruptive technology. He called the approach to discovering the emerging markets for disruptive technologies agnostic marketing, i.e., marketing under the implicit assumption that no one – not the company, not the customers – can know how or in what quantities a disruptive product can or will be used without the experience of using it.

In 1999, Constantinos Markides re-examined the nature of strategic planning. He described strategy formation and implementation as an ongoing, never-ending, integrated process requiring continuous reassessment and reformation. Strategic management is planned and emergent, dynamic and interactive.

J. Moncrieff stressed strategy dynamics. He claimed that strategy is partially deliberate and partially unplanned. The unplanned element comes from emergent strategies that result from the emergence of opportunities and threats in the environment and from "strategies in action" (ad hoc actions across the organization).

David Teece pioneered research on resource-based strategic management and the dynamic capabilities perspective, defined as "the ability to integrate, build, and reconfigure internal and external competencies to address rapidly changing environments". His 1997 paper (with Gary Pisano and Amy Shuen) "Dynamic Capabilities and Strategic Management" was the most cited paper in economics and business for the period from 1995 to 2005.

In 2000, Gary Hamel discussed strategic decay, the notion that the value of every strategy, no matter how brilliant, decays over time.

Strategy as Operational Excellence

Quality

A large group of theorists felt the area where western business was most lacking was product quality. W. Edwards Deming, Joseph M. Juran, A. Kearney, Philip Crosby and Armand Feignbaum suggested quality improvement techniques such total quality management (TQM), continuous improvement (kaizen), lean manufacturing, Six Sigma, and return on quality (ROQ).

Contrarily, James Heskett, Earl Sasser, William Davidow, Len Schlesinger, A. Paraurgman, Len Berry, Jane Kingman-Brundage, Christopher Hart, and Christopher Lovelock, felt that poor customer service was the problem. They gave us fishbone diagramming, service charting, Total Customer Service (TCS), the service profit chain, service gaps analysis, the service encounter, strategic service vision, service mapping, and service teams. Their underlying assumption was that there is no better source of competitive advantage than a continuous stream of delighted customers.

Process management uses some of the techniques from product quality management and some of the techniques from customer service management. It looks at an activity as a sequential process. The objective is to find inefficiencies and make the process more effective. Although the procedures have a long history, dating back to Taylorism, the scope of their applicability has been greatly widened, leaving no aspect of the firm free from potential process improvements. Because of the broad applicability of process management techniques, they can be used as a basis for competitive advantage.

Carl Sewell, Frederick F. Reichheld, C. Gronroos, and Earl Sasser observed that businesses were spending more on customer acquisition than on retention. They showed how a competitive advantage could be found in ensuring that customers returned again and again. Reicheld broadened the concept to include loyalty from employees, suppliers, distributors and shareholders. They developed techniques for estimating customer lifetime value (CLV) for assessing long-term relationships. The concepts begat attempts to recast selling and marketing into a long term endeavor that created a sustained relationship (called relationship selling, relationship marketing, and customer relationship management). Customer relationship management (CRM) software became integral to many firms.

Reengineering

Michael Hammer and James Champy felt that these resources needed to be restructured. In a process that they labeled reengineering, firm's reorganized their assets around whole processes rather than tasks. In this way a team of people saw a project through, from inception to completion. This avoided functional silos where isolated departments seldom talked to each other. It also eliminated waste due to functional overlap and interdepartmental communications.

In 1989 Richard Lester and the researchers at the MIT Industrial Performance Center identified seven best practices and concluded that firms must accelerate the shift away from the mass production of low cost standardized products.

The seven areas of best practice were:

- Simultaneous continuous improvement in cost, quality, service, and product innovation.
- Breaking down organizational barriers between departments.
- Eliminating layers of management creating flatter organizational hierarchies.

- Closer relationships with customers and suppliers.
- Intelligent use of new technology.
- Global focus.
- Improving human resource skills.

The search for best practices is also called benchmarking. This involves determining where you need to improve, finding an organization that is exceptional in this area, then studying the company and applying its best practices in your firm.

Other Perspectives on Strategy

Strategy as Problem Solving

Professor Richard P. Rumelt described strategy as a type of problem solving in 2011. He wrote that good strategy has an underlying structure called a kernel. The kernel has three parts: 1) A diagnosis that defines or explains the nature of the challenge; 2) A guiding policy for dealing with the challenge; and 3) Coherent actions designed to carry out the guiding policy. President Kennedy outlined these three elements of strategy:

1. Diagnosis: "This Government, as promised, has maintained the closest surveillance of the Soviet military buildup on the island of Cuba. Within the past week, unmistakable evidence has established the fact that a series of offensive missile sites is now in preparation on that imprisoned island. The purpose of these bases can be none other than to provide a nuclear strike capability against the Western Hemisphere."
2. Guiding Policy: "Our unswerving objective, therefore, must be to prevent the use of these missiles against this or any other country, and to secure their withdrawal or elimination from the Western Hemisphere."
3. Action Plans: First among seven numbered steps was the following: "To halt this offensive buildup a strict quarantine on all offensive military equipment under shipment to Cuba is being initiated. All ships of any kind bound for Cuba from whatever nation or port will, if found to contain cargoes of offensive weapons, be turned back."

Active strategic management required active information gathering and active problem solving. In the early days of Hewlett-Packard (HP), Dave Packard and Bill Hewlett devised an active management style that they called management by walking around (MBWA). Senior HP managers were seldom at their desks. They spent most of their days visiting employees, customers, and suppliers. This direct contact with key people provided them with a solid grounding from which viable strategies could be crafted. Some Japanese managers employ a similar system, which originated at Honda, and is sometimes called the 3 G's (Genba, Genbutsu, and Genjitsu, which translate into "actual place", "actual thing", and "actual situation").

Creative vs Analytic Approaches

In 2010, IBM released a study summarizing three conclusions of 1500 CEOs around the world: 1) complexity is escalating, 2) enterprises are not equipped to cope with this complexity, and 3) creativity is now the single most important leadership competency. IBM said that it is needed in all aspects of leadership, including strategic thinking and planning. Similarly, McKeown argued that over-reliance on any particular approach to strategy is dangerous and that multiple methods can be used to combine the creativity and analytics to create an "approach to shaping the future", that is difficult to copy.

Non-strategic Management

A 1938 treatise by Chester Barnard, based on his own experience as a business executive, described the process as informal, intuitive, non-routinized and involving primarily oral, 2-way communications. Bernard says "The process is the sensing of the organization as a whole and the total situation relevant to it. It transcends the capacity of merely intellectual methods, and the techniques of discriminating the factors of the situation. The terms pertinent to it are "feeling", "judgement", "sense", "proportion", "balance", "appropriateness". It is a matter of art rather than science."

In 1973, Mintzberg found that senior managers typically deal with unpredictable situations so they strategize in *ad hoc*, flexible, dynamic, and implicit ways. He wrote, "The job breeds adaptive information-manipulators who prefer the live concrete situation. The manager works in an environment of stimulus-response, and he develops in his work a clear preference for live action."

In 1982, John Kotter studied the daily activities of 15 executives and concluded that they spent most of their time developing and working a network of relationships that provided general insights and specific details for strategic decisions. They tended to use "mental road maps" rather than systematic planning techniques. Daniel Isenberg's 1984 study of senior managers found that their decisions were highly intuitive. Executives often sensed what they were going to do before they could explain why. He claimed in 1986 that one of the reasons for this is the complexity of strategic decisions and the resultant information uncertainty.

Zuboff claimed that information technology was widening the divide between senior managers (who typically make strategic decisions) and operational level managers (who typically make routine decisions). She alleged that prior to the widespread use of computer systems, managers, even at the most senior level, engaged in both strategic decisions and routine administration, but as computers facilitated (She called it "deskilled") routine processes, these activities were moved further down the hierarchy, leaving senior management free for strategic decision making.

In 1977, Abraham Zaleznik distinguished leaders from managers. He described leaders as visionaries who inspire, while managers care about process. He claimed that the rise of managers was the main cause of the decline of American business in the 1970s and 1980s. Lack of leadership is most damaging at the level of strategic management where it can paralyze an entire organization.

According to Corner, Kinichi, and Keats, strategic decision making in organizations occurs at two levels: individual and aggregate. They developed a model of parallel strategic decision making. The model identifies two parallel processes that involve getting attention, encoding information, storage and retrieval of information, strategic choice, strategic outcome and feedback. The individual and organizational processes interact at each stage. For instance, competition-oriented objectives are based on the knowledge of competing firms, such as their market share.

Strategy as Marketing

The 1980s also saw the widespread acceptance of positioning theory. Although the theory originated with Jack Trout in 1969, it didn't gain wide acceptance until Al Ries and Jack Trout wrote their classic book Positioning: The Battle For Your Mind. The basic premise is that a strategy should not be judged by internal company factors but by the way customers see it relative to the competition. Crafting and implementing a strategy involves creating a position in the mind of the collective consumer. Several techniques enabled the practical use of positioning theory. Perceptual mapping for example, creates visual displays of the relationships between positions. Multidimensional scaling, discriminant analysis, factor analysis and conjoint analysis are mathematical techniques used to determine the most relevant characteristics (called dimensions or factors) upon which positions should be based. Preference regression can be used to determine vectors of ideal positions and cluster analysis can identify clusters of positions.

In 1992 Jay Barney saw strategy as assembling the optimum mix of resources, including human, technology and suppliers, and then configuring them in unique and sustainable ways.

James Gilmore and Joseph Pine found competitive advantage in mass customization. Flexible manufacturing techniques allowed businesses to individualize products for each customer without losing economies of scale. This effectively turned the product into a service. They also realized that if a service is mass-customized by creating a "performance" for each individual client, that service would be transformed into an "experience". Their book, The Experience Economy, along with the work of Bernd Schmitt convinced many to see service provision as a form of theatre. This school of thought is sometimes referred to as customer experience management (CEM).

Information- and Technology-driven Strategy

Many industries with a high information component are being transformed. For example, Encarta demolished Encyclopædia Britannica (whose sales have plummeted 80% since their peak of $650 million in 1990) before it was in turn, eclipsed by collaborative encyclopedias like Wikipedia. The music industry was similarly disrupted. The technology sector has provided some strategies directly. For example, from the software development industry agile software development provides a model for shared development processes.

Peter Drucker conceived of the "knowledge worker" in the 1950s. He described how fewer workers would do physical labor, and more would apply their minds. In 1984, John Naisbitt theorized that the future would be driven largely by information: companies that managed information well could obtain an advantage, however the profitability of what he called "information float" (information that the company had and others desired) would disappear as inexpensive computers made information more accessible.

Daniel Bell examined the sociological consequences of information technology, while Gloria Schuck and Shoshana Zuboff looked at psychological factors. Zuboff distinguished between "automating technologies" and "informating technologies". She studied the effect that both had on workers, managers and organizational structures. She largely confirmed Drucker's predictions about the importance of flexible decentralized structure, work teams, knowledge sharing and the knowledge worker's central role. Zuboff also detected a new basis for managerial authority, based on knowledge (also predicted by Drucker) which she called "participative management".

Maturity of Planning Process

McKinsey & Company developed a capability maturity model in the 1970s to describe the sophistication of planning processes, with strategic management ranked the highest. The four stages include:

- Financial planning, which is primarily about annual budgets and a functional focus, with limited regard for the environment;
- Forecast-based planning, which includes multi-year budgets and more robust capital allocation across business units;
- Externally oriented planning, where a thorough situation analysis and competitive assessment is performed;
- Strategic management, where widespread strategic thinking occurs and a well-defined strategic framework is used.

PIMS Study

The long-term PIMS study, started in the 1960s and lasting for 19 years, attempted to understand the Profit Impact of Marketing Strategies (PIMS), particularly the effect of market share. The initial conclusion of the study was unambiguous: the greater a company's market share, the greater their rate of profit. Market share provides economies of scale. It also provides experience curve advantages. The combined effect is increased profits.

The benefits of high market share naturally led to an interest in growth strategies. The relative advantages of horizontal integration, vertical integration, diversification, franchises, mergers and acquisitions, joint ventures and organic growth were discussed. Other research indicated that a low market share strategy could still be very profitable. Schumacher, Woo and Cooper, Levenson, and later Traverso showed how smaller niche players obtained very high returns.

Other Influences on Business Strategy

Military Strategy

In the 1980s business strategists realized that there was a vast knowledge base stretching back thousands of years that they had barely examined. They turned to military strategy for guidance. Military strategy books such as The Art of War by Sun Tzu, On War by von Clausewitz, and The Red Book by Mao Zedong became business classics. From Sun Tzu, they learned the tactical side of military strategy and specific tactical prescriptions. From von Clausewitz, they learned the dynamic and unpredictable nature of military action. From Mao, they learned the principles of guerrilla warfare.

The four types of business warfare theories are:

- Offensive marketing warfare strategies.
- Defensive marketing warfare strategies.
- Flanking marketing warfare strategies.
- Guerrilla marketing warfare strategies.

The marketing warfare literature also examined leadership and motivation, intelligence gathering, types of marketing weapons, logistics and communications. By the twenty-first century marketing warfare strategies had gone out of favour in favor of non-confrontational approaches. In 1989, Dudley Lynch and Paul L. Kordis published Strategy of the Dolphin: Scoring a Win in a Chaotic World. "The Strategy of the Dolphin" was developed to give guidance as to when to use aggressive strategies and when to use passive strategies. A variety of aggressiveness strategies were developed.

In 1993, J. Moore used a similar metaphor. Instead of using military terms, he created an ecological theory of predators and prey, a sort of Darwinian management strategy in which market interactions mimic long term ecological stability.

Author Phillip Evans said in 2014 that "Henderson's central idea was what you might call the Napoleonic idea of concentrating mass against weakness, of overwhelming the enemy. What Henderson recognized was that, in the business world, there are many phenomena which are characterized by what economists would call increasing returns—scale, experience. The more you do of something, disproportionately the better you get. And therefore he found logic for investing in such kinds of overwhelming mass in order to achieve competitive advantage. And that was the first introduction of essentially a military concept of strategy into the business world. It was on those two ideas, Henderson's idea of increasing returns to scale and experience, and Porter's idea of the value chain, encompassing heterogenous elements, that the whole edifice of business strategy was subsequently erected."

Traits of Successful Companies

Like Peters and Waterman a decade earlier, James Collins and Jerry Porras spent years conducting empirical research on what makes great companies. Six years of research uncovered a key underlying principle behind the 19 successful companies that they studied: They all encourage and preserve a core ideology that nurtures the company. Even though strategy and tactics change daily, the companies, nevertheless, were able to maintain a core set of values. These core values encourage employees to build an organization that lasts. In Built To Last they claim that short term profit goals, cost cutting, and restructuring will not stimulate dedicated employees to build a great company that will endure. In 2000 Collins coined the term "built to flip" to describe the prevailing business attitudes in Silicon Valley. It describes a business culture where technological change inhibits a long term focus. He also popularized the concept of the BHAG (Big Hairy Audacious Goal).

Arie de Geus undertook a similar study and obtained similar results. He identified four key traits of companies that had prospered for 50 years or more. They are:

- Sensitivity to the business environment – the ability to learn and adjust.
- Cohesion and identity – the ability to build a community with personality, vision, and purpose.
- Tolerance and decentralization – the ability to build relationships.
- Conservative financing.

A company with these key characteristics he called a living company because it is able to perpetuate itself. If a company emphasizes knowledge rather than finance, and sees itself as an ongoing community of human beings, it has the potential to become great and endure for decades. Such an organization is an organic entity capable of learning (he called it a "learning organization") and capable of creating its own processes, goals, and persona.

Will Mulcaster suggests that firms engage in a dialogue that centres around these questions:

- Will the proposed competitive advantage create Perceived Differential Value?"
- Will the proposed competitive advantage create something that is different from the competition?"

- Will the difference add value in the eyes of potential customers?" – This question will entail a discussion of the combined effects of price, product features and consumer perceptions.
- Will the product add value for the firm?" – Answering this question will require an examination of cost effectiveness and the pricing strategy.

BUSINESS ANALYSIS

Business analysis is a research discipline of identifying business needs and determining solutions to business problems. Solutions often include a software-systems development component, but may also consist of process improvement, organizational change or strategic planning and policy development. The person who carries out this task is called a business analyst or BA. Business analysts do not work solely on developing software systems. Those who attempt to do so run the risk of developing an incomplete solution.

Although there are different role definitions, depending upon the organization, there does seem to be an area of common ground where most business analysts work. The responsibilities appear to be:

- To investigate business systems, taking a holistic view of the situation. This may include examining elements of the organisation structures and staff development issues as well as current processes and IT systems.
- To evaluate actions to improve the operation of a business system. Again, this may require an examination of organisational structure and staff development needs, to ensure that they are in line with any proposed process redesign and IT system development.
- To document the business requirements for the IT system support using appropriate documentation standards.

In line with this, the core business analyst role could be defined as an internal consultancy role that has the responsibility for investigating business situations, identifying and evaluating options for improving business systems, defining requirements and ensuring the effective use of information systems in meeting the needs of the business.

Sub-disciplines

Business analysis as a discipline includes requirements analysis, sometimes also called requirements engineering. It focuses on ensuring the changes made to an organisation are aligned with its strategic goals. These changes include changes to strategies, structures, policies, business rules, processes, and information systems.

Examples of business analysis include:

Enterprise Analysis or Company Analysis

Focuses on understanding the needs of the business as a whole, its strategic direction, and identifying initiatives that will allow a business to meet those strategic goals. It also includes:

- Creating and maintaining the business architecture;
- Conducting feasibility studies;
- Identifying new business opportunities;
- Scoping and defining new business opportunities;
- Preparing the business case;
- Conducting the initial risk assessment.

Requirements Planning and Management

Involves planning the requirements development process, determining which requirements are the highest priority for implementation, and managing change.

Requirements Elicitation

Describes techniques for collecting requirements from stakeholders in a project. Techniques for requirements elicitation include:

- Brainstorming
- Document analysis
- Focus group
- Interface analysis
- Interviews/Questionnaire
- Workshops
- Reverse engineering
- Surveys
- User task analysis
- Process mapping
- Observation/job shadowing
- Design thinking

Requirements Analysis and Documentation

Describes how to develop and specify requirements in enough detail to allow them to be successfully implemented by a project team.

Analysis

The major forms of analysis are:

- Architecture analysis
- Business process analysis
- Object-oriented analysis
- Structured analysis
- Data warehouse analysis, storage and databases analysis.

Documentation

Requirements documentation can take several forms:

- Textual – for example, stories that summarize specific information;
- Matrix – for example, a table of requirements with priorities;
- Diagrams – for example, how data flows from one structure to the other;
- Wireframe – for example, how elements are required in a website;
- Models – for example, 3-D models that describes a character in a computer game.

Requirements Communication

Describes techniques for ensuring that stakeholders have a shared understanding of the requirements and how they will be implemented.

Solution Assessment and validation

Describes how the business analyst can perform correctness of a proposed solution, how to support the implementation of a solution, and how to assess possible shortcomings in the implementation.

Techniques

There are a number of generic business techniques that a business analyst will use when facilitating business change.

PESTLE

This is used to perform an external environmental analysis by examining the many different external factors affecting an organization.

The six attributes of PESTLE:

- Political (current and potential influences from political pressures);
- Economic (the local, national and world economy impact);
- Sociological (the ways in which a society can affect an organization);
- Technological (the effect of new and emerging technology);
- Legal (the effect of national and world legislation);
- Environmental (the local, national and world environmental issues).

Heptalysis

This is used to perform an in-depth analysis of early stage businesses/ventures on seven important categories:

- Market opportunity
- Product/solution
- Execution plan
- Financial engine
- Human capital
- Potential return
- Margin of safety

Steer

It is an analysis that puts into consideration – the following:

- Socio-cultural
- Technological
- Economic
- Ecological
- Regulatory Factors

MOST

This is used to perform an internal environmental analysis by defining the attributes of MOST to ensure that the project you are working on is aligned to each of the four attributes.

The four attributes of MOST are:

- Mission (where the business intends to go)
- Objectives (the key goals which will help achieve the mission)
- Strategies (options for moving forward)
- Tactics (how strategies are put into action)

SWOT

SWOT is used to help focus activities into areas of strength and where the greatest opportunities lie. This is used to identify the dangers that take the form of weaknesses and both internal and external threats.

The four attributes of SWOT analysis are:

- Strengths – What are the advantages? What is currently done well? (e.g. key area of best-performing activities of your company).
- Weaknesses – What should be improved? What is there to overcome? (e.g. key area where you are performing unsatisfactorily).
- Opportunities – What good opportunities face the organization? (e.g. key area where your competitors are performing poorly).
- Threats – What obstacles does the organization face? (e.g. key area where your competitor will perform well).

CATWOE

This is used to prompt thinking about what the business is trying to achieve. Business perspectives help the business analyst to consider the impact of any proposed solution on the people involved.

There are six elements of CATWOE:

- Customers – Who are the beneficiaries of the highest level business process and how does the issue affect them?
- Actors – Who is involved in the situation, who will be involved in implementing solutions and what will impact their success?
- Transformation Process – What processes or systems are affected by the issue?

- World View – What is the big picture and what are the wider impacts of the issue?
- Owner – Who owns the process or situation being investigated and what role will they play in the solution?
- Environmental Constraints – What are the constraints and limitations that will impact the solution and its success?

de Bono's Six Thinking Hats

This is often used in a brainstorming session to generate and analyse ideas and options. It is useful to encourage specific types of thinking and can be a convenient and symbolic way to request someone to "switch gears". It involves restricting the group to only thinking in specific ways – giving ideas & analysis in the "mood" of the time. Also known as the Six Thinking Hats.

- White: Pure facts, logical
- Green: Creative
- Yellow: Bright, optimistic, positive
- Black: Negative, devil's advocate
- Red: Emotional
- Blue: Cold, control.

Not all colors/moods have to be used.

Five Whys

Five Whys is used to get to the root of what is really happening in a single instance. For each answer given a further 'why' is asked.

MoSCoW

This is used to prioritize requirements by allocating an appropriate priority, gauging it against the validity of the requirement itself and its priority against other requirements.

MoSCoW comprises:

- Must have – or else delivery will be a failure;
- Should have – otherwise will have to adopt a workaround;
- Could have – to increase delivery satisfaction;
- Won't have this time – useful to the exclude requirements from this delivery timeframe.

VPEC-T

This technique is used when analysing the expectations of multiple parties having different views of a system in which they all have an interest in common, but have different priorities and different responsibilities.

- Values – constitute the objectives, beliefs and concerns of all parties participating. They may be financial, social, tangible and intangible;
- Policies – constraints that govern what may be done and the manner in which it may be done;
- Events – real-world proceedings that stimulate activity;
- Content – the meaningful portion of the documents, conversations, messages, etc. that are produced and used by all aspects of business activity;
- Trust – between users of the system and their right to access and change information within it.

SCRS

The SCRS approach in business analysis claims that the analysis should flow from the high-level business strategy to the solution, through the current state and the requirements. SCRS stands for:

- Strategy
- Current State
- Requirements
- Solution

Business Analysis Canvas

The Business Analysis Canvas is a tool that enables Business Analyst to quickly present a high level view of the activities that will be completed as part of the business analysis work allocation. The Business Analysis Canvas is broken into several topics.

- Project Objective
- Stakeholder
- Deliverable
- Impact to Target Operating Model
- Communication Approach

- Responsibilities
- Scheduling
- Key Dates

The Canvas has activities and questions the Business analyst can ask the organization to help build out the content.

Roles of Business Analysts

As the scope of business analysis is very wide, there has been a tendency for business analysts to specialize in one of the three sets of activities which constitute the scope of business analysis, the primary role for business analysts is to identify business needs and provide solutions to business problems these are done as being a part of following set of activities.

Strategist

Organizations need to focus on strategic matters on a more or less continuous basis in the modern business world. Business analysts, serving this need, are well-versed in analyzing the strategic profile of the organization and its environment, advising senior management on suitable policies, and the effects of policy decisions.

Architect

Organizations may need to introduce change to solve business problems which may have been identified by the strategic analysis, referred to above. Business analysts contribute by analyzing objectives, processes and resources, and suggesting ways by which re-design (BPR), or improvements (BPI) could be made. Particular skills of this type of analyst are "soft skills", such as knowledge of the business, requirements engineering, stakeholder analysis, and some "hard skills", such as business process modeling. Although the role requires an awareness of technology and its uses, it is not an IT-focused role.

Three elements are essential to this aspect of the business analysis effort: the redesign of core business processes; the application of enabling technologies to support the new core processes; and the management of organizational change. This aspect of business analysis is also called "business process improvement" (BPI), or "reengineering".

IT-systems Analyst

There is the need to align IT development with the business system as a whole. A long-standing problem in business is how to get the best return from IT investments, which are generally very expensive and of critical, often strategic, importance. IT departments, aware of the problem, often create a business analyst role to better understand

and define the requirements for their IT systems. Although there may be some overlap with the developer and testing roles, the focus is always on the IT part of the change process, and generally this type of business analyst gets involved only when a case for change has already been made and decided upon.

In any case, the term "analyst" is lately considered somewhat misleading, insofar as analysts (i.e. problem investigators) also do design work (solution definers).

The key responsibility areas of a business analyst are to collate the client's software requirements, understand them, and analyze them further from a business perspective. A business analyst is required to collaborate with and assist the business and assist them.

Function within the Organizational Structure

The role of business analysis can exist in a variety of structures within an organizational framework. Because business analysts typically act as a liaison between the business and technology functions of a company, the role can be often successful either aligned to a line of business, within IT, or sometimes both.

Business Alignment

When business analysts work at the business side, they are often subject matter experts for a specific line of business. These business analysts typically work solely on project work for a particular business, pulling in business analysts from other areas for cross-functional projects. In this case, there are usually business systems analysts on the IT side to focus on more technical requirements.

IT Alignment

In many cases, business analysts work solely within IT and they focus on both business and systems requirements for a project, consulting with various subject matter experts (SMEs) to ensure thorough understanding. Depending on the organizational structure, business analysts may be aligned to a specific development lab or they might be grouped together in a resource pool and allocated to various projects based on availability and expertise. The former builds specific subject matter expertise while the latter provides the ability to acquire cross-functional knowledge.

Practice Management

In a large organizations, there are centers of excellence or practice management groups who define frameworks and monitor the standards throughout the process of implementing the change in order to maintain the quality of change and reduce the risk of changes to organization. Some organizations may have independent centers of excellence for individual streams such as project management, business analysis or quality assurance.

A practice management team provides a framework by which all business analysts in an organization conduct their work, usually consisting of processes, procedures, templates and best practices. In addition to providing guidelines and deliverables, it also provides a forum to focus on continuous improvement of the business analysis function.

Goals

Ultimately, business analysis wants to achieve the following outcomes:

- Create solutions;
- Give enough tools for robust project management;
- Improve efficiency and reduce waste;
- Provide essential documentation, such as project initiation documents.

One way to assess these goals is to measure the return on investment (ROI) for all projects. According to Forrester Research, more than $100 billion is spent annually in the U.S. on custom and internally developed software projects. For all of these software development projects, keeping accurate data is important and business leaders are constantly asking for the return or ROI on a proposed project or at the conclusion of an active project. However, asking for the ROI without sufficient data of where value is created or destroyed may result in inaccurate projections.

Reduce Waste and complete Projects on Time

Project delays are costly in several ways:

- Project costs – For every month of delay, the project team costs and expenses continue to accumulate. When a large part of the development team has been outsourced, the costs will start to add up quickly and are very visible if contracted on a time and materials basis (T&M). Fixed price contracts with external parties limit this risk. For internal resources, the costs of delays are not as readily apparent, unless time spent by resources is being tracked against the project, as labor costs are essentially 'fixed' costs.
- Opportunity costs – Opportunity costs come in two types – lost revenue and unrealized expense reductions. Some projects are specifically undertaken with the purpose of driving new or additional revenues to the bottom line. For every month of delay, a company foregoes a month of this new revenue stream. The purpose of other projects is to improve efficiencies and reduce costs. Again, each month of failure postpones the realization of these expense reductions by another month. In the vast majority of cases, these opportunities are never captured or analyzed, resulting in misleading ROI calculations. Of the two opportunity costs, the lost revenue is the most egregious – and the effects are greater and longer lasting.

On a lot of projects (particularly larger ones) the project manager is the one responsible for ensuring that a project is completed on time. The BA's job is more to ensure that if a project is not completed on time then at least the highest priority requirements are met.

Document the Right Requirements

Business analysts want to make sure that they define the requirements in a way that meets the business needs, for example, in IT applications the requirements need to meet end-users' needs. Essentially, they want to define the right application. This means that they must document the right requirements through listening carefully to 'customer' feedback, and by delivering a complete set of clear requirements to the technical architects and coders who will write the program. If a business analyst has limited tools or skills to help him elicit the right requirements, then the chances are fairly high that he will end up documenting requirements that will not be used or that will need to be re-written – resulting in rework as discussed below. The time wasted to document unnecessary requirements not only impacts the business analyst, it also impacts the rest of the development cycle. Coders need to generate application code to perform these unnecessary requirements and testers need to make sure that the wanted features actually work as documented and coded. Experts estimate that 10% to 40% of the features in new software applications are unnecessary or go unused. Being able to reduce the amount of these extra features by even one-third can result in significant savings. An approach of minimalism or "Keep it Simple" and minimum technology supports a reduced cost number for the end result and on-going maintenance of the implemented solution.

Improve Project Efficiency

Efficiency can be achieved in two ways: by reducing rework and by shortening project length. Rework is a common industry headache and it has become so common at many organizations that it is often built into project budgets and time lines. It generally refers to extra work needed in a project to fix errors due to incomplete or missing requirements and can impact the entire software development process from definition to coding and testing. The need for rework can be reduced by ensuring that the requirements gathering and definition processes are thorough and by ensuring that the business and technical members of a project are involved in these processes from an early stage.

Shortening project length presents two potential benefits. For every month that a project can be shortened, project resource costs can be diverted to other projects. This can lead to savings on the current project and lead to earlier start times of future projects (thus increasing revenue potential).

Goal Setting

Goal setting involves the development of an action plan designed to motivate and guide a person or group toward a goal. Goal setting can be guided by goal-setting criteria (or rules) such as SMART criteria. Goal setting is a major component of personal-development and management literature. Studies by Edwin A. Locke and his colleagues have shown that more specific and ambitious goals lead to more performance improvement than easy or general goals. The goals should be specific, time constrained and difficult. Difficult goals should be set ideally at the 90th percentile of performance assuming that motivation and not ability is limiting attainment of that level of performance. As long as the person accepts the goal, has the ability to attain it, and does not have conflicting goals, there is a positive linear relationship between goal difficulty and task performance.

The theory states that the simplest most direct motivational explanation of why some people perform better than others is because they have different performance goals. The essence of the theory is fourfold. First, difficult specific goals lead to significantly higher performance than easy goals, no goals, or even the setting of an abstract goal such as urging people to do their best. Second, holding ability constant, as this is a theory of motivation, and given that there is goal commitment, the higher the goal the higher the performance. Third, variables such as praise, feedback, or the involvement of people in decision-making only influences behavior to the extent that it leads to the setting of and commitment to a specific difficult goal. Fourth, goal-setting, in addition to affecting the three mechanisms of motivation, namely, choice, effort, and persistence, can also have a cognitive benefit. It can influence choice, effort, and persistence to discover ways to attain the goal.

Concept

Goals that are difficult to achieve and specific tend to increase performance more than goals that are not. A goal can be made more specific by:

- Quantification (that is, making it measurable), such as by pursuing "increase productivity by 50%" instead of "increase productivity",
- Enumeration, such as by defining tasks that must be completed to achieve the goal instead of only defining the goal.

Setting goals can affect outcomes in four ways:

- Choice: Goals may narrow someone's attention and direct their efforts toward goal-relevant activities and fromward goal-irrelevant actions.
- Effort: Goals may make someone more effortful. For example, if someone usually produces 4 widgets per hour but wants to produce 6 widgets per hour, then they may work harder to produce more widgets than without that goal.
- Persistence: Goals may make someone more willing to work through setbacks.
- Cognition: Goals may cause someone to develop and change their behavior.

Goal Commitment

People perform better when they are committed to achieving certain goals. Through an understanding of the effect of goal setting on individual performance, organizations are able to use goal setting to benefit organizational performance. Locke and Latham have indicated three moderators that indicate goal setting success:

1. The importance of the expected outcomes of goal attainment,
2. Self-efficacy: one's belief that they are able to achieve the goals,
3. Commitment to others: promises or engagements to others can strongly improve commitment.

Expanding the three from above, the level of commitment is influenced by external factors. Such as the person assigning the goal, setting the standard for the person to achieve/perform. This influences the level of commitment by how compliant the individual is with the one assigning the goal. An external factor can also be the role models of the individual. Say if they strive to be like their favorite athlete, the individual is more likely to put forth more effort to their own work and goals.

Internal factors can derive from their participation level in the work to achieve the goal. What they expect from themselves can either flourish their success, or destroy it. Also, the individual may want to appear superior to their peers or competitors. They want to achieve the goal the best and be known for it. The self-reward of accomplishing a goal, is usually one of the main keys that keep individuals committed.

Goal–performance Relationship

Locke and colleagues examined the behavioral effects of goal-setting, concluding that 90% of laboratory and field studies involving specific and challenging goals led to higher performance than did easy or no goals.

Locke and Latham argue that it is not sufficient to urge employees to "do their best". "Doing one's best" has no external referent, which makes it useless in eliciting specific behavior. To elicit some specific form of behavior from another person, it is important that this person has a clear view of what is expected from him/her. A goal is thereby of vital importance because it helps an individual to focus his or her efforts in a specified direction. In other words, goals canalize behavior. (However, when faced with complex tasks and directions that are difficult to specify, telling someone to "do their best", with a focus on learning, can sometimes lead to the discovery of better strategies whereby specific goals can then be set.

Feedback

Without proper feedback channels it is impossible for employees to adapt or adjust to the required behavior. Managers should keep track of performance to allow employees to see how effective they have been in attaining their goals. Providing feedback on short-term objectives helps to sustain motivation and commitment to the goal and without it, goal setting is unlikely to be successful. Feedback should be provided on the strategies followed to achieve the goals and the final outcomes achieved, as well. Feedback on strategies used to obtain goals is very important, especially for complex work, because challenging goals put focus on outcomes rather than on performance strategies, so they impair performance. Properly delivered feedback is also very essential, and the following hints may help for providing a good feedback:

- Create a positive context for feedback.
- Use constructive and positive language.
- Focus on behaviors and strategies.
- Tailor feedback to the needs of the individual worker.
- Make feedback a two-way communication process.

Advances in technology can facilitate providing feedback. Systems analysts have designed computer programs that track goals for numerous members of an organization. Such computer systems may maintain every employee's goals, as well as their deadlines. Separate methods may check the employee's progress on a regular basis, and other systems may require perceived slackers to explain how they intend to improve. More difficult goals require more cognitive strategies and well-developed skills. Thc more difficult the tasks, the smaller the group of people who possess the necessary skills and strategies. From an organizational perspective, it is thereby more difficult to successfully attain more difficult goals, since resources become more scarce.

Honing Goal Setting using Temporal Motivation Theory

Locke and Latham note that goal setting theory lacks "the issue of time perspective". Taking this into consideration, Steel and Konig utilize their temporal motivation theory (TMT) to account for goal setting's effects, and suggest new hypotheses regarding a pair of its moderators: goal difficulty and proximity. The effectiveness of goal setting can be explained by two aspects of TMT: the principle of diminishing returns and temporal discounting. Similar to the expression "the sum of the parts can be greater than the whole", a division of a project into several, immediate, subgoals appears to take advantage of these two elements.

Employee Motivation

The more employees are motivated, the more they are stimulated and interested in accepting goals. These success factors are interdependent. For example, the expected outcomes of goals are positively influenced when employees are involved in the goal setting process. Not only does participation increase commitment in attaining the goals that are set, participation influences self-efficacy as well. Additionally, feedback is necessary to monitor one's progress. When feedback is not present, an employee might think (s)he is not making enough progress. This can reduce self-efficacy and thereby harm the performance outcomes in the long run.

- Goal-commitment: the most influential moderator, becomes especially important when dealing with difficult or complex goals. If people lack commitment to goals, they lack motivation to reach them. To commit to a goal, one must believe in its importance or significance.
- Attainability: individuals must also believe that they can attain—or at least partially reach—a defined goal. If they think no chance exists of reaching a goal, they may not even try.
- Self-efficacy: the higher someone's self-efficacy regarding a certain task, the more likely they will set higher goals, and the more persistence they will show in achieving them.

In Business

In business, goal setting encourages participants to put in substantial effort. Also, because every member has defined expectations for their role, little room is left for inadequate, marginal effort to go unnoticed. Managers cannot constantly drive motivation, or keep track of an employee's work on a continuous basis. Goals are therefore an important tool for managers, since goals have the ability to function as a self-regulatory mechanism that helps employees prioritize tasks.

Four mechanisms through which goal setting can affect individual performance are:

1. Goals focus attention toward goal-relevant activities and away from goal-irrelevant activities.
2. Goals serve as an energizer: Higher goals induce greater effort, while low goals induce lesser effort.
3. Goals affect persistence; constraints with regard to resources affect work pace.
4. Goals activate cognitive knowledge and strategies that help employees cope with the situation at hand.

Limitations

Goal-setting has limitations. In an organization, a goal of a manager may not align with the goals of the organization as a whole. In such cases, the goals of an individual may come into direct conflict with the employing organization. Without clearly aligning goals between the organization and the individual, overall performance may suffer. Additionally, there is evidence that suggests that goal-setting can foster unethical behavior when people do not achieve their desired goals. Goal setting also may impair performance in certain situations. Such situations include when an individual becomes overly focused on accomplishing a previously-set goal that they end up under performing on current tasks.

Goal setting may have the drawback of inhibiting implicit learning: goal setting may encourage simple focus on an outcome without openness to exploration, understanding, or growth. A solution to this limitation is to set learning goals as well as performance goals, so that learning is expected as part of the process of reaching goals.

Developments in Theory

Goal Choice

Self-efficacy, past performance, and various other social factors influence goal setting. Failure to meet previous goals often leads to setting lower (and more likely achievable) goals.

Learning Goals

There are times when having specific goals is not a best option; this is the case when the goal requires new skills or knowledge. Tunnel vision is a consequence of specific goals; if a person is too focused on attaining a specific goal, he or she may ignore the need to learn new skills or acquire new information. This concept is illustrated well by the "basketball game task" study in which observers watched a video of a group of people wearing white shirts and black shirts who are passing a basketball back and forth, and the observers were instructed to count the number of times a basketball is passed between only the players wearing white shirts. During the video, a woman carrying an open umbrella walks across the screen. Of 28 observers who were focused on counting the number of passes between only the players wearing white shirts, only 6 reported noticing the woman carrying the umbrella. When observers watched the video without focusing on a specific task, all of the observers noticed the umbrella woman. In situations where the risk of tunnel vision is high, the best option is to set a learning goal. A learning goal is a generalized goal to achieve knowledge in a certain topic or field, but it can ultimately lead to better performance in specific goals related to the learning goals.

Locke and Latham attribute this response to metacognition. They believe that "a learning goal facilitates or enhances metacognition—namely, planning, monitoring, and evaluating progress toward goal attainment". This is necessary in environments with little or no guidance and structure. Although jobs typically have set goals, individual goals and achievement can benefit from metacognition.

Framing

Framing, or how goals are viewed, influences performance. When one feels threatened and or intimidated by a high goal they perform poorer than those who view the goal as a challenge. The framing of a goal as a gain or a loss influences one's eventual performance.

Affect

Realization of goals has an effect on affect—that is, feelings of success and satisfaction. Achieving goals has a positive effect, and failing to meet goals has negative consequences. However, the effect of goals is not exclusive to one realm. Success in one's job can compensate for feelings of failure in one's personal life.

Group Goals

The relationship between group goals and individual goals influences group performance; when goals are compatible there is a positive effect, but when goals are incompatible the effects can be detrimental to the group's performance. There is another factor at work in groups, and that is the sharing factor; a positive correlation exists between sharing information within the group and group performance. In the case of group goals, feedback needs to be related to the group, not individuals, in order for it to improve the group's performance.

Goals and Traits

On a basic level, the two types of goals are learning goals and performance goals; each possesses different traits associated with the selected goal. Learning goals involve tasks where skills and knowledge can be acquired, whereas performance goals involve easy-to-accomplish tasks that will make one appear successful (thus tasks where error and judgment may be possible are avoided).

A more complex trait-mediation study is the one conducted by Lee, Sheldon, and Turban, which yielded the following results:

- Amotivated orientation (low confidence in one's capabilities) is associated with goal-avoidance motivation, and more generally, associated with lower goals levels and lower performance.
- Control orientation (extrinsic motivation) is associated with both avoidance and approach goals. Approach goals are associated with higher goal levels and higher performance.
- Autonomy goals (intrinsic motivation) lead to mastery goals, enhanced focus, and therefore enhanced performance.

Macro-level Goals

Macro-level goals refer to goal setting that is applied to the company as a whole. Cooperative goals reduce the negative feelings that occur as a result of alliances and the formation of groups. The most common parties involved are the company and its suppliers. The three motivators for macro-level goals are: self-efficacy, growth goals, and organizational vision.

Goals and Subconscious Priming

The effects of subconscious priming and conscious goals are independent, although a conscious goal has a larger effect. The interaction effect is that priming can enhance the effects of difficult goals, but it has no effect on easy goals. There is also the situation in which priming and conscious goals conflict with one another, and in this situation the conscious goals have a greater effect on performance.

General Action and Inaction Goals

Action goals are believed to promote the sense of action, whereas inaction goals are considered to reduce people's tendency to take actions. Common action goals can be to do something, perform a certain act, or to go someplace, whereas typical inaction goals can take the form of having a rest or to stop doing something.

Goal-regulated overall activity and inactivity tendency result from both biological conditions and social-cultural environment. Recent research revealed that most nations hold more favorable attitude towards action rather than inaction, even though some countries value action and inaction slightly differently than others. Recent research suggested that people tend to choose inaction goals when they are making decisions among choices where uncertainty could result in negative outcomes, but they prefer action over inaction in their daily behaviors when no deliberation is needed. Timothy D. Wilson and colleagues found that many people "preferred to administer electric shocks to themselves instead of being left alone with their thoughts".

PLANNING

Planning is needed to grow or start a business. The main source of planning for a company is the business plan. A business plan is a document that details the strategy of business owners on how they intend to run their business. There are several objectives that should be covered in a business plan from what the company's goals are to how many employees are going to be hired. Business plans provide a road map for where the owners want to take their businesses. It is also necessary to have if owners want to secure financing.

Benefits

Business plans are guides for owners to run their businesses. Problems facing owners while running their businesses (slow sales, not enough customers or clients) may be solved by analyzing the information detailed in their business plans. It can help owners focus marketing efforts and get back to basics when the business begins to expand. This breeds confidence into the business owner as they continue to grow their business.

Features

A detailed business plan touches on several key areas. Business plans cover the company's vision, names of management and how many employees are/will be hired, a description of the company and what product(s) or service(s) it provides. Business plans also outline the marketing research done to analyze the profitability of the company, marketing and sales strategies and financial projections, competition, records, funding amount requests and how the money will be used.

Considerations

There are several types of business plans that are used for different situations. The main difference between plans is the amount of details that's produced. Some plans outline just the bare facts (mini-plans) while others, such as working plans, which are viewed internally by company management, and presentation plans, which are produced for investors and lenders, detail more facts and data. Business plans should be error free and tailored for the situation. Investors looking for graphs, charts and financial projections to make a final decision won't be satisfied with a mini-plan.

Significance

Not only do business plans breed confidence in owners, but in lenders as well. Business plans are one of the main requirements for owners to have when they're applying for business loans. Some lenders require business plans along with other documents such as bank statements as part of their business loan application. Detailed business plans prove to lenders that owners are very knowledgeable and serious about their businesses. If the rest of the application meets their approval, the business plan could be the difference for the owner to secure a business loan.

Misconceptions

Although a business plan was created at the start of the business venture, it is necessary to review it from time to time and make changes as the company evolves. A yearly review or a review when the company undergoes growth or significant changes is needed. The same objectives that were important two years ago may not be significant when new goals have replaced old ones. Owners should update their business plans by incorporating changes as much as possible to keep them current.

Scheduling

A schedule may also involve the completion of a project with which the public has no interaction public prior to its completion. In project management, a formal schedule will often be created as an initial step in carrying out a specific project, such as the construction of a building, development of a product, or launch of a program. Establishing a project management schedule involves listing milestones, activities, and deliverables with intended start and finish dates, of which the scheduling of employees may be an element. A production process schedule is used for the planning of the production or the operation, while a resource schedule aids in the logistical planning for sharing resources among several entities.

In such cases, a schedule "is obtained by estimating the duration of each task and noting any dependencies amongst those tasks". Dependencies, in turn, are tasks that must be completed in order to make other tasks possible, such as renting a truck before loading materials on the truck (since nothing can be loaded until the truck is available for things to be loaded on). Scheduling of projects, therefore, requires the identification of all of the tasks necessary to complete the project, and the earliest time at which each task can be completed. In creating a schedule, a certain amount of time is usually set aside as a contingency against unforeseen days. This time is called scheduling variance, or float, and is a core concept for the critical path method.

Strategic Planning

Every organisation or major part of a complex organisation occasionally has to make some momentous decisions- the sort of decisions that affect the entire destiny of the organisation for years into the future. These decisions are designed to address the really biggest and most important issues facing an organisation-issues so significant we might call them 'strategic elephants'.

Such decisions are not simply about small adjustments to activity levels, but are the kind of decisions that may lead to a substantially different organisational structure, or major changes in the relationships among key stakeholders, competitive position, or strategic partners of the organization.

Sometimes the outside world forces such decisions on the organisation. Such forces may include major shifts in the market, big changes in government policy, and radical moves by competing organisations. Sometimes, it is something inside the organisation that demands a major reappraisal. Technological change driving new methods of carrying out its work, or weakening of its financial structure, or a change in the senior management of the organisation requiring a large re-organisation are examples of such internal forces.

Organisations have always faced such pressures to make huge decisions. In recent years, the pressure has risen to the point where a systematic yet flexible process of dealing with such decisions is called for. Such a process is variously and sometimes confusingly described as: corporate planning, strategic planning, business planning, and variations such as corporate strategic planning, or strategic business planning. Other labels make the subject more industry specific such as military strategic planning, hospital strategic planning, and in some jurisdictions what others know as urban and regional planning is sometimes called strategic planning.

As its name implies simply-strategic-planning.com will focus primarily on 'strategic planning'. By this we have in mind any plan which looks forward several years and which is concerned with massive factors only. The focus of the decisions in the plan are the organisation as a whole in its environment as a whole.

Strategic Planning is Different from Business Planning

A definition of strategic planning must be based on understanding that a strategic plan differs from a Business Plan in three ways:

- It looks much further ahead;
- It consists largely of words with just a few figures to indicate the scale of the planners' intentions. A business plan, on the other hand, consists largely of figures. Because these are often unreliable beyond a few months, managers are reluctant to look ahead as far as they may need to. Strategic plans can look further ahead because so few figures are employed;
- What few figures they do contain are tested by risk analysis techniques.

A systematic, formally documented process for deciding what is the handful of key decisions that an organisation, viewed as a corporate whole must get right in order to thrive over the next few years. The process results in the production of a corporate strategic plan.

Strategic Plan

A set of statements describing the purpose and ethical conduct for an organisation together with the specific strategies designed to achieve the targets set for each of these. The importance of strategic planning is in the small number and the long term impact of the decisions embodied in the strategic plan. These decisions are those required in facing up to the most important challenges facing an organization. It helps in coming up with a clear definition of strategic planning to understand the purpose of strategic planning. These strategic planning issues are characterized by the size of their possible impact on organizational performance and the time span of the impact.

The geographic scope and impact may also set issues apart as strategic. Many more organizations of all types and sizes have to consider this matter in an international context. Global strategic planning is a process adopted by organizations that operate internationally in order to formulate an effective global strategy.

An effective strategic choice process positions an organization for making sustainable strategic decisions. Learn about the five simple components of strategic planning that reduce risk and dramatically improve long-term performance of your organisation. Use strategic planning principles to keep your corporate strategic planning process on track. Formal strategic planning as a group decision making process benefits greatly from formalizing of the procedures involved.

Strategic planning and business planning are separate and related, and the idea of merging them under the umbrella strategic business planning is not useful. It is important to be clear about different forms of planning, and in particular the differences between operational and strategic planning. Another unhelpful suggestion is when people oppose strategic planning and strategic thinking, as if somehow planning did not involve thinking.

A persistent problem for some organizations is the difficulty of getting strategic plans implemented. Applied strategic planning blends strategy formulation with the means of managing strategy implementation. Useful strategic planning models include clear procedures for objective setting, option generation, results monitoring, issue clarification, and participant engagement. Corporate level strategy covers the strategic scope of the organization as a whole, and for most organizations is the only strategic plan required.

Strategic planning is important to an organization because it provides a sense of direction and outlines measurable goals. Strategic planning is a tool that is useful for guiding day-to-day decisions and also for evaluating progress and changing approaches when moving forward. In order to make the most of strategic planning, your company should give careful thought to the strategic objectives it outlines, and then back up these goals with realistic, thoroughly researched, quantifiable benchmarks for evaluating results.

The Mission

Strategic planning starts with defining a company mission. A mission is important to an organization because it synthesizes and distils the overarching idea linking its practical strategies, enabling management and employees to align the specifics of their actions and decisions with a clearly defined vision and direction. Define your strategic mission in a way that is broad enough to guide both management and employees, and narrow enough to focus their efforts. "To help humanity," is too broad a mission, even for a non-profit. "To feed the hungry by connecting home gardeners with food banks," is a mission that is both general and actionable.

Setting Goals

The nuts and bolts of the strategic planning process are expressed in measurable goals. Measurable goals set specific, concrete objectives expressed in terms of quantities and timelines. Measurable goals are important to an organization because they enable managers and employees to evaluate progress and pace developments. "To grow substantially during the next few years" is not a measurable goal, but "To increase sales by 30 percent during the upcoming year" provides a concrete objective to be achieved in a specific time frame.

Evaluating Progress

Strategic objectives are of necessity based on the best information you have at the time and your most realistic assessments of what your company can achieve. Organizations also benefit from building a stage into the strategic planning process that involves evaluating goals and progress after an elapsed period of time in light of the company's success in achieving these goals and developments that have arisen in the interim. For example, if you plan to grow your hardware store business 20 percent during a specific year, but a formidable competitor opens a superstore down the road, you'll probably redefine your objectives and evaluate progress in terms of preserving market share.

The Strategic Planning Process

The process of strategic planning can be as important to an organization as the results. Strategic planning can be an especially valuable process when it includes employees in all departments and at all levels of responsibility thinking about how their activities and responsibilities fit into the larger picture, and about their potential contributions.

APPROACHES

Centralisation and Decentralisation

Centralization is said to be a process where the concentration of decision making is in a few hands. All the important decision and actions at the lower level, all subjects and actions at the lower level are subject to the approval of top management. According to Allen, "Centralization" is the systematic and consistent reservation of authority at central points in the organization. The implication of centralization can be:

1. Reservation of decision making power at top level.
2. Reservation of operating authority with the middle level managers.
3. Reservation of operation at lower level at the directions of the top level.

Under centralization, the important and key decisions are taken by the top management and the other levels are into implementations as per the directions of top level. For example, in a business concern, the father & son being the owners decide about the important matters and all the rest of functions like product, finance, marketing, personnel, are carried out by the department heads and they have to act as per instruction and orders of the two people. Therefore in this case, decision making power remain in the hands of father & son.

On the other hand, Decentralization is a systematic delegation of authority at all levels of management and in all of the organization. In a decentralization concern, authority in retained by the top management for taking major decisions and framing policies concerning the whole concern. Rest of the authority may be delegated to the middle level and lower level of management. The degree of centralization and decentralization will depend upon the amount of authority delegated to the lowest level. According to Allen, "Decentralization refers to the systematic effort to delegate to the lowest level of authority except that which can be controlled and exercised at central points.

Decentralization is not the same as delegation. In fact, decentralization is all extension of delegation. Decentralization pattern is wider is scope and the authorities are diffused to the lowest most level of management. Delegation of authority is a complete process and takes place from one person to another. While decentralization is complete only when fullest possible delegation has taken place. For example, the general manager of a company is responsible for receiving the leave application for the whole of the concern. The general manager delegates this work to the personnel manager who is now responsible for receiving the leave applicants. In this situation delegation of authority has taken place. On the other hand, on the request of the personnel manager, if the general manager delegates this power to all the departmental heads at all level, in this situation decentralization has taken place. There is a saying that "Everything that increasing the role of subordinates is decentralization and that decreases the role is centralization". Decentralization is wider in scope and the subordinate's responsibility increase in this case. On the other hand, in delegation the managers remain answerable even for the acts of subordinates to their superiors.

Implications of Decentralization

1. There is less burden on the Chief Executive as in the case of centralization.
2. In decentralization, the subordinates get a chance to decide and act independently which develops skills and capabilities. This way the organization is able to process reserve of talents in it.
3. In decentralization, diversification and horizontal can be easily implanted.
4. In decentralization, concern diversification of activities can place effectively since there is more scope for creating new departments. Therefore, diversification growth is of a degree.
5. In decentralization structure, operations can be coordinated at divisional level which is not possible in the centralization set up.
6. In the case of decentralization structure, there is greater motivation and morale of the employees since they get more independence to act and decide.
7. In a decentralization structure, co-ordination to some extent is difficult to maintain as there are lot many department divisions and authority is delegated to maximum possible extent, i.e., to the bottom most level delegation reaches. Centralization and decentralization are the categories by which the pattern of authority relationships became clear. The degree of centralization and de-centralization can be affected by many factors like nature of operation, volume of profits, number of departments, size of a concern, etc. The larger the size of a concern, a decentralization set up is suitable in it.

Advantages and Disadvantages

There are some very good reasons why companies choose to centralize their management, but also big disadvantages to going too far.

Advantages

The upper management at a centralized company will have complete control over training, products they offer, and are more likely to ensure the company's core objectives and values are maintained. A centralized management style also has the potential to improve the organization as a whole instead of just one smaller branch at a time.

Centralized management usually keeps its external communication, like Business to Business relationships, controlled down to just a few individuals, which helps keep the company's messaging consistent and more efficient. Centralization also helps standardize products and materials, which in turn helps speed up preparation and procurement.

McDonald's is a prime example of centralized management and standardization. The exact same number of pickles is put on each burger no matter where you are in the world. Airlines do this too – you will get the exact same brand of bottled water on every airplane in the same brand. Companies often centralize when they want to improve the consistency of their product quality, and standardize production.

Disadvantages

Centralized management strategies limit the creativity to the top management that makes the majority of the decisions. This can lead to problems for the company trying to adapt to a changing market. Heavily centralized organizations involved in a fast-paced product and rapidly-changing industries are not able to react quickly to changing demands of their customers.

An example of this retail stores selling trendy clothing. The sales and staff managers often receive feedback from shoppers that would be vitally important for the purchasing department to cater to the needs of the customer. This information needs to be relayed through the line of upper management, usually through weekly or monthly reports, putting a huge delay on the changes that impact the storefront.

Decentralized Management

Decentralization avoids some of the biggest drawbacks of centralized management, but it has pitfalls of its own for managers to avoid.

Advantages

Decentralization has a broader immediate contact with customers by allowing management to have more decision-making ability. This can give more efficient managerial decisions because lower-level managers have more direct control over their day-to-day tasks and can reward/discipline employees as needed. It allows managers to have a clear view of performance-related results among their employees. Giving the lower levels of the organization more flexibility to make decisions, it also increases job satisfaction, and gives awareness of how significant their job is to the whole company.

Disadvantages

A decentralized organization has a lot riding on the decisions made by many employees. This means that if some of those lower-level managers lack training, experience, education, or competence, it can damage the organization as a whole. Smaller organizations are the least-likely decentralize their organization successfully, since having many low-level managers making their own decisions can be costly. Larger companies with strong upper management are the most successful at successfully using decentralized organizational styles, simply by having a large pool of talented middle managers to give more responsibility.

Providing Accountability

When a company suffers from low employee efficiency, the biggest culprit is usually "job ambiguity". This is where individual employees do not have their roles in the organization clearly defined. Employees need precise job descriptions to be liable for their performance – by reducing uncertainty, employees can develop skills to better perform their job, and gives managers more accurate ways to measure performance.

As companies centralize and decentralize, the main question is how exactly the role of each manager and employee being defined is. If individuals are given too many unrelated tasks, it becomes harder to measure their overall efficiency. On the other hand, if the company centralizes decisions to the point where employees have very little flexibility, they may feel their hands are tied and their efficiency is held back by "red tape".

Autonomy in the workplace has shown to create a sense of job empowerment, allowing employees to not only take on more responsibility but to also give them the freedom to make decisions that affect their performance. This allows managers to delegate responsibility and hold employees accountable for their results and focus less on the process of how the desired outcomes were achieved.

Management by Objectives

Management by objectives (MBO), also known as management by results (MBR), was first popularized by Peter Drucker in his 1954 book The Practice of Management. Management by objectives is the process of defining specific objectives within an organization that management can convey to organization members, then deciding on how to achieve each objective in sequence. This process allows managers to take work that needs to be done one step at a time to allow for a calm, yet productive work environment. This process also helps organization members to see their accomplishments as they achieve each objective, which reinforces a positive work environment and a sense of achievement. An important part of MBO is the measurement and comparison of an employee's actual performance with the standards set. Ideally, when employees themselves have been involved with the goal-setting and choosing the course of action to be followed by them, they are more likely to fulfill their responsibilities. According to George S. Odiorne, the system of management by objectives can be described as a process whereby the superior and subordinate jointly identify common goals, define each individual's major areas of responsibility in terms of the results expected of him or her, and use these measures as guides for operating the unit and assessing the contribution of each of its members.

Concept and Framework

Management by objectives at its core is the process of employers/supervisors attempting to manage their subordinates by introducing a set of specific goals that both the employee and the company strive to achieve in the near future, and working to meet those goals accordingly.

Five steps:

- Review organizational goal
- Set worker objective
- Monitor progress
- Evaluation
- Give reward.

Features and Advantages

The principle of MBO is for employees to have a clear understanding of their roles and the responsibilities expected of them, so they can understand how their activities relate to the achievement of the organization's goals. MBO also places importance on fulfilling the personal goals of each employee.

Proponents argue that benefits of MBO include:

1. Motivation – Involving employees in the whole process of goal setting and increasing employee empowerment. This increases employee job satisfaction and commitment.
2. Better communication and coordination – Frequent reviews and interactions between superiors and subordinates help to maintain harmonious relationships within the organization and also to solve problems.

3. Clarity of goals.
4. Subordinates tend to have a higher commitment to objectives they set for themselves than those imposed on them by another person.
5. Managers can ensure that objectives of the subordinates are linked to the organization's objectives.
6. Common goal for whole organization means it is a unifying, directive principle of management.

Application in Practice

There are endless ways to exercise management by objectives. One must simply find specific goals to aim for in an organization or business. Many noteworthy companies have used MBO. The management at the computer company Hewlett-Packard (HP) has said that it considers the policy a huge component of its success. Many other corporations praise the effectiveness of MBO, including Xerox, DuPont, Intel, and countless others. Companies that use MBO often report greater sales rates and productiveness within the organization. Objectives can be set in all domains of activities, such as production, marketing, services, sales, R&D, human resources, finance, and information systems. Some objectives are collective, and some can be goals for each individual worker. Both make the task at hand seem attainable and enable the workers to visualize what needs to be done and how.

In the MBO paradigm, managers determine the mission and the strategic goals of the enterprise. The goals set by top-level managers are based on an analysis of what can and should be accomplished by the organization within a specific period of time. The functions of these managers can be centralised by appointing a project manager who can monitor and control activities of the various departments. If this cannot be done or is not desirable, each manager's contributions to the organizational goal should be clearly spelled out.

In many large Japanese corporations, beginning in the late 1990s MBO was used as the basis of "the performance-based merit system" (seika-shugi) which used clear numerical targets to measure performance in contrast to the previous system of non-specific contracts in Japanese companies.

Objectives need quantifying and monitoring. Reliable management information systems are needed to establish relevant objectives and monitor their "reach ratio" in an objective way. Pay incentives (bonuses) are often linked to results in reaching the objectives.

The mnemonic S.M.A.R.T. is associated with the process of setting objectives in this paradigm. "SMART" objectives are:

- Specific - Target a specific area for improvement.

- Measurable - Quantify or suggest an indicator of progress.
- Assignable - Specify who will do it.
- Realistic - State what results can realistically be achieved, given available resources.
- Time-bound - Specify when the result(s) can be achieved.

The aphorism "what gets measured gets done", is aligned with the MBO philosophy.

Arguments Against

MBO has its detractors and attention notably among them W. Edwards Deming, who argued that a lack of understanding of systems commonly results in the misapplication of objectives. Additionally, Deming stated that setting production targets will encourage workers to meet those targets through whatever means necessary, which usually results in poor quality.

Point 7 of Deming's key principles encourages managers to abandon objectives in favour of leadership because he felt that a leader with an understanding of systems was more likely to guide workers to an appropriate solution than the incentive of an objective. Deming also pointed out that Drucker warned managers that a systemic view was required and felt that Drucker's warning went largely unheeded by the practitioners of MBO.

There are limitations in the underlying assumptions about the impact of management by objectives:

1. It over-emphasizes the setting of goals over the working of a plan as a driver of outcomes.
2. It under-emphasizes the importance of the environment or context in which the goals are set.

That context includes everything from the availability and quality of resources, to relative buy-in by leadership and stake-holders. As an example of the influence of management buy-in as a contextual influencer, in a 1991 comprehensive review of thirty years of research on the impact of Management by Objectives, Robert Rodgers and John Hunter concluded that companies whose CEOs demonstrated high commitment to MBO showed, on average, a 56% gain in productivity. Companies with CEOs who showed low commitment only saw a 6% gain in productivity.

When this approach is not properly set, agreed and managed by organizations, self-centered employees might be prone to distort results, falsely representing achievement of targets that were set in a short-term, narrow fashion. In this case, managing by objectives would be counterproductive.

BUSINESS PROCESS MODELING

Business process modeling (or) process modeling, is the analytical representation or put simply an illustration of an organization's business processes. Modeling processes is a critical component for effective business process management. Process modeling software gives an analytical representation of 'as-is' processes in an organization and contrasts it with 'to-be' processes for making them more efficient.

Many business process modeling tools end up producing something like this:

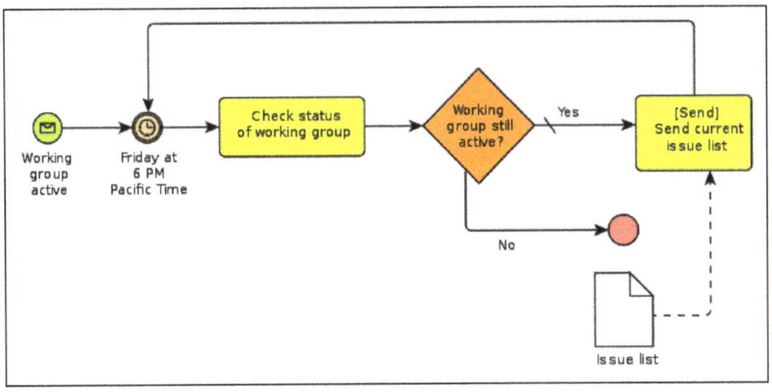

Significance of Business Process Modeling

Your first step in modeling is actually pen and paper. However, to actually run a business process, you will need to digitize that process in a way that a workflow engine can understand. Business process modeling software allows you to represent your process in a digital way that can then be transferred to a live automated process.

There are many benefits to business process modeling:

- Gives everyone a clear understanding of how the process works;
- Provides consistency and controls the process;
- Identifies and eliminates redundancies and inefficiencies;
- Sets a clear starting and ending to the process.

Business process modeling can also help you group similar processes together and anticipate how they should operate. The primary objective of business process modeling tools is to analyze how things are right now and simulate how they should be carried out to achieve better results.

Business Process Modeling Techniques

Business process modeling can be expressed through flowcharts, programs, hypertext, or scripts. The most common business process modeling techniques:

Business Process Modeling Notation (BPMN)

BPMN 2.0 has become something of a standard syntax used by process analysts and those who create business modeling tools. It is a relatively simple usage of lines, arrows, and geometric shapes that all communicate the flow and nuances of the process. A process consultant can look at a BPMN 2.0 model and know exactly how it should function.

However, BPMN 2.0 is still a learned language, and although relatively simple, isn't immediately intuitive for the regular business user. It is a great tool for process consultants, but not helpful for those looking to create their own applications.

Universal Process Notation

Instead of having a new language to learn, a more intuitive system is Universal Process Notation or UPN. UPN provides a simple box for each task to be completed. The box shows what happens, who is assigned to it, and when it happens in the sequence. It is extremely useful for IT to design and analyze processes, for management to comply to business norms, and - more importantly - for end business users to understand processes as intended.

Flowchart Technique

Flowcharts explain complex process flows in a simple yet effective way. They illustrate process steps in their sequential order, going from inputs to actual process to outputs. In fact, flowcharts provide the basic framework for BPMN to display advanced process flows.

Gantt Charts

Rather than showing the steps sequentially, Gantt charts are able to show the entire process using 'time taken' as one of the main axes. It does a better job of showing the overall time taken to complete a project than other options.

Petri-nets

Traditionally a modeling technique in mathematics, petri-nets are also useful for modeling business processes. Petri-nets classify or color-code complex workflow steps, users, and routes in different colors.

Need of Process Modeling Software

Most BPM Suites include business process modeling tools in them. However, some have the modeler as a separate application. The modeler is one of the most important elements in a BPMS.

Great business modeling tools should:

- Be easy to learn for the business departments;

- Be simple for IT teams to communicate with other departments;
- Be inexpensive and industry compliant;
- Have an integrated workflow editor tool with graphic interface;
- Be able to simulate workflow before implementing.

References

- Laszlo, C. & Zhexembayeva, N. (2011). Embedded Sustainability: The Next Big Competitive Advantage. Stanford, CA: Stanford University Press. ISBN 0-804-77554-0
- Strategy-definition: managementstudyguide.com, Retrieved 09 March, 2019
- Shalley, Christina E. (April 1995), "Effects of coaction, expected evaluation, and goal setting on creativity and productivity", Academy of Management Journal, 38 (2): 483–503 (501), doi:10.2307/256689, JSTOR 256689
- Business-environment, business-environment, strategy: toppr.com, Retrieved 14 June, 2019
- Definition-business-planning-2527: smallbusiness.chron.com, Retrieved 15 August, 2019
- Stajkovic, Alex; Sergent, Kayla (2019). Management and Leadership: What Can MBA Do in My Workday?. Research Paradigms Applied. p. 33. ISBN 978-1-7338275-0-8
- Strategic-planning-important-organization-4103: yourbusiness.azcentral.com, Retrieved 11 July, 2019
- Centralization-decentralization: managementstudyguide.com, Retrieved 30 August, 2019
- Steel, Piers; König, Cornelius J. (October 2006). "Integrating theories of motivation" (PDF). Academy of Management Review. 31 (4): 889–913. CiteSeerX 10.1.1.196.3227. doi:10.5465/AMR.2006.22527462
- Centralized-and-decentralized-management-explained, finance-knowledge: content.personalfinancelab.com, Retrieved 08 April, 2019

8

Entrepreneurship and Small Business Management

The process of designing, launching and then running a new business is known as entrepreneurship. The new business is generally a small business, with lesser number of employees than a regular-sized business. This chapter closely examines the key concepts related to entrepreneurship and the management of small businesses to provide an extensive understanding of the subject.

ENTREPRENEURSHIP

Entrepreneurship refers to the process of creating a new enterprise and bearing any of its risks, with the view of making the profit. It is an act of seeking investment and production opportunity, developing and managing a business venture, so as to undertake production function, arranging inputs like land, labour, material and capital, introducing new techniques and products, identifying new sources for the enterprise.

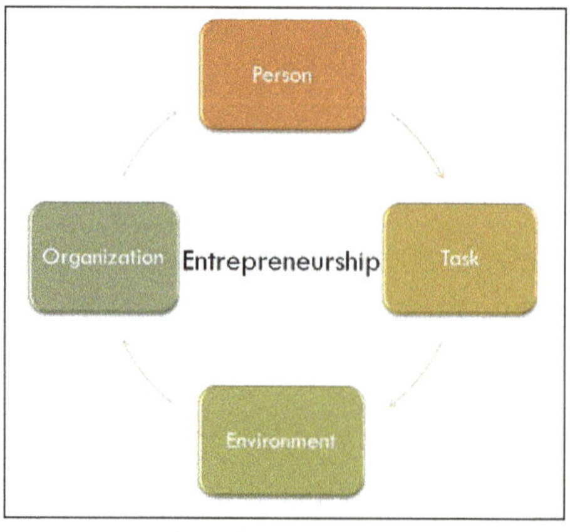

Conceptual model of entrepreneurship.

The person who creates a new enterprise and embraces every challenge for its development and operation is known as an entrepreneur. And the undertaking or organisation, typically a startup company, set up by the entrepreneur is called enterprise.

Characteristics of Entrepreneurship

- Economic Activity: Entrepreneurship is an economic activity, as it involves designing, launching and running new business enterprises in order to earn the profit, by ensuring best possible use of resources.
- Creativity and innovation: It involves discovering new ideas and implementing it in business. The entrepreneur continuously evaluates current modes of running a business and identifies new methods and techniques for operating the business more efficiently and effectively.
- Profit: The activity of entrepreneurship is undertaken with the sole objective of making the profit. It is also the reward of the efforts made and risk taken by the entrepreneur.
- Risk Bearing: "Willingness to assume the risk" is the essence of entrepreneurship without which he/she cannot succeed. It occurs due to the creation and implementation of new ideas. Such ideas are often uncertain, and so the result may or may not be positive and instant.

Skills Required in Entrepreneurship

- Technical Skills: Oral Communication, ability to organise, productive ability, technical business management, coaching, network building, monitoring environment, ability to spot new trends, active listening, writing and interpersonal skills.
- Business Management Skills: Forecasting, planning, budgeting, decision making, negotiation, goal setting, human relations, marketing, finance, etc.
- Personal Skills: Ability to manage change, leadership, persistence, self-reliance, foresightedness, innovativeness, risk taking, self-reflection, disciplinc, self-confidence, honesty, patience, intelligence, tactfulness, emotional stability, etc.

Entrepreneurship Ecosystem

Entrepreneurship operates under an ecosystem called as entrepreneurship ecosystem. The ecosystem comprises of government programs and schemes which encourage entrepreneurship, non-governmental organisations that provide advisory services to entrepreneurs, and other organisations which promote and support entrepreneurship directly or indirectly. Entrepreneurship is not confined to starting a new business but it about facing challenges at each step. It is an important tool for bridging the gap between science and marketplace, wherein a new enterprise is formed and new products and services are brought to thc markct.

SMALL BUSINESS

Small businesses on Dalrymple Street.

Small businesses are privately owned corporations, partnerships, or sole proprietorships that have fewer employees and less annual revenue than a regular-sized business or corporation. Businesses are defined as "small" in terms of being able to apply for government support and qualify for preferential tax policy varies depending on the country and industry. Small businesses range from fifteen employees under the Australian Fair Work Act 2009, fifty employees according to the definition used by the European Union, and fewer than five hundred employees to qualify for many U.S. Small Business Administration programs. While small businesses can also be classified according to other methods, such as annual revenues, shipments, sales, assets, or by annual gross or net revenue or net profits, the number of employees is one of the most widely used measures.

Small businesses in many countries include service or retail operations such as convenience stores, small grocery stores, bakeries or delicatessens, hairdressers or tradespeople (e.g., carpenters, electricians), restaurants, guest houses, photographers, very small-scale manufacturing, and Internet-related businesses such as web design and computer programming. Some professionals operate as small businesses, such as lawyers, accountants, dentists and medical doctors (although these professionals can also work for large organizations or companies). Small businesses vary a great deal in terms of size, revenues and regulatory authorization, both within a country and from country to country. Some small businesses, such as a home accounting business, may only require a business license. On the other hand, other small businesses, such as day cares, retirement homes and restaurants serving liquor are more heavily regulated, and may require inspection and certification from various government authorities.

Characteristics

Researchers and analysts of small or owner-managed businesses generally behave as if nominal organizational forms (e.g., partnership, sole-trader, or corporation), and the consequent legal and accounting boundaries of owner-managed firms are consistently meaningful. However, owner-managers often do not delineate their behavior to accord with the implied separation between their personal and business interests. Lenders also often contract around organizational (corporate) boundaries by seeking personal guarantees or accepting privately held assets as collateral. Because of this behavior, researchers and analysts may wish to be cautious in the way they assess the organizational types and implied boundaries in contexts relating to owner-managed firms. These include analyses that use traditional accounting disclosures, and studies that view the firm as defined by some formal organizational structure.

Small businesses in the Central Zone of São Paulo.

Small Business, Self-employment, Entrepreneurship and Startup

The concepts of small business, self-employment, entrepreneurship, and startup overlap to certain degree but also carry important distinctions. These four concepts often conflated with each other.

Portici di Sottoripa, Genova, Italy Galleries tend to form clusters of small business owners over time.

Below are the key differences of these concepts in summary:

- Self-employment: an organization created with the primarily intention to give a job to the founders, i.e. Sole proprietor operations.
- Entrepreneurship: all new organizations.

- Startup: a temporary new organization created with the intention to be bigger (at least have employees).
- Small business: an organization that is small (few employees) and may or may not have the intention to be bigger.

From the summaries, we can see that many small businesses are sole proprietor operations consisting solely of the owner, but small businesses can have a small number of employees. When big firms start out, they are known as startups, but not all small businesses are startups that aim to become bigger. Many of these small businesses offer an existing product, process or service, and they do not aim at growth. In contrast, startups aim for growth and often offer an innovative product, process or service, and the entrepreneurs of startups typically aim to scale up the company by adding employees, seeking international sales, and so on, a process which is financed by venture capital and angel investments. Successful entrepreneurs have the ability to lead a business in a positive direction by proper planning, to adapt to changing environments and understand their own strengths and weakness. Spectacular success stories stem from startups that expanded in growth. Examples would be Microsoft, Genentech, and Federal Express which all embody the sense of new venture creation on small business.

Self-employment provides works primarily for the founders. Entrepreneurship refers all new businesses, including self-employment and businesses that never intend to grow big or become registered, but startups refer to new businesses that intend to grow beyond the founders, to have employees, and grow large.

The legal definition of "small business" varies by country and by industry. In addition to number of employees, methods used to classify small companies include annual sales (turnover), value of assets and net profit (balance sheet), alone or as a combination of factors.

- In the United States, the Small Business Administration establishes small business size standards on an industry-by-industry basis, but generally specifies a small business as having fewer than 500 employees for manufacturing businesses and less than $7.5 million in annual receipts for most non-manufacturing businesses. The definition can vary by circumstance—for example, a small business having fewer than 25 full-time equivalent employees with average annual wages below $50,000 qualifies for a tax credit under the health care reform bill Patient Protection and Affordable Care Act. By comparison, a medium-sized business or mid-sized business has fewer than 500 employees.
- The European Union generally defines a small business as one that has fewer than fifty employees and either turnover or balance sheet less than 10 m. but the European Commission is undertaking a review of this definition. By comparison, a medium-sized business has fewer than 250 employees and either turnover less than 50 m. or balance sheet less than 43 m.

- In Australia, a small business is defined by the *Fair Work Act 2009* as one with fewer than fifteen employees. By comparison, a medium-sized business or mid-sized business has fewer than two hundred employees.
- In South Africa, the National Small Business Amendment Act defines businesses in a variety of ways using five categories previously established by the National Small Business Act, namely, standard industrial sector and subsector classification, size of class, equivalent of paid employees, turnover and asset value excluding fixed property.

Small businesses are usually not dominant in their field of operation. The table below serves as a useful guide to business size nomenclature.

Business Size by Number of Employees

	AUS	US	CAN	EU
Minute/Micro	1-2	1-6	1-4	<10
Small	<15	<250	1-99	<50
Medium	<200	<500	100-499	<250
Large	<500	<1000	>500	<1000
Enterprise	>500	>1000	N/A	>1000

- Most cells reflect sizes not defined in legislation,
- Some definitions are multi-parameter, e.g., by industry, revenue or market share.

Demographics

In 2016 a study that examined the demographic of small business owners was published. The study showed that the median American small business owners were above the age of 50. The ages were distributed as: 51% over 50 years old, 33% between the ages 35–49, and 16% being under the age of 35. As for sex: 55% were owned by males, 36% by females, and 9% being equal ownership of both males and females. As for race: 72% were white/Caucasian, 13.5% were Latinos, 6.3% were African American, 6.2% were Asian, and 2% as other. As for educational background: 39% had obtained a bachelor's degree or higher, 33% had some college background, and 28% received at least a high school diploma.

The United States census data for the years 2014 and 2015 shows the women's ownership share of small businesses by firm size. The data explains percentages owned by women along with the number of employees including the owner. Generally, the smaller the business, the more likely to be owned by a woman. The data shows that about 22% of small businesses with 100-500 employees were owned by women, a percentage that rises the smaller the business. 41% of businesses with just 2-4 employees were run by women, and in businesses with just one person, that person was a woman 51% of the time.

Franchise Businesses

Franchising is a way for small business owners to benefit from the economies of scale of the big corporation (franchiser). McDonald's and Subway are examples of a franchise. The small business owner can leverage a strong brand name and purchasing power of the larger company while keeping their own investment affordable. However, some franchisees conclude that they suffer the "worst of both worlds" feeling they are too restricted by corporate mandates and lack true independence. It is an assumption that small business are just franchisees, but the truth is many franchisers are also small businesses, Although considered to be a successful way of doing business, literature has proved that there is a high failure rate in franchising as well, especially in UK, where research indicates that out of 1658 franchising companies operating in 1984, only 601 remained in 1998, a mere 36%.

Retailers' Cooperative

A retailers' cooperative is a type of cooperative which employs economies of scale on behalf of its retailer members. Retailers' cooperatives use their purchasing power to acquire discounts from manufacturers and often share marketing expenses. They are often recognized as "local groups" because they own their own stores within the community. It is common for locally owned grocery stores, hardware stores, and pharmacies to participate in retailers' cooperatives. Ace Hardware, True Value, and NAPA are examples of retailers' cooperative. Retail cooperatives also allow consumers to supply their own earnings and gain bargaining power outside of the business sector. Retail cooperatives mainly reside within small communities where local businesses are often shut down.

Advantages

One of the claimed advantages of small business owners is the ability to serve market niches not served by mass production industries. Consider how few major corporations would be willing to deal the risks and uncertainty that small antique store deals with: buying and selling non-standardized items and making quick assessments of the value of rare items.

Many small businesses can be started at a low cost and on a part-time basis, while a person continues a regular job with an employer or provides care for family members in the home. In developing countries, many small businesses are sole-proprietor operations such as selling produce at a market stall or preparing hot food to sell on the street, that provide a small income. In the 2000s, a small business is also well suited to Internet marketing; because, it can easily serve specialized niches, something that would have been more difficult prior to the Internet revolution which began in the late 1990s. Internet marketing gives small businesses the ability to market with smaller budgets. Adapting to change is crucial in business and particularly small business; not being tied to the bureaucratic inertia associated with large corporations, small businesses can respond to changing marketplace demand more quickly. Small business proprietors tend to be in closer personal contact with their customers and clients than large corporations, as small business owners see their customers in person each week.

One study showed that small, local businesses are better for a local economy than the introduction of new chain stores. By opening up new national level chain stores, the profits of locally owned businesses greatly decrease and many businesses end up failing and having to close. This creates an exponential effect. When one store closes, people lose their jobs, other businesses lose business from the failed business, and so on. In many cases, large firms displace just as many jobs as they create.

Independence is another advantage of owning a small business. A small business owner does not have to report to a supervisor or manager. In addition, many people desire to make their own decisions, take their own risks, and reap the rewards of their efforts. Small business owners possess the flexibility and freedom to making their own decisions within the constraints imposed by economic and other environmental factors. However, entrepreneurs have to work for very long hours and understand that ultimately their customers are their bosses.

Several organizations in the United States also provide help for the small business sector, such as the Internal Revenue Service's Small Business and Self-Employed One-Stop Resource. Small businesses (often carried out by family members) adjust quicker to the changing conditions; however, they are closed to the absorption of new knowledge and employing new labor from outside.

Challenges

Small businesses often face a variety of problems, some of which are related to their size. A frequent cause of bankruptcy is under capitalization. This is often a result of poor planning rather than economic conditions. It is a common "rule of thumb" that the entrepreneur should have access to a sum of money at least equal to the projected revenue for the first year of business in addition to his or her anticipated expenses. For example, if the prospective owner thinks that he or she will generate $100,000 in revenues in the first year with $150,000 in start-up expenses, then he or she should have not less than $250,000 available. Start-up expenses are often grossly underestimated adding to the burden of the business. Failure to provide this level of funding for the company could leave the owner liable for all of the company's debt should he or she end up in bankruptcy court, under the theory of under capitalization.

In addition to ensuring that the business has enough capital, the small business owner must also be mindful of contribution margin (sales minus variable costs). To break even, the business must be able to reach a level of sales where the contribution margin equals fixed costs. When they first start out, many small business owners under price their products to a point where even at their maximum capacity, it would be impossible to break even. Cost controls or price increases often resolve this problem.

In the United States, some of the largest concerns of small business owners are insurance costs (such as liability and health), rising energy costs, taxes, and tax compliance. In the United Kingdom and Australia, small business owners tend to be more concerned with excessive governmental red tape.

Contracting fraud has been an ongoing problem for small businesses in the United States. Small businesses are legally obligated to receive a fair portion (23 percent) of the total value of all the government's prime contracts as mandated by the Small Business Act of 1953. Since 2002, a series of federal investigations have found fraud, abuse, loopholes, and a lack of oversight in federal small business contracting, which has led to the diversion of billions of dollars in small business contracts to large corporations.

Another problem for many small businesses is termed the 'Entrepreneurial Myth' or E-Myth. The mythic assumption is that an expert in a given technical field will also be expert at running that kind of business. Additional business management skills are needed to keep a business running smoothly. Some of this misunderstanding arises from the failure to distinguish between small business managers as entrepreneurs or capitalists. While nearly all owner-managers of small firms are obliged to assume the role of capitalist, only a minority will act as entrepreneur. The line between an owner-manager and an entrepreneur can be defined by whether or not their business is growth oriented. In general, small business owners are primarily focused on surviving rather than growing; therefore, not experiencing the five stages of the corporate life cycle (birth, growth, maturity, revival, and decline) like an entrepreneur would.

Another problem for many small businesses is the capacity of much larger businesses to influence or sometimes determine their chances for success. Business networking and social media has been used as a major tool by small businesses in the UK, but most of them just use a "scatter-gun" approach in a desperate attempt to exploit the market which is not that successful. Over half of small firms lack a business plan, a tool that is considered one of the most important factors for a venture's success. Business planning is associated with improved growth prospects. Funders and investors usually require a business plan. A plan also serves as a strategic planning document for owners and CEOs, which can be used as a "bible" for decision-making.

An international trade survey indicated that the British share of businesses which are exporting rose from 32% in 2012 to 39% in 2013. Although this may seem positive, in reality the growth is slow, as small business owners shy away from exporting due to actual and perceived barriers. Learning the basics of a foreign language could be the solution to open doors to new trade markets it is a reality that not all foreign business partners speak English. China is stated to grow by 7.6% in 2013 and still sadly 95% of business owners who want to export to China have no desire and no knowledge to learn their local language.

Bankruptcy

When small business fails, the owner may file for bankruptcy. In most cases, this can be handled through a personal bankruptcy filing. Corporations can file bankruptcy, but if it is out of business and valuable corporate assets are likely to be repossessed by secured creditors, there is little advantage to going to the expense of a corporate bankruptcy. Many states offer exemptions for small business assets so they can continue to operate during and after personal bankruptcy. However, corporate assets are normally not exempt; hence, it may be more difficult to continue operating an incorporated business if the owner files bankruptcy. Researchers have examined small business failures in some depth, with attempts to model the predictability of failure.

Social Responsibility

Small businesses can encounter several problems related to engaging in corporate social responsibility, due to characteristics inherent in their size. Owners of small businesses often participate heavily in the day-to-day operations of their companies. This results in a lack of time for the owner to coordinate socially responsible efforts, such as supporting local charities or not-for-profit activities. Additionally, a small business owner's expertise often falls outside the realm of socially responsible practices, which contributing to a lack of participation. Small businesses also face a form of peer pressure from larger forces in their respective industries, making it difficult to oppose and work against industry expectations. Furthermore, small businesses undergo stress from shareholder expectations. Because small businesses have more personal relationships with their patrons and local shareholders, they must also be prepared to withstand closer scrutiny if they want to share in the benefits of committing to socially responsible practices or not.

Job Quality

While small businesses employ over half the workforce in the US and have been established as a main driving force behind job creation, the quality of the jobs these businesses create has been called into question. Small businesses generally employ individuals from the Secondary labour market. As a result, in the U.S., wages are 49% higher for employees of large firms. Additionally, many small businesses struggle or are unable to provide employees with benefits they would be given at larger firms. Research from the U.S.

Small Business Administration indicates that employees of large firms are 17% more likely to receive benefits including salary, paid leave, paid holidays, bonuses, insurance, and retirement plans. Both lower wages and fewer benefits combine to create a job turnover rate among U.S. small businesses that is three times higher than large firms. Employees of small businesses also must adapt to the higher failure rate of small firms, which means that they are more likely to lose their job due to the firm going under. In the U.S. 69% of small businesses last at least two years, but this percentage drops to 51% for firms reaching five years in operation. The U.S. Small Business Administration counts companies with as much as $35.5 million in sales and 1,500 employees as "small businesses", depending on the industry. Outside government, companies with less than $7 million in sales and fewer than five hundred employees are widely considered small businesses.

Cyber Crime

Cyber crime, in the business world can be broken down into 4 main categories. They include loss of reputation and consumer confidence, cost of fixing the issue, loss of capital and assets, and legal difficulties that can come from these problems. Loss of reputation and consumer confidence can be impacted greatly after one attack. Many small businesses will struggle to gain confidence and trust in their customers after being known for having problems prior. Cost of fixing the cyber attack would require experts outside of their field to further the investigation and find the problem. Being down for a business means losing money at the same time. This could halt the online operations and mean the business could potentially be down for a long period of time. Loss of capital and assets ties well in with the cost of fixing the issue. During a cyber attack, a business may lose their funds for that business. Worst-case scenario, a business may actually lose all their working capital and funds. The legal difficulties involved with cyber crime can become pricy and hurt the business itself for not having standard security measures and standards. Security not only for the business but more importantly the customer should be number one priority when dealing with security protocol.

The monetary dollar damage caused by cyber crime in 2016 equalled out to be over 1.33 billion dollars in the United States alone. In 2016, California alone had over 255 million dollars reported to the IC3. The average company this year in the United States amounted to 17.36 million dollars in cyber crime attacks. Certain cyber attacks can vary on how long it takes to solve a problem. It can take upwards to 69 days for an average everyday attack on a business. The types of attacks include viruses and malware issues. Employee activities within the workspace can also render a cyber attack. Employees using mobile devices or remote work access off the job make it easier for a cyber attack to occur.

Marketing

Although small businesses have close relationships with their existing customers, finding new customers and reaching new markets is a major challenge for small business owners. Small businesses typically find themselves strapped for time to do marketing, as they have to run the day-to-day aspects of the business. To create a continual stream of new business and find new clients and customers, they must work on marketing their business continuously. Low sales (result of poor marketing) is one of the major reasons of small business failure. Common marketing techniques for small business include business networking (e.g., attending Chamber of Commerce events or trade fairs), "word of mouth" promotion by existing customers, customer referrals, Yellow pages directories, television, radio, and outdoor ads (e.g., roadside billboards), print ads, and Internet marketing. TV ads can be quite expensive, so they are normally intended to create awareness of a product or service. Another means by which small businesses can advertise is through the use of "deal of the day" websites such as Groupon and Living Social. These Internet deals encourage customers to patronize small businesses.

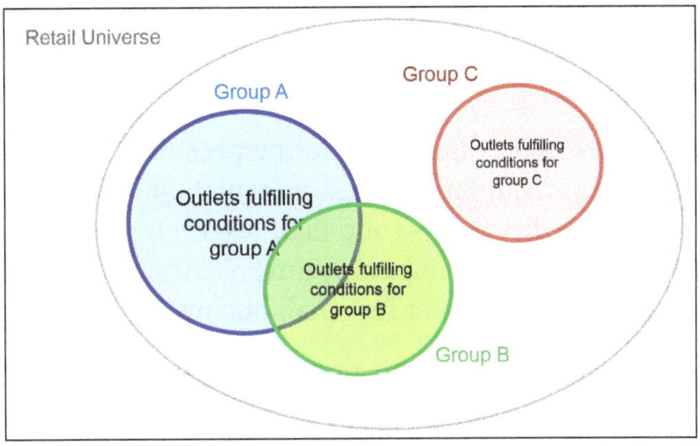

Example of keyword analysis based on market competition.

Many small business owners find internet marketing more affordable. Google AdWords and Yahoo, Search Marketing are two popular options of getting small business products or services in front of motivated web searchers. Social media has also become an affordable route of marketing for small business. It is a fraction of the cost of traditional marketing and small businesses are able to do it themselves or find small social marketing agencies that they can hire out for a small fee. Statistically, social media marketing has a higher lead-to-close rate than traditional media. Successful online small business marketers are also adept at utilizing the most relevant keywords in their website content. Advertising on niche websites that are frequented by potential customers can also be effective, but with the long tail of the Internet, it can be time intensive to advertise on enough websites to garner an effective reach.

Creating a business website has become increasingly affordable with many do-it-yourself programs now available for beginners. A website can provide significant marketing exposure for small businesses when marketed through the Internet and other channels. Some popular services are WordPress, Joomla Squarespace, Wix and EXAI. Social media has proven to be very useful in gaining additional exposure for many small businesses. Many small business owners use Facebook and Twitter as a way to reach out to their loyal customers to give them news about specials of the day or special coupons, generate repeat business and reach out to new potential clients. The relational nature of social media, along with its immediacy and twenty-four-hour presence lend intimacy to the relationships small businesses can have with their customers, while making it more efficient for them to communicate with greater numbers. Facebook ads are also a very cost-effective way for small businesses owners to reach a targeted audience with a very specific message. In addition to the social networking sites, blogs have become a highly effective way for small businesses to position themselves as experts on issues that are important to their customers. This can be done with a proprietary blog and/or by using a back-link strategy wherein the marketer comments on other blogs and leaves a link to the small business' own website. Posting to a blog about the company's business or service area regularly can increase web traffic to a company website.

Marketing Plan

- Market research – To produce a marketing plan for small businesses, research needs to be done on similar businesses, which should include desk research (done online or with directories) and field research. This gives an insight in the target group's behavior and shopping patterns. Analyzing the competitor's marketing strategies makes it easier for small business to gain market share.

- Marketing mix – Marketing mix is a crucial factor for any business to be successful. Especially for a small business, examining a competitor's marketing mix can be very helpful. An appropriate market mix, which uses different types of marketing, can help to boost sales.

- Product life cycle – After the launch of the business, crucial points of focus should be the growth phase (adding customers, adding products or services, and/or expanding to new markets) and working towards the maturity phase. Once the business reaches maturity stage, an extension strategy should be in place. Re-launching is also an option at this stage. Pricing strategy should be flexible and based on the different stages of the product life cycle.

- Promotion techniques – It is preferable to keep promotion expenses as low as possible. 'Word of mouth', 'email marketing', 'print-ads' in local newspapers etc. can be effective.

- Channels of distribution – Selecting an effective channel of distribution may reduce the promotional expenses as well as overall expenses for a small business.

Contribution to the Economy

In the US, small businesses (fewer than five hundred employees) account for more than half the non-farm, private GDP and around half the private sector employment.

Regarding small business, the top job provider is those with fewer than ten employees, and those with ten or more but fewer than twenty employees comes in as the second, and those with twenty or more but fewer than one hundred employees comes in as the third (interpolation of data from the following references). The most recent data shows firms with fewer than twenty employees account for slightly more than 18% of the employment.

According to "The Family Business Review," "There are approximately seventeen million sole-proprietorship in the US. It can be argued that a sole-proprietorship (an unincorporated business owned by a single person) is a type of family business" and "there are twenty-two million small businesses (fewer than five hundred employees) in the US and approximately 14,000 big businesses." Also, it has been found that small businesses created the newest jobs in communities, "In 1979, David Birch published the first empirical evidence that small firms (fewer than 100 employees) created the most new jobs", and Edmiston claimed that "perhaps the greatest generator of interest in entrepreneurship and small business is the widely held belief that small businesses in the United States create most new jobs. The evidence suggests that small businesses indeed create a substantial majority of net new jobs in an average year." The U.S. Small Business Administration has found small businesses have created two-thirds of net new private sector jobs in the US since 2007. Local businesses provide competition to each other and also challenge corporate giants. Of the 5,369,068 employer firms in 1995, 78.8 percent had fewer than ten employees, and 99.7 percent had fewer than five hundred employees.

Sources of Funding

Small businesses use various sources available for start-up capital:

- Self-financing by the owner through cash savings, equity loan on his or her home, and or other assets.
- Loans or financial gifts from friends or relatives.

- Grants from private foundations, government or other sources.
- Private stock issue.
- Forming partnerships.
- Angel investors.
- Loans from banks, credit unions, or other financial institutions.
- SME finance, including collateral-based lending and venture capital, given sufficiently sound business venture plans.

Some small businesses are further financed through credit card debt—usually a poor choice, given that the interest rate on credit cards is often several times the rate that would be paid on a line of credit at a bank or a bank loan. Recent research suggests that the use of credit scores in small business lending by community banks is surprisingly widespread. Moreover, the scores employed tend to be the consumer credit scores of the small business owners rather than the more encompassing small business credit scores that include data on the firms as well as on the owners. Many owners seek a bank loan in the name of their business; however, banks will usually insist on a personal guarantee by the business owner.

In the United States, the Small Business Administration (SBA) runs several loan programs that may help a small business secure loans. In these programs, the SBA guarantees a portion of the loan to the issuing bank, and thus, relieves the bank of some of the risk of extending the loan to a small business. The SBA also requires business owners to pledge personal assets and sign as a personal guarantee for the loan. The 8(a) Business Development Program assists in the development of small businesses owned and operated by African Americans, Hispanics, and Asians. Canadian small businesses can take advantage of federally funded programs and services. Alejandro Cremades and Tanya Prive founded the first equity crowdfunding platform for small businesses in history as an alternative source of financing. The platform operates under the name of Rock the Post.

Business Networks and Advocacy Groups

Small businesses often join or come together to form organizations to advocate for their causes or to achieve economies of scale that larger businesses benefit from, such as the opportunity to buy cheaper health insurance in bulk. These organizations include local or regional groups such as Chambers of Commerce and independent business alliances, as well as national or international industry-specific organizations. Such groups often serve a dual purpose, as business networks to provide marketing and connect members to potential sales leads and suppliers, and also as advocacy groups, bringing together many small businesses to provide a stronger voice in regional or national politics. In the case of independent business alliances, promoting the value of locally owned, independent business (not necessarily small) through public education campaigns is integral to their work.

The largest regional small business group in the United States is the Council of Smaller Enterprises, located in Greater Cleveland. United Kingdom trade and Investment gives out research in different markets around the world, also research in program planning and promotional activities to exporters. The BEXA (British Exporters Association) role is to connect new exporters to expert services, it can provide details about regional export contacts, who could be made informally to discuss issues. Trade associations and all major banks could often provide links to international groups in foreign markets, some could also help set up joint venture, trade fairs etc.

A number of youth organizations, including 4-H, Junior Achievement, and Scouting have special interactive programs and training to help young people run their own small business under adult supervision.

SMALL BUSINESS MANAGEMENT

Small business owners are responsible for managing all aspects of their company. Management is commonly defined as the alignment and coordination of multiple activities in an organization. Business owners use management skills to accomplish the goals and objectives of their company. Small business management requires business owners to use a mix of education, knowledge and expertise to run their company.

Styles

Autocratic, paternalistic, democratic and laissez-faire are a few common styles of management. Autocratic management allows a business owner to be the main individual responsible for making decisions and driving the company through the business environment. Paternalistic management looks to create the best work environment for every employee. Business owners use a democratic management style when they allow employees to have input or feedback on business decisions. Laissez-faire creates the most employee autonomy, and allows decisions to be made with little business owner oversight.

Facts

Business owners usually represent the most visible individual in an organization. Business owners are responsible for creating business relationships to advance their company's operations. Vendors, suppliers, distributors and warehouse companies are a few external companies business owners may work with in the business environment. Business owners coordinate the activities involving these organizations to ensure that their company has sufficient economic resources. Economic resources represent the raw materials and supply chain needed to produce and distribute goods in the business environment.

Features

Small business management requires business owners to provide oversight for several functions in the business. Purchasing, human resources, sales, customer service, marketing and product development are a few major departments or functions business owners must manage. Larger business organizations often have more departments or divisions to manage. Business owners in large organizations often delegate management responsibilities to employees. Delegation ensures individuals provide oversight for business functions in accordance with the business owner's management style.

Tools

Business owners often use management tools to help them manage their small business. Accounting, finance tools and performance management represent a few universal small business management tools. Business owners use accounting to record and report their company's financial information. Finance tools can help business owners forecast production output, potential sales and the amount of external financing needed for business operations. Business owners use performance management to gauge the effectiveness and efficiency of their company's operations.

Business technology allows business owners to improve their company's business operations. Business owners can use technology to create a management information system. This system transfers information electronically to the business owner or other managers in the company. Business owners and managers can make real-time decisions based on current information collected from business operations. Although expensive to purchase and implement, business owners should consider using a management information systems to aid them when making decisions.

BENEFITS OF SMALL BUSINESS MANAGEMENT

Small business management is a process entrepreneurs use when running their business operations. Small business management often requires entrepreneurs to have a wide variety of knowledge or understanding relating to business topics. Entrepreneurs may need to understand how to manage employees, accurately report financial information, acquire economic resources or business assets, and make various business decisions. Entrepreneur and business owners are usually required to complete these functions because they may not have enough capital to pay someone else to complete this work.

Presenting Single Vision

Small business management allows an entrepreneur or business owner to present a single vision for his organization. Many small businesses are started as hobbies or side jobs, and grown into full-fledged, professional organizations. Entrepreneurs often start a business so they can work in an environment where they believe in what they do. They can also manage their operations and decide how to select opportunities or expand operations consistent with their personal vision. Entrepreneurs may also limit their hiring practices to individuals who share and understand their vision.

Ensures Goals Achieved

Entrepreneurs use small business management to ensure their organizations goals are achieved in a timely manner and in a way consistent with the entrepreneur's desires. Although entrepreneurs are solely responsible for achieving goals early in the small business' existence, expanding the organization and hiring new employees requires the entrepreneur to achieve goals with other individuals. Small business owners must learn to manage business operations through people, not around them. This can be a difficult concept for entrepreneurs to learn in the small business management process as they may have been completing goals themselves for a long time.

Deeper Understanding of Business

Small business owners often use the management process to gain a deeper understanding about various business topics. Many entrepreneurs do not have all of the skills required to run a business. Entrepreneurs often need to learn these skills as they go along and experience new situations in the business environment. Accounting, marketing, business financing and other business topics relating to small business may be a few areas entrepreneurs learn about during small business management.

Ability to Remain Flexible

Entrepreneurs may use their small business management skills to remain flexible in the business environment. Using a single individual to make business decisions shortens the process for reviewing and analyzing situations regarding new business opportunities. This flexibility allows entrepreneurs to make quick decisions for improving business operations and creating a competitive advantage in the business environment. Entrepreneurs may also use this flexibility to create specific work schedules that allow them to create a work schedule based around their personal life.

References

- Longenecker, Justin G.; Carlos W. Moore; J. William Petty; Leslie E. Palich (2008). Small business management : launching and growing entrepreneurial ventures (14th ed.). Cengage Learning. p. 768. ISBN 978-0-324-56972-8. OCLC 191487420
- Entrepreneurship: businessjargons.com, Retrieved 11 April, 2019

- Shailer, Gregory E. P. (1 September 1993). "The irrelevance of organisational boundaries of owner-managed firms". Small Bus Econ. 5 (3): 229–237. doi:10.1007/BF01531920
- Benefits-small-business-management-67: smallbusiness.chron.com, Retrieved 25 May, 2019
- Richbell, S. M.; Wardle, P.; Watts, H. D. (2006). "Owner-managers and Business Planning in the Small Firm". International Small Business Journal. 24 (5): 496–514. doi:10.1177/0266242606067275

Permissions

All chapters in this book are published with permission under the Creative Commons Attribution Share Alike License or equivalent. Every chapter published in this book has been scrutinized by our experts. Their significance has been extensively debated. The topics covered herein carry significant information for a comprehensive understanding. They may even be implemented as practical applications or may be referred to as a beginning point for further studies.

We would like to thank the editorial team for lending their expertise to make the book truly unique. They have played a crucial role in the development of this book. Without their invaluable contributions this book wouldn't have been possible. They have made vital efforts to compile up to date information on the varied aspects of this subject to make this book a valuable addition to the collection of many professionals and students.

This book was conceptualized with the vision of imparting up-to-date and integrated information in this field. To ensure the same, a matchless editorial board was set up. Every individual on the board went through rigorous rounds of assessment to prove their worth. After which they invested a large part of their time researching and compiling the most relevant data for our readers.

The editorial board has been involved in producing this book since its inception. They have spent rigorous hours researching and exploring the diverse topics which have resulted in the successful publishing of this book. They have passed on their knowledge of decades through this book. To expedite this challenging task, the publisher supported the team at every step. A small team of assistant editors was also appointed to further simplify the editing procedure and attain best results for the readers.

Apart from the editorial board, the designing team has also invested a significant amount of their time in understanding the subject and creating the most relevant covers. They scrutinized every image to scout for the most suitable representation of the subject and create an appropriate cover for the book.

The publishing team has been an ardent support to the editorial, designing and production team. Their endless efforts to recruit the best for this project, has resulted in the accomplishment of this book. They are a veteran in the field of academics and their pool of knowledge is as vast as their experience in printing. Their expertise and guidance has proved useful at every step. Their uncompromising quality standards have made this book an exceptional effort. Their encouragement from time to time has been an inspiration for everyone.

The publisher and the editorial board hope that this book will prove to be a valuable piece of knowledge for students, practitioners and scholars across the globe.

Index

A

Advertising Agency, 23, 60

Autocratic Management, 9, 237

B

Behavioral Finance, 56-57

Board of Directors, 6, 13-15, 18, 20, 23, 131

Brand Audit, 57-58

Brand Development Index, 65-66

Business Intelligence, 104-110

C

C-suite, 24-25

Capacity Utilization, 93-94

Capital Structure, 51-53

Career Planning, 7, 21

Cash Flow, 52, 55

Chief Marketing Officer, 25

Commanding, 37

Competitive Advantage, 7, 44, 58, 61-62, 69-72, 126, 143, 168-175, 179, 183, 186, 189, 221, 239

Competitive Intelligence, 57, 104, 108

Controlling Function, 38

Cooperative Behavior, 6, 21

Coordination, 28, 31, 35-36, 38, 70, 93, 173, 216, 237

Corporate Culture, 25-26, 61, 167, 181

Corporate Finance, 49, 51-53, 55

Corporation Sole, 13

Customer Lifetime Value, 79, 183

Customer Relationship Management, 60, 183

Customer Service, 42, 58, 87, 183, 238

D

Decision-making Process, 4, 40, 159

Dynamic Process, 36, 38

F

Financial Management, 39, 49, 52

Financial Markets, 55

First-level Managers, 7, 21

Functional Management, 22-23

G

Generic Competitive Strategy, 69-70

H

Human Capital, 44, 46, 193

Human Resource Management, 39, 44-47

I

Industrial Revolution, 40, 44, 82, 84-85

Information Technology, 25, 30, 39-41, 43, 48, 108, 151, 156, 176, 185, 187

Inventory Control, 35, 81, 86-87, 94, 102-103

Investment Management, 52

J

Joint-stock Company, 14

K

Knowledge Management, 107, 110, 137, 160

L

Labor Relations, 44-47

Laissez-faire, 9, 237

Lean Manufacturing, 86, 93, 95, 97, 147-148, 182

Legal Entity, 11, 13-14, 18

Limited Liability, 2, 11-12, 14-16

Line Manager, 27, 29

Lower Management, 6, 20-21, 30

M

Management Skills, 4, 223, 230, 237, 239

Market Development, 73, 76

Market Research, 1, 57, 59, 63, 159-160, 174, 234

Market Share, 59, 66, 75-78, 169-170, 172, 186, 188, 212, 227, 234

Marketing Management, 39, 57, 59-62, 104, 167

Marketing Mix, 59-60, 76, 78, 80, 234

Middle Management, 27, 29-31

Middle-level Managers, 6, 20-21

N

Non-profit Organization, 16-17, 19

O

Organizational Behavior, 1, 45, 89, 140

P

Parent Company, 13

Payroll, 22, 25, 44

Personal Finance, 49, 51, 53

Pest Analysis, 67-68, 175

Process Management, 7-8, 60, 108, 110, 149-150, 152, 155-158, 183, 219

Product Development, 25, 60, 64, 73, 77, 134, 238

Product Differentiation, 57, 159, 172, 179

Production Management, 89, 98, 101-104

Q

Quality Control, 31, 35, 100, 102-103, 134, 144

R

Rate Of Return, 49-50, 52

S

Semi-executive Position, 29

Share Capital, 12-13

Sole Proprietorship, 1-2, 12, 14, 16

Staffing, 3, 7-8, 33-34, 36, 47, 105-106, 133, 146

Strategic Planning, 8, 10-11, 61-63, 67, 76, 79, 161, 165, 167, 169, 174-175, 182, 190, 209-212, 230

Supervisory Board, 15

Supply Chain, 60, 88, 91, 101, 124, 126-127, 178, 237

Swot Analysis, 57, 66, 68, 168, 175, 194

T

Talent Management, 44, 46

Target Market, 59, 71, 76, 159

Tax Liability, 18, 51

Tax Planning, 50

Top-level Managers, 6, 20-21, 217

U

Upper Management, 23-24, 214-215

V

Value Chain Analysis, 57, 66

Vertical Integration, 57, 74-75, 91, 188

W

Working Capital, 52, 54, 232

CPSIA information can be obtained
at www.ICGtesting.com
Printed in the USA
LVHW060908030122
707669LV00002B/403

9 781647 260767